# Lecture Notes in Computer Science 10137

Commenced Publication in 1973
Founding and Former Series Editors:
Gerhard Goos, Juris Hartmanis, and Jan van Leeuwen

More information about this series at http://www.springer.com/series/7408

Yuliya Lierler · Walid Taha (Eds.)

# Practical Aspects of Declarative Languages

19th International Symposium, PADL 2017
Paris, France, January 16–17, 2017
Proceedings

 Springer

*Editors*
Yuliya Lierler
University of Nebraska
Omaha, NE
USA

Walid Taha
Halmstad University
Halmstad
Sweden

ISSN 0302-9743 ISSN 1611-3349 (electronic)
Lecture Notes in Computer Science
ISBN 978-3-319-51675-2 ISBN 978-3-319-51676-9 (eBook)
DOI 10.1007/978-3-319-51676-9

Library of Congress Control Number: 2016961275

LNCS Sublibrary: SL2 – Programming and Software Engineering

Printed on acid-free paper

This Springer imprint is published by Springer Nature
The registered company is Springer International Publishing AG
The registered company address is: Gewerbestrasse 11, 6330 Cham, Switzerland

# Preface

This volume contains the papers presented at 19th International Symposium on Practical Aspects of Declarative Languages (PADL 2017) held January 16–17, 2017, in Paris, France. The symposium was colocated with the 44th ACM SIGPLAN Symposium on Principles of Programming Languages (POPL 2017).

PADL is a forum for researchers and practitioners to present original work emphasizing novel applications and implementation techniques for all forms of declarative languages, including but not limited to logic, constraint, and functional languages. Declarative languages have been successfully applied to many different real-world situations, ranging from database management to active networks, software engineering, and decision support systems. New developments in theory and implementation have opened up new application areas. At the same time, applications of declarative languages to novel problems raise numerous interesting research questions. Examples include designing for scalability, language extensions for application deployment, and programming environments. We continue to see that attention to applications and practical challenges simultaneously benefits from research progress and helps steer attention to timely challenges.

This year there were 27 submissions. Each submission was reviewed by at least three Program Committee members. The committee decided to accept 14 papers based on the merit of each submission and irrespective of any scheduling or space constraints. The program also included an invited talk. Two of the papers were nominated for the Best Paper Award:

- "Boltzmann Samplers for Closed Simply-Typed Lambda Terms" by Maciej Bendkowski, Katarzyna Grygiel and Paul Tarau (Best Student Paper Award)
- "Canonicalizing High-Level Constructs in Picat" by Neng-Fa Zhou and Jonathan Fruhman (Most Practical Paper Award)

Springer sponsored 250 euro for these awards. The authors were encouraged to submit the long versions of their work for the rapid publication track to the journal of Theory and Practice of Logic Programming.

We would like to express thanks to the Association of Logic Programming for their continuous support of the symposium and Springer for their longstanding, successful cooperation with the PADL series. We are also grateful to the 31 members of the PADL 2017 Program Committee and external reviewers. The chairs of POPL 2017 were of great help in steering the organizational details of the event. The conference was managed with the help of EasyChair.

November 2016

Yuliya Lierler
Walid Taha

# Organization

## Program Committee

| | |
|---|---|
| Erika Abraham | RWTH Aachen University, Germany |
| Marcello Balduccini | Drexel University, USA |
| Lars Bergstrom | Mozilla Research |
| Bart Bogaerts | KU Leuven, Belgium |
| Edwin Brady | University of St. Andrews, UK |
| Martin Brain | University of Oxford, UK |
| Mats Carlsson | SICS |
| Manuel Carro | Technical University of Madrid (UPM) and IMDEA Software Institute, Spain |
| Stefania Costantini | Università dell'Aquila, Italy |
| Marc Denecker | KU Leuven, Belgium |
| Thomas Eiter | Vienna University of Technology, Austria |
| Esra Erdem | Sabanci University, Turkey |
| Thom Fruehwirth | University of Ulm, Germany |
| Marco Gavanelli | University of Ferrara, Italy |
| Martin Gebser | University of Potsdam, Germany |
| Jeremy Gibbons | University of Oxford, UK |
| Hai-Feng Guo | University of Nebraska at Omaha, USA |
| Jurriaan Hage | Universiteit Utrecht, The Netherlands |
| Yuliya Lierler | University of Nebraska at Omaha, USA |
| Geoffrey Mainland | Drexel University, USA |
| Henrik Nilsson | University of Nottingham, UK |
| Enrico Pontelli | New Mexico State University, USA |
| Ricardo Rocha | University of Porto, Portugal |
| Peter Schüller | Marmara University, Turkey |
| Peter Sestoft | IT University of Copenhagen, Denmark |
| Martin Sulzmann | Karlsruhe University of Applied Sciences, Germany |
| Walid Taha | Halmstad and Rice Universities, USA |
| Paul Tarau | University of North Texas, USA |
| Kazunori Ueda | Waseda University, Japan |
| Niki Vazou | University of California, San Diego, USA |
| Philip Wadler | University of Edinburgh, UK |
| Daniel Winograd-Cort | University of Pennsylvania, USA |
| Neng-Fa Zhou | CUNY Brooklyn College and Graduate Center, USA |
| Lukasz Ziarek | SUNY Buffalo, USA |

## Additional Reviewers

Correas Fernández, Jesús

Dao-Tran, Minh

Gall, Daniel

Jansen, Joachim

Kaminski, Roland

Mantadelis, Theofrastos

Mariño, Julio

Morales, Jose F.

Ontañón, Santiago

Ostrowski, Max

Redl, Christoph

Stollenwerk, Andre

Van den Eynde, Tim

You, Jia-Huai

Zaki, Amira

# Contents

# Eliminating Irrelevant Non-determinism in Functional Logic Programs

Sergio Antoy[1] and Michael Hanus[2(⊠)]

[1] Computer Science Department, Portland State University, Oregon, USA
antoy@cs.pdx.edu
[2] Institut Für Informatik, CAU Kiel, 24098 Kiel, Germany
mh@informatik.uni-kiel.de

**Abstract.** Functional logic programming languages support non-deterministic search and a flexible use of defined operations by applying them to unknown values. The use of these features has the risk that equal values might be computed several times or I/O computations could fail due to non-deterministic subcomputations. To detect such problems at compile time, we present a method to locate non-deterministic operations. If the non-determinism caused by some operation is semantically not relevant, the programmer can direct the compiler to produce only one result of a computation. If all the results of the computations are equal, this directive preserves the semantics and improves the operational behavior of programs. We define the declarative meaning of such annotations and propose both testing and verification techniques that respectively increase the confidence or formally prove that the non-determinism of an operation is irrelevant.

## 1  Introduction

Functional logic languages combine the most important features of functional and logic programming in a single language (see [7,18] for recent surveys). In particular, the functional logic language Curry conceptually extends Haskell with common features of logic programming, i.e., non-determinism, free variables, and constraint solving. Non-determinism is useful in programming to write a specification of a task instead of coding all the details of the task's solution. For instance, consider the selection sort algorithm where the smallest element is placed in front of the sorted remaining elements. In Curry, one can easily specify the smallest element of a list of integers by

```
min :: [Int]  → Int
min xs@(_ ++ [x] ++ _) | all (x <=) xs = x
```

Here we use a *functional pattern*, i.e., an expression with evaluable functions at pattern positions [4], to express that x is any element of the input list, and an *as pattern* (known from Haskell) to refer to the complete input list by xs. If the condition that x is not greater than any element of the input list xs is satisfied, we return the selected element x as the smallest one. Operation min shows an example of don't care non-determinism. Its definition through a

© Springer International Publishing AG 2017
Y. Lierler and W. Taha (Eds.): PADL 2017, LNCS 10137, pp. 1–18, 2017.
DOI: 10.1007/978-3-319-51676-9_1

functional pattern is elegant and declarative, but a consequence is that if there are repeated occurrences of the minimum in the argument, the minimum is returned multiple times. Of course, we don't care which occurrence is returned since they are all equal.

With this definition of min, the implementation of sorting a list is straight-forward (delete x xs returns the list xs without the first occurrence of x):

```
selSort []        = []
selSort xs@(_:_) = m : selSort (delete m xs) where m = min xs
```

Although this implementation of sorting a list is correct, it has a potential draw-back when used in larger applications. To ensure a declarative style of computa-tions, Curry adopts the monadic I/O approach of Haskell. Hence, an application program computes an I/O action, i.e., a transformation on a state of a "world" (including physical resources like a terminal or file system), that is applied to a concrete world when the program is executed. Since it is impossible to copy the world to apply a non-deterministic I/O action to these copies, the computed I/O action must be unique [18]. For instance, the execution of the call ("?" denotes a non-deterministic choice between two values)

```
print 1 ? print 2
```

leads to a run-time error ("non-determinism in I/O"). This is intended, since it is intentionally unspecified whether one should show 1 or 2 on the display. As a con-sequence, non-deterministic computations need to be encapsulated when using them in applications performing I/O. Encapsulating non-determinism means producing the set of every possible non-deterministic result of a computation, hence a deterministic result. Thus, if the call "print (selSort [1,3,2,1])" is evaluated without encapsulating the argument, we obtain a non-determinism error. This is due to the fact that the list contains two smallest elements so that the auxiliary operation min yields two (equal) results.

The same problem might occur even if only one non-deterministic branch of a computation leads to a result. For instance, consider the computation of the last element of a list by an inverse use of list concatenation:

```
last (_ ++ [x]) = x
```

Although last yields at most one result for a given list, its use in the context of an I/O operation causes a run-time error since one cannot decide which of the alternative I/O actions eventually yields a result.

These are not artificial examples. Such problems occurred to us several times when putting together applications consisting of more than one hun-dred modules and thousands of operations. As known from lazy functional languages, the source of run-time errors is not easy to locate from the run-time stack available when an error actually occurs. Therefore, we propose a compile-time analysis to locate potential calls to non-deterministic operations from a main operation. In this way, a programmer can examine these operations. If an operation computes, for a given argument, a single result multiple times, we propose to annotate such operations as *deterministic*. This information is used by a compiler to return the result only once since any recomputation would provide no additional information. This yields an improved operational behavior (reduction of the computation space) and avoids the kinds of non-determinism errors sketched above. In our·example, we simply annotate the operation min as deterministic to avoid the non-determinism error. By the use of determinism annotations, we combine the compact and comprehensible specification of operations with a reasonable operational behavior.

This paper investigates the source of non-determinism in a program, introduces a new concept of deterministic operation and defines its semantics. The semantic properties of deterministic operations allow us to implement them more efficiently. Moreover, we discuss methods to check these properties.

## 2   Functional Logic Programming and Curry

We briefly review those elements of functional logic languages and Curry that are necessary to understand the contents of this paper. Curry is a declarative multi-paradigm language combining in a seamless way features from functional and logic programming. The syntax of Curry is close to Haskell. In addition to Haskell, Curry allows *free (logic) variables* in conditions and right-hand sides of rules. These variables must be explicitly declared unless they are anonymous. Function calls can contain free variables, in particular variables without a value at call time. These calls are evaluated lazily where free variables as demanded arguments are non-deterministically instantiated [3].

Moreover, the patterns of a defining rule are expanded with respect to traditional functional languages. As a matter of convenience, patterns can be non-linear, i.e., they might contain multiple occurrences of some variable, which is an abbreviation for equalities between these occurrences. Patterns can also be *functional* [4] to more easily and directly define functions. A functional pattern is a pattern containing defined operations (and not only data constructors and variables) occurring in an argument of the left-hand side of a rule. Such a pattern abbreviates the set of all standard patterns to which the functional pattern can be evaluated (by narrowing). Details about their semantics and a constructive implementation of functional patterns by a demand-driven unification procedure can be found in [4].

*Example 1.* The following simple program shows the functional and logic features of Curry. It defines an operation "++" to concatenate two lists, which is identical to the Haskell encoding. The second operation, dup, returns some list element having at least two occurrences:

```
(++) :: [a]  → [a]  → [a]      dup :: [a]  → a
[]      ++ ys = ys             dup xs | xs == _ ++ [x] ++ _ ++ [x] ++ _
(x:xs) ++ ys = x : (xs ++ ys)         = x     where x free
```

The condition of the rule defining dup is solved by instantiating x and the anonymous free variables "_". This evaluation method corresponds to narrowing, but Curry narrows with possibly non-most-general unifiers to ensure the optimality of computations [3]. Using a functional pattern, the definition of dup is simply phrased as:

```
dup (_++[x]++_++[x]++_) = x
```

Note that `dup` is a *non-deterministic operation* since it might deliver more than one result for a given argument, e.g., the evaluation of `dup [1,2,2,1]` yields the values 1 and 2. Non-deterministic operations, which are interpreted as mappings from values into sets of values [16], are an important feature of contemporary functional logic languages. Hence, there is also a predefined *choice* operation:

```
x ? _ = x
_ ? y = y
```

Thus, the expression "0 ? 1" evaluates to 0 and 1 with the value non-deterministically chosen.

*Default rules*, which have recently been proposed [8], are useful in combination with functional patterns in order to express cases where a functional pattern, which often corresponds to an infinite set of standard patterns, is not applicable. Any operation can have a single default rule. To avoid syntactic extensions, default rules are marked by adding the suffix `'default` to the operation's name. The default rule is applied if no standard rule is applicable (see [8] for a precise definition in the context of non-deterministic values and free variables). For instance, by slightly modifying the operation `dup`, we can easily define a predicate `isSet` which checks whether a given list represents a set, i.e., does not contain duplicates:

```
isSet (_++[x]++_++[x]++_) = False
isSet'default _           = True
```

*Set functions* [6] allow the encapsulation of non-deterministic computations in a strategy-independent manner. For each defined function $f$, $f_S$ denotes the corresponding set function. $f_S$ encapsulates the non-determinism caused by evaluating $f$ apart from the non-determinism originating from the evaluation of the arguments to which $f$ is applied. For instance, consider the operation `decOrInc` defined by

```
decOrInc x = (x-1) ? (x+1)
```

Then "`decOrInc`$_S$ 3" evaluates to (an abstract representation of) the set $\{2,4\}$, i.e., the non-determinism caused by `decOrInc` is encapsulated into a set. However, "`decOrInc`$_S$ (2?5)" evaluates to two different sets $\{1,3\}$ and $\{4,6\}$, i.e., the non-determinism caused by the argument is not encapsulated.

## 3   Location of Non-deterministic Operations

To avoid potential problems with non-deterministic operations, first we have to locate them in a source program. In this section we present our method for this.

**Definition 1 (NDD operation).** *An operation is* non-deterministically *defined (NDD) if its defining rules are not inductively sequential[1] or some of the defining rules contain free variables.*

---

[1] The defining rules are inductively sequential if their patterns are just case distinctions on the constructors (see [2] for a precise definition). A consequence of this definition is that operations defined by functional patterns are NDD.

The operation dup defined in Example 1 shows why the occurrence of free variables in rules might lead to non-deterministic operations even if the left-hand sides are inductively sequential. This is due to the fact that free variables are equivalent to non-deterministic operations that generate all the values [5] of a given type. For instance, the choice operator "?" defined above by rules with overlapping left-hand sides can also be defined by rules with non-overlapping left-hand sides and a free variable:

```
x ? y = choose b x y          choose True  x y = x
        where b free          choose False x y = y
```

Note that Definition 1 only approximates non-deterministic evaluations. For instance, the use of the operation f defined by

```
f = if True then [] else ys++ys where ys free
```

will never lead to a choice in a computation, although we classify it as non-deterministically defined. However, our approximation is syntactically decidable.

If NDD operations are not invoked during a functional logic computation, then this computation is deterministic, i.e., there is no alternative outcome for the same initial expression. This can be easily proved by induction on the steps of an evaluation sequence, e.g., using the small-step operational semantics defined in [1]. Hence, in order to detect the sources of potentially non-deterministic computations, we have to find NDD operations. However, in a large application with many libraries, not all NDD operations are relevant since they might not be called or their calls are encapsulated in set functions. It would not be helpful to report all NDD operations occurring in a program. Instead, we want to know only those NDD operations that are called (directly or indirectly) from the main expression starting the application. For this purpose, we need a dependency analysis which assigns to each operation the set of all relevant NDD operations.

**Definition 2 (Relevant NDD operations).** *Let $\mathcal{F}$ be the set of all defined operations in a program. For all $f \in \mathcal{F}$ we denote by $f^{\mathcal{R}} \subseteq \mathcal{F}$ the set of NDD operations that are* relevant *for $f$: $f^{\mathcal{R}}$ is the smallest set such that the following properties hold:*

- *If $f$ is an NDD operation, then $f^{\mathcal{R}} = \{f\}$.*
- *If $f$ is a set function, then $f^{\mathcal{R}} = \varnothing$.*
- *Otherwise: $g^{\mathcal{R}} \subseteq f^{\mathcal{R}}$ for all $g \in \mathcal{F}$ occurring in some rule defining $f$.*

The first property ignores further NDD operations called by $f$ if $f$ itself is NDD. Hence, we return only the "first" NDD operation. In all our practical examples (see Sect. 5.2), this is sufficient to spot the NDD operation that is actually relevant for the overall non-deterministic behavior. Our implementation supports also the computation of the transitive closure of relevant NDD operations, but this often returns too much information.

Relevant NDD operations can be computed by a standard fixpoint analysis. The fixpoint computation always terminates since $\mathcal{F}$ is finite so that the abstract domain is finite. The implementation and practical results of this analysis are discussed in Sect. 5.

# 4   Deterministic Operations

When we locate a relevant NDD operation in an application, we can avoid its non-deterministic behavior if it is semantically not relevant, like in the operations min or isSet defined above. We call operations with semantically irrelevant non-determinism *deterministic*. Informally, an operation is deterministic if *different* values cannot be obtained for the *same* input. However, the operation can compute the same value multiple times. Deterministic operations can also fail if the input is not appropriate. For instance, the operation head defined as

```
head (x:xs) = x
```

is deterministic, although it does not yield a result for the empty list.

In order to mark a defined operation as deterministic, we annotate its determinism status in the last arrow of its type signature (this is partially inspired by the notation of deterministic and non-deterministic operations used in the semantic models of functional logic programming in [16]). Thus, we express the determinism status of the operations min and last by the following type signatures:

```
min  :: [Int] →DET Int              last :: [a] →DET a
```

From a declarative point of view, such an annotation is correct, i.e., an operation is deterministic, if all the results computed by this operation for a given input are equal. Since we are in a context of a lazy non-deterministic language where arguments, even if they are ground expressions, might denote several or also infinite values, a precise definition needs more care. For instance, consider the identity operation

```
id :: a  → a
id x = x
```

Intuitively, id is a deterministic operation since it does not introduce any non-determinism. However, the ground (i.e., variable free) call id (0?1) yields two different results: 0 and 1. Note that these non-deterministic results are caused by the arguments and not by id itself.

In order to deal with such subtleties, we need a formal model of the semantics of functional logic programs. The difficulties of combining non-deterministic operations with a demand-driven evaluation model have been pioneered in [16]. The authors proposed the *call-time choice* semantics as a reasonable model, which has been adapted to contemporary functional logic languages. The authors defined the rewriting logic CRWL as a logical foundation for declarative programming with non-strict and non-deterministic operations. Conceptually, values of arguments of an operation are determined before the operation is evaluated. In a lazy strategy, this is naturally obtained by sharing. Since standard term rewriting does not conform to the intended call-time choice semantics, other notions of rewriting are necessary to formalize this idea. In this paper we use the simple reduction relation of [22] which we review in the following.

*Expressions* occurring in a program contain *operations*, *constructors* (introduced in data type declarations), and *variables* (arguments of operations or free variables). The goal of a computation is to obtain a value of some expression, where a *value* is an expression that does not contain any operation. To cover demand-driven or non-strict computations, expressions can also contain the special symbol $\perp$ to represent an *undefined or unevaluated value*. A *partial value* is a value which might contain occurrences of $\perp$. A *partial constructor substitution* is a substitution that replaces variables by partial values. A *context* $C[\cdot]$ is an expression with some "hole". Then the reduction relation we use throughout this paper is defined as follows:

$$C[\sigma(f\ t_1 \ldots t_n)] \ \twoheadrightarrow \ C[\sigma(r)] \quad (f\ t_1 \ldots t_n = r \text{ program rule, } \sigma \text{ partial constr. subst.})$$
$$C[e] \ \twoheadrightarrow \ C[\perp] \qquad (e \text{ expression})$$

The first rule models call-time choice: if a rule is applied, the actual arguments of the operation must have been evaluated to partial values. The second rule models non-strictness by allowing the evaluation of any subexpression to an undefined value (which is intended if the value of this subexpression is not demanded). As usual, $\twoheadrightarrow^*$ denotes the reflexive and transitive closure of this reduction relation. The equivalence of this rewrite relation and CRWL is shown in [22]. We recall that two expressions $e_1$ and $e_2$ are *equal* iff they can be reduced to the same *value*, i.e., there exists a value $t$ such that $e_1 \twoheadrightarrow^* t$ and $e_2 \twoheadrightarrow^* t$.

Now we can formally define the meaning of deterministic operations.

**Definition 3 (Deterministic operation).** *An n-ary operation f is* determin-*istic, i.e., a determinism annotation* $f :: \tau_1 \to \cdots \tau_n \to_{DET} \tau'$ *is correct, iff, for all partial values* $t_1, \ldots, t_n$ *and evaluations* $f\ t_1, \ldots, t_n \twoheadrightarrow^* r$ *and* $f\ t_1, \ldots, t_n \twoheadrightarrow^* r'$ *with values* $r$ *and* $r'$, $r = r'$ *holds.*

Clearly, the declaration "id :: a $\to_{DET}$ a" is correct, but "dup :: [a] $\to_{DET}$ a" (see Example 1) would not be correct, since "dup [1,2,2,1]" evaluates to 1 and 2. It is not obvious whether the annotation "min :: [Int] $\to_{DET}$ Int" is correct. We discuss methods to check the correctness of determinism annotations in Sect. 6.

Below, we motivate two crucial design decisions of the definition, namely why a deterministic operation must have unique result *values* and not just unique head normal forms or partial values and why arguments can be evaluated up to partial values rather then values, i.e., fully evaluated.

An alternative to unique *values* is unique head normal forms. Often, the latter is a target of computations in non-strict languages. Head normal form would be inappropriate since non-determinism may show up under the head, as in

    f x = [x, 0 ? 1]

The expression "f 0" evaluates to the single head normal form [0,0?1] but to two different values [0,0] and [0,1]. Hence, the number of different results of an expression might depend on the degree of its evaluation, which is unfortunate when reasoning about programs in a declarative manner, i.e., without considering an evaluation strategy. As a consequence of this design, we must evaluate a deterministic operation application completely, i.e., to normal form, before we omit all other alternative choices.

Likewise, unique partial values would be inappropriate since most expressions might have different partial result values. For example, consider the operation `id` defined above. Then "`id 1 →*  1`" and "`id 1 →*  ⊥`" are two derivations with different partial result values. Hence, if we change Definition 3 so that we require unique *partial* result values, `id` would not be deterministic.

The requirement that arguments can be partial values is appropriate since this allows us to prune the computation space even if an argument has not been fully evaluated. For instance, consider the following contrived non-deterministic definition of computing the first element of a list and the definition of an infinite list:

```
head (x:xs) = x                          ones = 1 : ones
head (x:xs) = id x
```

Note that `head` is a deterministic operation according to our definition. The evaluation of the expression `head ones` demands the head normal form of the argument, which is `1:ones`. If we apply the first rule of `head`, we obtain the result value `1` and any attempt to compute another value can be dropped because `1:ones →*  1:⊥` and `head` is deterministic. Requiring values for the arguments in Definition 3 would have the consequence that the evaluation of `head [1]` yields one result whereas the evaluation of `head ones` yields two identical results.

Nevertheless, to check deterministic operations, it is sufficient to consider their behavior on values provided that each data type is *sensible*, i.e., has at least one value:

**Proposition 1.** *Assume types are sensible and that $f$ is an $n$-ary operation such that, for all values $t_1, \ldots, t_n$ and evaluations $f\ t_1, \ldots, t_n \to^*  r$ and $f\ t_1, \ldots, t_n \to^*  r'$ with values $r$ and $r'$, $r = r'$ holds. Then $f$ is a deterministic operation.*

We could have used this property, where the requirements on arguments and results are more symmetric, as the definition of deterministic operations. However, this would unnecessarily restrict the cutting of the search space by deterministic operations, as discussed above.

Our notion of deterministic operations is intended to be a constructive approximation of determinism in functional logic programs. Hence, we do not cover all potential determinism, in particular for non-terminating operations. To see why we cut the search space only if we compute a result value (and not a partially evaluated expression), consider the operation

```
inf x = if p x then x : inf (x+1)
             else (42 ? x) : inf (x+1)
```

where $p$ is some predicate on integers. Intuitively, the operation `inf` does not branch if $p$ is always satisfied. If $p$ is not satisfied only on the argument 42, the evaluation of `inf` branches but does not compute different results. In other cases, `inf` might compute different results. In particular, the non-deterministic branching might occur "arbitrarily late" during the evaluation of a call to `inf` so that there is no point to cut the computation space during the computation of an infinite structure. Thus, we decided to restrict the determinism property to finite result values.

We demonstrate the advantages of determinism annotations for application programming by two further examples.

*Example 2.* We define an operation to sort a list by switching two adjacent elements which are out of order (a generalization of bubble sort):

```
bsort :: [Int] →DET [Int]
bsort (xs++[x,y]++ys) | x>y = bsort (xs++[y,x]++ys)
bsort'default xs = xs
```

The functional pattern in the first rule frees the programmer from specifying a concrete strategy to find a pair which should be swapped. Actually, the sort operation works with any strategy to select such pairs. The determinism annotation has the effect that all attempts to compute further values after the first sorted list are discarded. Without this annotation, we obtain 16 (equal) result values for the call `bsort [4,3,2,1]`, 768 results for `bsort [5,4,3,2,1]`, and 292864 results for `bsort [6,5,4,3,2,1]`.

*Example 3.* The simplification of symbolic arithmetic expressions has been used in [4] to demonstrate the power of functional patterns. The task is to simplify arithmetic expressions like $1*(x+0)$ to $x$. Based on the definition of a replacement operation `replace`, where "`replace e p t`" is equivalent to the notation $e[t]_p$ commonly used in term rewriting, and a non-deterministic operation `evalTo` which evaluates to expressions equivalent to the argument, [4] defines a one-step simplification operation as

```
simplifyStep (replace c p (evalTo x)) = replace c p x
```

The code for completely simplifying expressions, which is omitted in [4], becomes quite agile with default rules and determinism annotations:

```
simplify :: Exp →DET Exp
simplify (replace c p (evalTo t)) = simplify (replace c p t)
simplify'default e = e
```

The correctness of the determinism annotation of `simplify` depends on the confluence of the simplification rules specified by `evalTo`.

# 5 Practical Aspects

## 5.1 Implementation

We have implemented the analysis of relevant NDD operations described in Sect. 3 with the Curry analysis framework CASS [19]. CASS provides the infrastructure to analyze larger applications in a modular and incremental manner. Our actual analysis does not return only the relevant NDD operations but also the call sequence (limited to a fixed maximal length to keep the abstract domain finite) leading to relevant NDD operations from a main expression. This context information could be helpful to decide at which point non-determinism should be encapsulated.

To implement the reduction of the computation space by deterministic operations, we use existing features of functional logic languages. In particular, deterministic operations are implemented by a preprocessing approach that requires no language extension. The actual preprocessor is available and integrated into the compilation chain of the Curry systems PAKCS [20] and KiCS2 [10].

To support the possibility to annotate deterministic operations similarly to the notation used before, we introduce a type synonym:

```
type DET a = a
```

Hence, we can put the type constructor DET around any type without changing its meaning. For instance, we can write the type annotation of Example 3 as

```
simplify :: Exp ->DET Exp
```

Our preprocessor reads a Curry program and looks for such occurrences of DET. Since a deterministic operation is intended to compute only a single value for a given argument and ignore all others, we use set functions [6] to compute and select one value. Since the result sets are evaluated lazily, the computation of further elements is automatically precluded if we access only one element. Therefore, the following transformation is sufficient. If the preprocessor finds a function definition of the form (where $\overline{t_n}$ denotes a sequence of elements $t_1 \ldots t_n$)

$$f :: \tau_1 \rightarrow \ldots \rightarrow \tau_n \rightarrow_{\text{DET}} \tau$$
$$f\ \overline{t_n^1}\ |\ c_1\ =\ e_1$$
$$\vdots$$
$$f\ \overline{t_n^k}\ |\ c_k\ =\ e_k$$

then it is transformed into

$$f :: \tau_1 \rightarrow \cdots \rightarrow \tau_n \rightarrow \tau \qquad\qquad f^{ND} :: \tau_1 \rightarrow \cdots \rightarrow \tau_n \rightarrow \tau$$
$$f\ \overline{x_n}\ =\ \texttt{selectValue}\ (f^{ND}_\mathcal{S}\ \overline{x_n}) \qquad f^{ND}\ \overline{t_n^1}\ |\ c_1\ =\ e_1$$
$$\vdots$$
$$f^{ND}\ \overline{t_n^k}\ |\ c_k\ =\ e_k$$

where $f^{ND}$ is a new identifier and $\overline{x_n}$ are pairwise distinct variables. Hence, the original operation is replaced by a call to its set function where some element of the set is returned by the operation `selectValue`.[2] Due to this transformation, determinism annotations have similarities to strictness annotations ("seq") in Haskell: they change the semantics in order to get a more efficient operational behavior.

Note that if the arguments of a deterministic operations are non-deterministic and have several values, the search space is cut for each value separately. This is due to the fact that set functions encapsulate the non-determinism of the function definition but not the non-determinism of the arguments (see Sect. 2). For instance, consider the operation `list2set` which transforms a list into a set by removing duplicated elements (also known as `nub` in Haskell but specified without a concrete strategy to find duplicates):

```
list2set :: [a] →DET [a]
list2set (xs++[e]++ys++[e]++zs) = list2set (xs++[e]++ys++zs)
list2set'default xs = xs
```

---

[2] Note that this operation on value sets returns *some* value from the set and ignores the others, i.e., it implements "don't care" non-determinism.

Then the call

```
list2set [True, True?False, True]
```

evaluates to two results: `[True]` and `[True,False]`. Thanks to the determinism annotation, the result `[True]` is computed once whereas it would be computed three times without the determinism annotation. One can even call deterministic functions with unknown arguments. For instance, `list2set xs == [True,False]` is solved by non-deterministically instantiating `xs` to `[True,False]`, `[True,False,False]`, `[True,False,True]`, and so on.[3] This shows that a determinism annotation does not imply that the operation can only be used in a purely functional manner, i.e., to compute an output value from a given input value, but deterministic operations compute at most one result for each given input value, which can still be guessed. This makes deterministic operations more powerful than Prolog's cut operator.

## 5.2    Benchmarking

To evaluate our analysis on non-trivial examples, we applied it to some existing applications where I/O non-determinism errors occurred during their development. Since our analysis was not available at that time, we manually located them in a time-consuming process. For our current test, we re-introduced the problematic definitions (mainly due to the use of functional patterns) in these applications. Our current analysis precisely returned these NDD operations as relevant for the main operation of the applications. The applications we tested are the KiCS2 compiler, CurryCheck (discussed in Sect. 6.1), the Curry preprocessor (partially described above), and a web-based information system for the curricula in the department of computer science in Kiel. For the benchmarks, we used the Curry implementation KiCS2 (Version 0.5.1) [10] with the Glasgow Haskell Compiler (GHC 7.6.3, option -O2) as its back end on a Linux machine (Debian 8.5) with an Intel Core i7-4790 (3.60 Ghz) processor and 8 GiB of memory.

Figure 1 shows the size of these applications and their analysis times. The table shows the number of modules, the size (in KB) and the number of lines of the source code (including all imported libraries), the time to analyze the complete application for the first time, and the time to re-analyze the complete

| Application | # modules | program size | # source lines | initial | re-analysis |
|---|---|---|---|---|---|
| KiCS2 Compiler | 63 | 651 | 17521 | 7.72 | 2.36 |
| Curry Preprocessor | 110 | 1040 | 26085 | 12.58 | 2.69 |
| CurryCheck | 52 | 538 | 14357 | 5.33 | 1.80 |
| Curricula Web System | 97 | 1056 | 26634 | 15.27 | 7.42 |

**Fig. 1.** Benchmarks: analysis of relevant NDD operations

---

[3] This behavior is specific to KiCS2. PAKCS suspends on this equation since it has a more restricted implementation of set functions.

| Expression | nondet | det |
|---|---|---|
| isSet (take 200 (repeat [1..10])) | 1.46 | 0.00 |
| last [1..20000] | 0.05 | 0.24 |
| selSort ([1..10]++[1..10]) | 0.48 | 0.00 |
| bsort [5,4,3,2,1] | 2.25 | 0.00 |
| list2set [1,2,3,4,5,6,7,7,6,5,4,3,2,1] | 53.96 | 0.02 |
| simplify <expression with 17 nodes> | 4.33 | 0.00 |

**Fig. 2.** Benchmarks: assessing the effect of determinism annotations

application after fixing the problem (in seconds). Note that CASS performs a modular and incremental analysis, i.e., if some module has been analyzed, it stores the analysis information and re-analyzes a module only if the module or some of its (direct or indirect) imported modules have been changed. Hence, the initial analysis time is the worst-case analysis time which rarely occurs in practice. The re-analysis time clearly shows the advantage of this incremental analysis method. Altogether, the benchmarks demonstrate that our analysis method is effective and efficient enough for realistic applications.

In order to assess the practical consequences of determinism annotations, we compared the run times of some examples with and without determinism annotations on the same architecture used in the previous benchmarks. The timings were performed with the Unix *time* command measuring the execution time to compute all solutions (in seconds) of a compiled executable for each benchmark as a mean of three runs. The programs used for the benchmarks are the examples presented in the previous sections.

Figure 2 shows the execution times for evaluating the given expression without ("nondet" column) and with ("det" column) a determinism annotation (where "0.00" means less than 10 ms). Obviously, one can obtain arbitrarily large speedups by increasing the size of the input. Nevertheless, the numbers indicate that a non-deterministic implementation where we don't care about strategies to solve intermediate problems, like selecting appropriate list elements, is reasonable if the overall operation is deterministic. The example last shows that determinism annotations can also come with some cost since the machinery to encapsulate search with set functions is not for free. However, it should be noted that this comparison is also somehow artificial since a non-encapsulated top-level non-determinism is compared with an encapsulated computation. In practice, where the application program performs I/O operation on the top-level, all intermediate non-deterministic computations need to be encapsulated as discussed in Sect. 1.

## 6  Checking Deterministic Operations

If we add determinism annotations to operations that are not deterministic according to Definition 3, we lose completeness. Since the determinism property is undecidable in general, we cannot expect an automatic tool to verify this property.

On the other hand, accepting only those determinism annotations where the determinism property can be verified by some sufficient criteria would be too restrictive. Therefore, the preprocessor outputs for each operation with a determinism annotation a proof obligation as a reminder and puts the task of verifying this property into the hands of the programmer. In this section, we discuss some methods to check or verify the correctness of determinism annotations.

## 6.1 Testing Deterministic Operations

A first approach to get confidence in the correctness of determinism annotations is testing. Testing can be quite powerful if one tests program properties, i.e., predicates, with a lot of test data. A well known example of such a property-based test framework is Haskell's QuickCheck tool [13] which generates random test data to test given properties. CurryCheck is a similar new tool for Curry programs distributed with the Curry systems PAKCS and KiCS2. It uses Easy-Check [12] for test data generation but automates property testing with additional features. In particular, CurryCheck automatically tests the correctness of determinism annotations as follows. If CurryCheck finds an annotation

$$f :: \tau_1 \ \rightarrow \ \dots \ \rightarrow \ \tau_n \ \rightarrow_{\text{DET}} \ \tau$$

CurryCheck removes the determinism annotation (actually, it copies the code of $f$ without the determinism annotation, since the annotated operation might be used in some other property) and adds the following property (where the property "$e$ #< $n$" is satisfied if the *set* of all values of $e$ contains less than $n$ elements):

```
fIsDeterministic :: τ₁ → ⋯ → τₙ → Prop
fIsDeterministic x₁...xₙ = f x₁...xₙ #< 2
```

This property is tested by systematically enumerating values for $x_1, \dots, x_n$. Although this enumeration is exhaustive only for finite domains, checking determinism properties by testing is a quite useful tool in practice if the test cases are numerous and well distributed. These test cases are provided by the underlying EasyCheck library.

## 6.2 Proving Determinism Annotations

To show the correctness of determinism annotations also for infinite sets of input values, formal proofs are required. We discuss in this section methods to construct such proofs for particular examples.

A method to determine the determinism of an operation borrows from the theory of rewriting [24]. We denote by $\rightarrow$ the standard rewrite relation on terms and by $\rightarrow^*$ its reflexive and transitive closure. Then we can use the following proposition to verify determinism annotations by rewriting:

**Proposition 2.** *Assume that each data type is sensible and $f$ is an $n$-ary operation so that, for all values $t_1, \dots, t_n$ and rewrite derivations $f \ t_1, \dots, t_n \rightarrow^* r$ and $f \ t_1, \dots, t_n \rightarrow^* r'$ with values $r$ and $r'$, $r = r'$ holds. Then $f$ is deterministic.*

Note that the converse of this proposition does not hold: The operation f defined as

```
f x = square (x ? (0-x))  where square x = x*x
```

is deterministic in the sense of Definiton 3 but the expression f 3 has the following rewrite derivations (among others):

```
f 3 →* 3 * (3 ? (0-3))  → 3 * 3   → 9
f 3 →* 3 * (3 ? (0-3))  → 3 * -3  → -9
```

There are many cases where Proposition 2 can be applied to verify determinism annotations. For instance, within the context of rewriting, determinism coincides with *confluence*, the property that the end result of a complete sequence of applications of the rules does not depend on the order in which the rules were applied. *Weak orthogonality* is a sufficient condition to ensure confluence, hence determinism. First we briefly recall this concept, then we show its application to Example 3.

Given a binary relation $\rightarrow$ on a set $A$ of "objects" and an element $a \in A$, we say that $a$ is *confluent* iff for all $b, c \in A$, if $a \rightarrow^* b$ and $a \rightarrow^* c$ then there exists some $d \in A$ such that $b \rightarrow^* d$ and $c \rightarrow^* d$. If every element of $A$ is confluent, then $A$ is called confluent (or also Church-Rosser). Confluence captures determinism in that no element can have two distinct normal forms or values. When the objects of $A$ are terms, there is a simple syntactic condition, called weak orthogonality, that ensures confluence. A rewrite system $R$ is *weakly orthogonal* iff the following two conditions holds: (1) the rules of $R$ are *left-linear*, i.e., no variable in the left-hand side is repeated, and (2) any critical pair $(t, s)$ is trivial, i,.e. $t = s$ syntactically. We refer to [24, Defintion 2.7.9] for the definition of *critical pair*, which is quite technical, but in the following paragraph we show an application of these concepts to one of our examples.

The simplification of an expression, as in Example 3, can be seen as a rewrite computation. A rule, $l \rightarrow r$, of this computation is constructed as follows: $l$ is an alternative in the right-hand side of the definition of evalTo and $r$ is the variable $e$, for example Add (Lit 0) e $\rightarrow$ e. An inspection of the rules shows that they are left-linear. If the left-hand sides of two rules do not overlap, as in a rule simplifying addition and a rule simplifying multiplication, then the rules can be applied independently of each other and the order in which they are applied does not affect the result. If the left-hand sides overlap, then we consider their most general common instance and rewrite this instance with each rule. The two results form a critical pair. For example, the two rules of addition overlap, their most common general instance is Add (Lit 0) (Lit 0), and the critical pair is (Lit 0, Lit 0). Since the components of the pair are equal, the pair is trivial. Since all the critical pairs of this system are trivial, the system is weakly orthogonal, hence confluent, hence deterministic.

A second approach to ensure the determinism of an operation relies on the characteristics of the operation definition. For example, consider the sort operation bsort defined earlier. A call to bsort $t$, where $t$ is a list of elements, has either of two outcomes: (1) the call result in a recursive call bsort $t'$ where $t'$ is a permutation of $t$, or (2) the call outputs $t$, the argument of bsort. The latter occurs only when there are no elements out of order in the argument. Since there is only one permutation of $t$ with this property, this permutation is the only value that `bsort` $t$ can ever produce. Hence `bsort` is deterministic. The pattern exemplified by `bsort` is not uncommon, hence this is a simple and useful technique for determinism proofs.

One could also use proof assistants to show determinism properties. Due to the presence of (don't know) non-determinism in Curry programs, this requires the formal representation of the rewriting logic, as sketched in Sect. 4, in the logic of the proof assistant, as proposed in [14]. However, in simpler examples, it suffices to show properties about functional computations to show the correctness of determinism annotations. For instance, to show the determinism of the operation `last`, we have to show that every concatenation used in the pattern of `last` produces the same last element. This proof obligation can be formally written as

$$\forall l, l1, l2, x1, x2 : (l \mathrel{==} l1 \mathbin{++} [x1] \ \wedge \ l \mathrel{==} l2 \mathbin{++} [x2]) \implies x1 \mathrel{==} x2$$

Since the involved operations "==" and "++" are defined in a purely functional manner, we could apply proof assistants for functional programs to verify this property. Actually, we formally verified this property with Agda, a dependently typed functional programming language where proofs are written in a functional programming style [23]. The similarity of Agda with Haskell eases the translation of Curry programs into Agda. Actually, [9] describes a method to prove properties of non-deterministic computations by translating Curry programs into Agda programs. Using this method, one can mechanically prove that `min` (see Sect. 1) is deterministic by verifying its correspondence to a deterministic definition of a minimum function. Due to lack of space, the Agda proofs are omitted but they can be found in the long version of this paper.[4]

# 7   Related Work

The use of deterministic operations to improve the operational behavior of functional logic computations has a long history. For instance, the SLOG system [15] used simplification with program rules and inductive axioms to reduce the search space. Similarly, the more general language ALF exploited deterministic rewrite computations interspersed in narrowing steps to obtain efficient functional logic computations [17]. A more dynamic use of deterministic computations was proposed in [21] where the "dynamic cut" as an alternative to Prolog's static cut has been introduced. In contrast to the static cut operator in Prolog, all these proposals aim at keeping the completeness of functional logic computations. In contrast to our proposal, these older proposals did not characterize a separate set of deterministic operations since all operations are deterministic due to a confluence requirement of the involved programs.

This view changed with the introduction of a new semantic foundation of functional logic programming presented in [16]. There, the notion of non-deterministic

---

[4]   http://www.informatik.uni-kiel.de/~mh/papers.

functions was introduced in functional logic programs and deterministic and non-deterministic functions are distinguished on a semantic level. The authors used these two kinds of functions to define the intended models of functional logic programs. Deterministic functions characterize homomorphisms and interpret data constructors, whereas user-defined operations are always interpreted as non-deterministic functions so that they are evaluated in a non-deterministic manner.

Improving computations for deterministic operations in the presence of non-deterministic operations has also been addressed in [11]. The authors transferred the idea of dynamic determinism detection in functional logic programs introduced in [21] to functional logic programs with non-deterministic operations. Dynamic determinism detection is based on the idea to check variable bindings of actual arguments inside an operation and omit alternatives (as with Prolog's cut) if arguments are not bound during the evaluation of the operation. Although this has some similarities with our approach, it is less general. Due to the use of set functions, we can still call deterministic operations with free variables and compute bindings for them in order to cut the search space in computations with individual bindings. Moreover, [11,21] have strong criteria on operations where dynamic determinism detection is applied (in particular, no extra variables in right-hand sides) so that it is not applicable to most of our examples.

The declarative language Mercury[5] also supports monadic I/O as well as non-deterministic computations. To annotate predicates where only one of possibly several solutions are needed, the user can use committed choice annotations (`cc_nondet`, `cc_multi`) to suppress the computation of several solutions. Since the Mercury compiler checks these annotations, their usage is restricted in contrast to our semantic-based notion of deterministic operations.

## 8    Conclusions

We presented a method to detect relevant non-deterministic operations in Curry applications and proposed the use of deterministic operations to improve their operational behavior. We characterized deterministic operations semantically w.r.t. their input/output behavior, i.e., deterministic operations might yield multiple results under the standard semantics but all results are equal for a given input. We showed that one can exploit this property by cutting the computation space for such operations if the arguments are sufficiently evaluated. In this way, we do not only improve their operational behavior, but one can also avoid runtime problems if these operations are used inside I/O operations, which always require deterministic subcomputations.

We demonstrated with various examples that deterministic operations frequently occur in functional logic programs. Actually, they occur whenever a task like selecting list elements or subterms, or applying transformation rules can be more easily expressed in a non-deterministic manner.

We also discussed how determinism properties can be checked, since they are decidable only in simple cases. One can automatically test these properties with

---

[5] www.mercurylang.org.

advanced testing tools which might also prove a property if the set of possible argument values is finite. We sketched also proof techniques for determinism annotations. Developing better proof techniques with mechanical support is an interesting topic for future research.

**Acknowledgments.** This material is based in part upon work supported by the National Science Foundation under Grant No. 1317249.

# References

1. Albert, E., Hanus, M., Huch, F., Oliver, J., Vidal, G.: Operational semantics for declarative multi-paradigm languages. J. Symbolic Comput. **40**(1), 795–829 (2005)
2. Antoy, S.: Definitional trees. In: Kirchner, H., Levi, G. (eds.) ALP 1992. LNCS, vol. 632, pp. 143–157. Springer, Heidelberg (1992). doi:10.1007/BFb0013825
3. Antoy, S., Echahed, R., Hanus, M.: A needed narrowing strategy. J. ACM **47**(4), 776–822 (2000)
4. Antoy, S., Hanus, M.: Declarative programming with function patterns. In: Hill, P.M. (ed.) LOPSTR 2005. LNCS, vol. 3901, pp. 6–22. Springer, Heidelberg (2006). doi:10.1007/11680093_2
5. Antoy, S., Hanus, M.: Overlapping rules and logic variables in functional logic programs. In: Etalle, S., Truszczyński, M. (eds.) ICLP 2006. LNCS, vol. 4079, pp. 87–101. Springer, Heidelberg (2006). doi:10.1007/11799573_9
6. Antoy, S., Hanus, M.: Set functions for functional logic programming. In: Proceedings of PPDP 2009, pp. 73–82. ACM Press (2009)
7. Antoy, S., Hanus, M.: Functional logic programming. Commun. ACM **53**(4), 74–85 (2010)
8. Antoy, S., Hanus, M.: Default rules for Curry. In: Gavanelli, M., Reppy, J. (eds.) PADL 2016. LNCS, vol. 9585, pp. 65–82. Springer, Cham (2016). doi:10.1007/978-3-319-28228-2_5
9. Antoy, S., Hanus, M., Libby, S.: Proving non-deterministic computations in Agda. In: Proceedings of 24th International Workshop on Functional and Logic Programming (WFLP 2016), EPTCS (2016)
10. Braßel, B., Hanus, B., Peemöller, B., Reck, F.: KiCS2: a new compiler from Curry to Haskell. In: Kuchen, H. (ed.) WFLP 2011. LNCS, vol. 6816, pp. 1–18. Springer, Heidelberg (2011)
11. Caballero, R., López-Fraguas, F.J.: Improving deterministic computations in lazy functional logic languages. J. Funct. Logic Program. **2003** (2003)
12. Christiansen, J., Fischer, S.: EasyCheck — test data for free. In: Garrigue, J., Hermenegildo, M.V. (eds.) FLOPS 2008. LNCS, vol. 4989, pp. 322–336. Springer, Heidelberg (2008). doi:10.1007/978-3-540-78969-7_23
13. Claessen, K., Hughes, J.: QuickCheck: a lightweight tool for random testing of Haskell programs. In: Proceedings of ICFP 2000, pp. 268–279. ACM Press (2000)
14. Cleva, J.M., Leach, J., López-Fraguas, F.J.: A logic programming approach to the verification of functional-logic programs. In: Proceedings of PPDP 2004, pp. 9–19. ACM Press (2004)
15. Fribourg, L.: Slog: a logic programming language interpreter based on clausal superposition and rewriting. In: Proceedings of IEEE International Symposium on Logic Programming, pp. 172–184 (1985)

16. González-Moreno, J.C., Hortalá-González, M.T., López-Fraguas, F.J., Rodríguez-Artalejo, M.: An approach to declarative programming based on a rewriting logic. J. Logic Program. **40**, 47–87 (1999)

17. Hanus, M.: Efficient implementation of narrowing and rewriting. In: Boley, H., Richter, M.M. (eds.) PDK 1991. LNCS, vol. 567, pp. 344–365. Springer, Heidelberg (1991). doi:10.1007/BFb0013543

18. Hanus, M.: Functional logic programming: from theory to Curry. In: Voronkov, A., Weidenbach, C. (eds.) Programming Logics. LNCS, vol. 7797, pp. 123–168. Springer, Heidelberg (2013). doi:10.1007/978-3-642-37651-1_6

19. Hanus, M., Skrlac, F.: A modular and generic analysis server system for functional logic programs. In: Proceedings of PEPM 2014, pp. 181–188. ACM Press (2014)

20. Hanus, M. et al.: PAKCS: The Portland Aachen Kiel Curry System (2016). http://www.informatik.uni-kiel.de/~pakcs/

21. Loogen, R., Winkler, S.: Dynamic detection of determinism in functional logic languages. Theor. Comput. Sci. **142**, 59–87 (1995)

22. López-Fraguas, F.J., Rodríguez-Hortalá, J., Sánchez-Hernández, J.: A simple rewrite notion for call-time choice semantics. In: Proceedings of PPDP 2007, pp. 197–208. ACM Press (2007)

23. Stump, A.: Verified Functional Programming in Agda. ACM and Morgan & Claypool, New York (2016)

24. TeReSe: Term Rewriting Systems, vol. 55 of Cambridge Tracts in Theoretical Computer Science. Cambridge University Press, Cambridge (2003)

# Canonicalizing High-Level Constructs in Picat

Neng-Fa Zhou[1](✉) and Jonathan Fruhman[2]

[1] CUNY Brooklyn College and Graduate Center, New York, USA
zhou@sci.brooklyn.cuny.edu
[2] New York, USA

**Abstract.** Picat is a logic-based multi-paradigm dynamic language that integrates logic programming, functional programming, constraint programming, and scripting. The Picat language is underpinned by the core logic programming concepts, including logic variables, unification, and nondeterminism. Picat takes many constructs from other languages, among which functions, list and array comprehensions, loops, and assignments are convenient for scripting and modeling. This paper gives an overview of the language features of Picat, and shows how different language constructs are compiled into a canonical form.

## 1 Introduction

Picat is a simple, and yet powerful, logic-based multi-paradigm dynamic language. Picat was designed with the goal of creating a logic-based general-purpose programming language that overcomes the weaknesses of Prolog, is as powerful as Python and Ruby for scripting, and is on a par with OPL [6] and MiniZinc [10] for modeling combinatorial problems.

Like Prolog, Picat is based on the core logic programming concepts, including logic variables, unification, and nondeterminism realized through depth-first backtracking search. Picat departs from Prolog in many aspects. Picat uses pattern-matching rather than unification in the selection of rules. Unification might be a natural choice in Horn clause resolution for theorem proving [8], but its power is rarely needed for general programming tasks. In Picat, pattern-matching rules are fully indexed, while most Prolog implementations only index clauses on one argument; therefore, Picat can be more scalable than Prolog. Unification can be considered as an equation over terms [1], and just like constraints over finite domains, Picat supports unification as an explicit call.

Non-determinism, a powerful feature of logic programming, makes concise solutions possible for many problems, including the simulation of non-deterministic automata, the parsing of ambiguous grammars, and search problems. In Prolog, Horn clauses are backtrackable by default. As it is generally undecidable to detect determinism, programmers tend to excessively use the cut operator to prune unnecessary clauses. Picat supports explicit non-determinism, which renders the cut operator unnecessary. In Picat, rules are deterministic, unless they are explicitly annotated as backtrackable.

© Springer International Publishing AG 2017
Y. Lierler and W. Taha (Eds.): PADL 2017, LNCS 10137, pp. 19–33, 2017.
DOI: 10.1007/978-3-319-51676-9_2

Picat supports functions, like many other logic-based languages, such as Curry [5] and Ciao [7]. In Prolog, a predicate defines a relation, and may succeed multiple times. It is common for queries to fail in Prolog without the system providing any clue about the source of the failure. Functions should be used instead of relations, unless multiple answers are required. It is more convenient to use functions instead of predicates, because (1) functions are guaranteed to succeed with a return value; (2) function calls can be nested; and (3) the directionality of functions often enhances the readability.

Picat provides arrays and loops, which are probably the features that are most unlike those of Prolog. In Prolog, in order to describe repetitions, programmers mainly rely on recursion, and occasionally rely on failure-driven loops and higher-order extensions [15]. The lack of powerful loop constructs has arguably made Prolog less acceptable to programmers than other languages. The extension of Prolog to support constraints has further revealed the weakness of Prolog as a modeling language. Early attempts to introduce arrays and loops into Prolog for modeling failed to produce a satisfactory language: most noticeably, array accesses are only treated as functions in certain contexts, and loops require the declaration of global variables in ECLiPSe [11] and local variables in B-Prolog [17].

Picat allows list comprehensions to be included as special functions in expressions in order to declaratively construct lists. Picat also supports the assignment operator :=, whose original motive was to facilitate the compilation of list comprehensions. A list comprehension is easily translated into a `foreach` loop in which an assignment is utilized to accumulate the constructed list. The decision to make the assignment operator available to programmers is controversial but pragmatic. The assignment operator in Picat has earned fondness among programmers for its simple semantics and convenience.

All of the language constructs, including functions, loops, comprehensions, and assignments, are provided as syntactic sugar in Picat. They are compiled away at compile time. This paper gives an overview of the language constructs of Picat, and shows how they are compiled into canonical-form pattern-matching rules.

## 2    The Picat Language

The name "Picat" is an acronym, and the letters in the name summarize Picat's features: 'P' for pattern-matching, 'I' for intuitive programming, 'C' for constraints, 'A' for action rules, and 'T' for tabling. This section gives an overview of the language constructs of Picat. Some of Picat's features, such as action rules, tabling, and the tabling-based planner [18], are orthogonal to the language constructs, and will not be covered in this article. More details of the Picat language can be found in [20].

### 2.1    Data Types

Picat is a logic-based multi-paradigm programming language for general-purpose applications. Picat's core is underpinned by logic programming concepts, as seen in Prolog, including *logic variables*, *unification*, and *backtracking*. Logic variables, like variables in mathematics, are value holders. A logic variable can be bound to any term, including another logic variable. Figure 1 gives the types of terms in Picat. Picat is a dynamically-typed language, which means that type checking occurs at runtime.

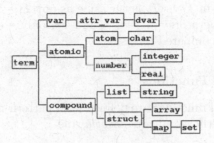

**Fig. 1.** Picat's data types

A variable name is an identifier that begins with a capital letter or the underscore; for example, X1 and _abc are variable names. The underscore itself _ is used for *anonymous variables*, and each occurrence of the underscore indicates a different variable.

An *atomic* value can be an *atom* or a *number*. An *atom* is a constant symbol. An atom name can be either unquoted or quoted. An unquoted name is an identifier that begins with a lower-case letter, followed by an optional string of letters, digits, and underscores. A quoted atom is a single-quoted sequence of arbitrary characters. For example, x1, x_1, '_abc', and 'a+b' are atom names. A number can be an *integer* or a *real number*. Picat supports big integers.

A *compound* value can be a *list* or a *structure*; for example, [a,b,c] is a list, and f(a,b,c) is a structure.[1] Lists are singly-linked lists. A *string* is a list of characters; for example, "a+b" is the same as [a,'+',b]. An *array* is a special structure; for example, {a,b,c} is an array. A *map* is a special structure that contains a set of key-value pairs, and a *set* is a special map that only contains keys; both are hash tables.

Each type provides a set of built-in functions and predicates. Each of the type names, except term and set, is a type-checking predicate. For example, list($L$) tests if $L$ is a list. Let $L$ be a compound term. The index notation $L[I]$ is a special function that returns the $I$th component of list $L$, with $L[1]$ referring to the first element of $L$. An index notation can take multiple subscripts. The *cons* operator $[H|T]$ builds a new list by adding $H$ to the front of $T$. The *concatenation* operator $L_1 ++ L_2$ returns the concatenated list of $L_1$ and $L_2$.

---

[1] A structure requires a preceding dollar symbol, as in $f(a,b,c), to distinguish the structure from a function call, unless the structure is special, or it occurs in a special context.

The equality test $T_1$ == $T_2$ is true if term $T_1$ and term $T_2$ are identical. The inequality test $T_1$ !== $T_2$ is the same as not $T_1$ == $T_2$. Note that two terms can be identical even if they are different terms stored in different memory locations. Also note that two terms of different types can be tested for equality, but they are never identical. The *unification* $T_1$ = $T_2$ is true if term $T_1$ and term $T_2$ are already identical, or if they can be made identical by instantiating the variables in the terms. The built-in $T_1$ != $T_2$ is the same as not $T_1$ = $T_2$. Note that among the four comparison operators ==, !==, =, and !=, only = can change the state of the variables in the compared terms.

## 2.2   Predicates and Functions

In Picat, predicates and functions are defined with pattern-matching rules. Picat has two types of rules: the *non-backtrackable* rule

> *Head, Cond* => *Body.*

and the *backtrackable* rule

> *Head, Cond* ?=> *Body.*

In a predicate definition, the *Head* takes the form $p(t_1, \ldots, t_n)$, where $p$ is a predicate name, and $n$ is the arity. The condition *Cond*, which is an optional goal, specifies a condition under which the rule is applicable. For a call $C$, if $C$ matches *Head* (i.e., there exists a substitution $\theta$ such that $Head\theta = C$) and *Cond* succeeds, then the rule is said to be *applicable* to $C$. When applying a rule to call $C$, Picat rewrites $C$ into *Body*. If the used rule is non-backtrackable, then the rewriting is a commitment, and the program can never backtrack to $C$. However, if the used rule is backtrackable, then the program will backtrack to $C$ once *Body* fails, meaning that *Body* will be rewritten back to $C$, and the next applicable rule will be tried on $C$. The backtrackable rule is semantically equivalent to:

> *Head* ?=> *Cond, Body.*

However, in-line tests that are written to the left of ?=> will be used by the compiler to index the rule.

The following defines the predicate member:

```
member(X, [Y|_]) ?=> X = Y.
member(X, [_|T]) => member(X, T).
```

Like the Prolog built-in member(X,L), this predicate can be utilized to check if X is a member of the list L, and it can also be utilized to retrieve an element of L through X by backtracking if X is a variable. Unlike Prolog's member(X,L), which can succeed an infinite number of times if L is a variable, the Picat definition can never succeed more times than the number of elements in L, since pattern-matching never changes call arguments.

A *function* is a special kind of a predicate that is defined by non-backtrackable rules. In a function definition, the *Head* takes the form $f(t_1, \ldots, t_n) = Term$, where $f$ is a function name and *Term* is a result to be returned. If *Cond* and *Body* are both true, then they can be omitted together with the => arrow.

The following gives two functions for reversing a list:

```
naive_reverse([]) = [].
naive_reverse([H|T]) = naive_reverse(T) ++ [H].

reverse(L) = reverse_aux(L, []).

reverse_aux([], Acc) = Acc.
reverse_aux([H|T], Acc) = reverse_aux(T, [H|Acc]).
```

For a list, if it is empty, then naive_reverse returns the empty list; otherwise, naive_reverse attaches the head H to the end of the reversed list of the tail T. The call naive_reverse(L) takes $O(n^2)$ time to reverse list L of length $n$. The function reverse calls reverse_aux, which scans the list while accumulating the reversed list in the second argument. The call reverse(L) takes linear time to reverse list L.

Picat, like functional programming languages, discourages the use of side effects in describing computations. All of the built-in functions in Picat's basic module are side-effect-free mathematical functions. Pure, side-effect-free functions are not dependent on the context in which they are applied. This purity can greatly enhance the readability and maintainability of programs.

Picat's dot notation makes calling a function look like calling a method on an object, as in X.to_string().reverse(). This *uniform function call syntax*[2] is convenient for chaining function calls in a readable way.

## 2.3 Loops and Comprehensions

Picat provides *loops* for describing repetitions and *comprehensions* for constructing lists and arrays. A foreach loop has the following general form:

```
foreach (E₁ in D₁, Cond₁, ..., Eₙ in Dₙ, Condₙ)
    Goal
end
```

The expression $E_i$ in $D_i$ is called an *iterator*, where $E_i$ is an iterating pattern, and $D_i$ is an expression that gives a compound value. Each $Cond_i$ is an optional condition on iterators $E_1$ through $E_i$. A loop statement forms a name *scope*: variables that occur in a loop, but do not occur before the loop in the outer scope, are local to each iteration of the loop.

A list comprehension has the following general form:

```
[Exp : E₁ in D₁, Cond₁, ..., Eₙ in Dₙ, Condₙ]
```

---

[2] http://dlang.org/spec/function.html.

where *Exp* is an expression, and the iterators and conditions have the same format as those used in the `foreach` loop. A list comprehension is a special functional notation for creating lists. It includes *Exp* as an element in the list for each possible combination of values in the iterators that satisfies the conditions. Like a loop, a list comprehension also forms a name scope.

An array comprehension has the following general form:

$$\{Exp : E_1 \text{ in } D_1, Cond_1, \ldots, E_n \text{ in } D_n, Cond_n\}$$

An array comprehension first creates a list, and then calls the function `to_array` to convert the list to an array.

The following gives an example that uses loops and comprehensions:

```
matrix_multi(A, B) = C =>
    C = new_array(A.length, B[1].length),
    foreach (I in 1..A.length, J in 1..B[1].length)
        C[I,J] = sum([A[I,K]*B[K,J] : K in 1..A[1].length])
    end.
```

The function `matrix_multi(A,B)` takes two matrices, A and B, that are represented as two-dimensional arrays, and returns the product A × B. All three of the variables A, B, and C, are non-local to the loop, because they occur before the loop. Note that, for an aggregate function, such as `sum` or `len`, that takes a list comprehension as the argument, the compiler generates a special function that computes the aggregate without actually building a list.

Loops are very convenient for scripting. The following gives an example program which recursively copies all of the files in a directory and its subdirectories to the current directory:

```
import os.

main =>
    WD = pwd(),
    flatten_dir(WD, WD).

flatten_dir(WD, Dir) =>
    Fs = listdir(Dir),
    foreach (F in Fs, F !==".", F !=="..")
        FullName = full_path(Dir, F),
        if directory(FullName) then
            flatten_dir(WD, FullName)
        else
            cp(FullName, full_path(WD, F))
        end
    end.

full_path(Dir, Name) =
    Dir ++ [separator()] ++ Name.
```

This program imports the `os` module, from which the built-ins `pwd`, `listdir`, `directory`, `cp`, and `separator` are used. The function `listdir(Dir)` returns a list Fs of files and directories in the directory Dir. For each item F in Fs, if F is neither "." nor "..", then the program calls full_path to construct the full name FullName of F. If FullName is a directory, then the program recursively calls flatten_dir on the directory; otherwise, it copies the file to the WD directory.

## 2.4   Assignments and While Loops

Picat variables are *single-assignment*, meaning that once a variable is bound to a value, the variable cannot be bound again, unless the value is a variable or the value contains variables. In order to simulate imperative language variables, Picat provides the assignment operator :=. An assignment takes the form

$$LHS := RHS$$

where $LHS$ is either a variable or an access of a compound value in the form $X[\ldots]$. When $LHS$ is a variable, the assignment does not actually assign the value of $RHS$ to $LHS$. Instead, it creates a new variable for $LHS$ to hold the value of $RHS$. After the assignment, whenever $LHS$ is accessed in the body, the new variable is accessed. When $LHS$ is an access in the form $X[I]$, the component of $X$ indexed $I$ is updated. This update is undone if execution backtracks over this assignment.

An assignment in the form X[I] := RHS has global side effects, since the compound term that is referenced by X is destructively updated, like an assignment in an imperative language. An assignment in the form X := RHS, where X is a variable, only has a side effect within the body of the rule in which the assignment occurs. Recall that the compiler introduces a new variable for X and replaces the remaining occurrences of $X$ by the new variable. Variable assignments do not have cross-predicate or cross-function side effects.

An assignment makes it possible to use a variable to hold values at different stages during computation without inventing new variable names. With assignments, Picat is able to provide while loops that repeat under a condition. A while loop has the form:

```
while (Cond)
    Goal
end
```

As long as $Cond$ succeeds, the loop will repeatedly execute $Goal$. A do-while loop has the form:

```
do
    Goal
while (Cond)
```

A do-while loop is similar to a while loop, except that a do-while loop executes $Goal$ one time before testing $Cond$. In order for a while loop to make sense,

*Goal* must contain assignments that change some variables in *Cond*, unless the loop is meant to be an infinite loop.[3]

## 2.5   Constraint Modeling

Picat provides three solver modules, `cp`, `sat`, and `mip`, for modeling and solving constraint satisfaction and optimization problems (CSPs). As a constraint programming language, Picat resembles CLP(FD) [3]: the operators `::` and `notin` are used for domain constraints, the operators `#=`, `#!=`, `#>`, `#>=`, `#<`, `#<=`, and `#=<` are used for arithmetic constraints, and the operators `#/\` (and), `#\/` (or), `#^` (xor), `#~` (not), `#=>` (if), and `#<=>` (iff) are used for Boolean constraints. Picat supports several global constraints, such as `all_different/1`, `element/3`, and `cumulative/4`. In addition to intensional constraints, Picat also provides two predicates for expressing extensional constraints: `table_in/2` and `table_notin/2`.

The following gives a solution for the Fashion Police problem, which was used in GCJ Round 1 C 2016.[4] You have brought along $J$ different jackets (numbered $1, \ldots, J$), $P$ different pairs of pants (numbered $1, \ldots, P$), and $S$ different shirts $(1, \ldots, S)$, $J \leq P \leq S$. Every day, you will pick one jacket, one pair of pants, and one shirt to wear as an outfit. You will be put into jail if you have worn the exact same outfit twice or if you have worn the same two-garment combination more than $K$ times in total for some input $K$. Determine the maximum number of days that you will be able to avoid being taken to jail. The problem entails finding a maximum subset of outfits that satisfies the cardinality limit. For example, for $J = 1$, $P = 1$, $S = 3$, and $K = 2$, the answer is 2, because (1,1,1) and (1,1,2) are possible outfits, while adding the third outfit (1,1,3) to the list will violate the cardinality limit.

```
import util, sat.

main =>
    T = read_line().to_int(),
    foreach (TC in 1..T)
        [J,P,S,K] = [to_int(Token) : Token in read_line().split()],
        not not do_case(TC,J,P,S,K)
    end.

do_case(TC,J,P,S,K) =>
    L = {{Ij,Ip,Is} : Ij in 1..J, Ip in 1..P, Is in 1..S},
    N = J * P * S,
    Bs = new_array(N),
    Bs :: 0..1,
    sum(Bs) #=< J * P * K,    % pigeonhole principle
    foreach (R1 in 1..N)
        L[R1] = {Ij,Ip,Is},
        if S > K then
```

---

[3] It is possible to write an infinite loop as `while (true)` *Goal* `end`.
[4] https://code.google.com/codejam/contest/4314486/dashboard#s=p2\&a=2.

```
        Bs[R1] #=> sum([Bs[R2] : R2 in 1..N, L[R2] = {Ij,Ip,_}]) #=< K
    end,
    if P > K then
        Bs[R1] #=> sum([Bs[R2] : R2 in 1..N, L[R2] = {Ij,_,Is}]) #=< K
    end,
    if J > K then
        Bs[R1] #=> sum([Bs[R2] : R2 in 1..N, L[R2] = {_,Ip,Is}]) #=< K
    end
end,
solve([$max(sum(Bs))],Bs),
printf("Case #%w: %w\n", TC,sum(Bs)),
foreach (R in 1..N, Bs[R] == 1, L[R] = {Ij,Ip,Is})
    printf("%w %w %w\n", Ij,Ip,Is)
end.
```

The `main` predicate first reads in an integer T, which is the number of test cases. For each test case TC in 1..T, the body of the loop reads in J, P, S, and K in one line. The call `do_case(TC,J,P,S,K)` solves the case.[5]

The `do_case` predicate creates an array L of all possible outfits, computes the number of possible outfits N, and creates an array Bs of N Boolean variables. Each outfit is associated with one Boolean variable, which indicates whether the outfit is in the subset. The constraint `sum(Bs) #=< J * P * K` encodes the pigeonhole principle.[6]

The `foreach` loop ensures that no pair of garments occurs in outfits more than K times in the subset. For an outfit number R1, let {Ij,Ip,Is} be the outfit. The constraint

```
Bs[R1] #=> sum([Bs[R2] : R2 in 1..N, L[R2] = {Ij,Ip,_}]) #=< K
```

ensures that, if the outfit {Ij,Ip,Is} is in the subset (Bs[R1] = 1), then the number of the jacket-pants pair {Ij,Ip} does not occur in the outfits more than K times in the subset. This constraint is only generated if S > K, because if S ≤ K, it is impossible to have more than K pairs of {Ij,Ip}. The `foreach` loop also generates cardinality constraints to ensure that the number of jacket-shirt pairs and the number of pants-shirt pairs do not exceed the limit.

The statement `solve([$max(sum(Bs))],Bs)` calls the SAT solver to solve the constraints such that the objective `sum(Bs)` is maximized.

GCJ problems normally require some amount of insight to solve, even for small datasets. This program is based on a straightforward model. Nevertheless, it solves the large dataset in 3 min, which is within the time limit of 8 min. This example demonstrates the use of Picat's language constructs, including arrays, loops, and list comprehensions, in modeling constraint problems.

## 3   Canonicalizing the Language Constructs

The Picat implementation adopts the virtual machine TOAM [17], which is a redesign of the Warren Abstract Machine [16] for fast software emulation. TOAM

---

[5] The double negation `not not` is used here to discard the generated constraints after the case is done.

[6] Since $J \leq P \leq S$, $\min(J \times P \times K, P \times S \times K, J \times S \times K)$ equals $J \times P \times K$.

provides instructions for encoding pattern-matching rules. An extended TOAM, which supports tabling and constraint propagation, is described in [17]. The Picat implementation reuses codes from the B-Prolog system, except the parser, the preprocessor, and many library built-ins. An early implementation of the SAT compiler, which translates high-level constraints into CNF, is given in [19].

Picat translates programs into a canonical form, which is further compiled into TOAM. This section describes the canonical form and the translation of Picat's different language constructs into the form. The compilation of the canonical form into TOAM is detailed in [17].

## 3.1 Canonical-Form Rules

A *canonical-form* rule takes one of the following forms:

$$Head, Cond \Rightarrow Body.$$
$$Head, Cond \text{ ?=> } Body.$$

A canonical-form rule is different from the source-language rule in that *Cond* and *Body* do not include functions, comprehensions, loops, or assignments; all of these constructs are compiled away by Picat's preprocessor.

## 3.2 Transformation of Functions

Picat replaces a function call $f(t_1, \ldots, t_n)$ by a new variable $V$, and inserts a new predicate call $p(t_1, \ldots, t_n, V)$ before the goal in which the function call occurs. For a rule in the definition of $f/n$

$$f(t_1, \ldots, t_n) = Exp, Cond \Rightarrow Body.$$

Picat translates it into the following predicate rule:

$$p(t_1, \ldots, t_n, V), Cond \Rightarrow Body, V = Exp.$$

Picat employs an optimization to generate a tail-recursive rule if *Exp* is a list.

Consider, for example, the following function conc, which concatenates two lists:

```
conc([], Ys) = Ys.
conc([X|Xs], Ys) = [X | conc(Xs, Ys)].
```

Picat translates it into the following predicate:

```
conc_p([], Ys, Zs) => Zs = Ys.
conc_p([X|Xs], Ys, Zs) =>
    Zs = [X|Zs1],
    conc_p(Xs, Ys, Zs1).
```

The Picat compiler incorporates the *tail-recursion optimization*, which translates tail-recursive deterministic predicates into iteration. A call to conc_p only allocates one frame on the stack, no matter how long the list is.

### 3.3    Transformation of Comprehensions

Picat translates a list comprehension into a `foreach` loop that uses := to accumulate values. The list comprehension

$$[Exp : E_1 \text{ in } D_1, Cond_1, \ldots, E_n \text{ in } D_n, Cond_n]$$

is replaced by a new variable L, and the following statements are inserted into the context:

```
L = Tail,
foreach (E₁ in D₁, Cond₁, ..., Eₙ in Dₙ, Condₙ)
    Tail = [Exp|NewVar],
    Tail := NewVar,
end,
Tail = []
```

Initially, `Tail` is a free variable. In the body of the loop, the call

```
Tail = [Exp|NewVar]
```

binds `Tail` to the term `[Exp|NewVar]`, and the assignment `Tail := NewVar` lets `Tail` reference the new tail. After the loop, the call `Tail = []` binds `Tail` to `[]`, completing the list. An alternative translation is possible, which begins with an empty list, and attaches each value to the end of the list. However, this translation is not efficient, since it takes linear time to add a value to the end of a list.

List comprehensions that occur in aggregate functions, including `sum(L)`, `min(L)`, `max(L)`, and `len(L)`, are compiled in such a way that an aggregate value is computed, rather than a list. For example, the function call

```
sum([f(I) : I in 1..100])
```

is replaced by a new variable Sum, and the following statements are inserted into the context:

```
S = 0,
foreach (I in 1..100)
    S := S + f(I)
end,
Sum = S
```

### 3.4    Transformation of Pure `foreach` Loops

Picat translates loops into tail-recursive predicates. Consider pure `foreach` loops that do not contain assignments. Without loss of generality, consider a `foreach` loop that has only one iterator:

```
foreach (E in D)
    Goal
end
```

The general form of the `foreach` loop can be converted into this form by introducing if-then statements and nested loops into the loop goal. For a loop statement that has nested loops, the inner-most loop is transformed first.

Let $V_1$, $V_2$, ..., $V_n$ be the global variables in *Goal*, i.e., variables that occur before the loop in the context. If $D$ is a list, then the loop is replaced by a predicate call in the form $p(V_1, V_1, \ldots, V_n, D)$, where $p$ is a newly generated predicate:

```
p(V₁,V₁,...,Vₙ,[]) => true.
p(V₁,V₁,...,Vₙ,[E|T]) => Goal, p(V₁,V₁,...,Vₙ,T).
```

Note that local variables in *Goal* are not passed to predicate $p$, and are naturally localized. If $D$ is an array or a range in the form `LB..Step..UB`, then the generated predicate takes extra arguments for iterating over the array or the range using recursion.

## 3.5    Transformation of Assignments

An assignment that updates a compound value is transformed into a built-in predicate called `segarg`. This subsection shows how to transform assigned variables.

For an assignment $LHS := RHS$ that occurs in a conjunction of goals, Picat introduces a new variable for $LHS$ that holds the value of $RHS$. For example, consider the following rule:

```
test => X = 0, X := X + 1,  X := X + 2, write(X).
```

Picat creates a new variable, say X1, to hold the value of X after the assignment X := X + 1. Picat replaces X by X1 on the LHS of the assignment. All occurrences of X after the assignment are replaced by X1. When encountering X1 := X1 + 2, Picat creates another new variable, say X2, to hold the value of X1 after the assignment, and replaces the remaining occurrences of X1 by X2. When `write(X2)` is executed, the value held in X2 is printed. After preprocessing, the rule is translated into the following:

```
test => X = 0, X1 = X + 1, X2 = X1 + 2, write(X2).
```

For an assignment that occurs in if-then-else, Picat introduces a new predicate. Consider the following example:

```
go(Z) =>
    X = 1, Y = 2,
    if Z > 0 then
        X := X * Z
    else
        Y := Y + Z
    end,
    println([X,Y]).
```

Picat translates the program into the following:

```
go(Z) =>
    X = 1, Y = 2,
    p(X, Xout, Y, Yout, Z),
    println([Xout,Yout]).

p(Xin, Xout, Yin, Yout, Z), Z > 0 =>
    Xout = Xin * Z,
    Yout = Yin.
p(Xin, Xout, Yin, Yout, Z) =>
    Xout = Xin,
    Yout = Yin + Z.
```

One rule is generated for each branch of the if-then-else statement. For each variable V that occurs on the LHS of an assignment that is inside of the if-then-else statement, predicate p is passed two arguments, Vin and Vout. In the above example, X and Y each occur on the LHS of an assignment. Therefore, predicate p is passed the parameters Xin, Xout, Yin, and Yout.

Similarly, for an assignment that occurs in a loop, Picat passes two variables to the predicate for the loop: one variable holds the value before the loop goal is executed, and the other holds the value after the loop goal is executed. Consider the following example:

```
sum_list(L, Sum) =>
    S = 0,
    foreach (E in L)
        S := S + E
    end,
    Sum = S.
```

Picat translates the program into the following:

```
sum_list(L, Sum) =>
    S = 0,
    p(L, S, Sout),
    Sum = Sout.

p([], Sin, Sout) =>
    Sout = Sin.
p([E|T], Sin, Sout) =>
    St = Sin + E,
    p(T, St, Sout).
```

In addition to the list L, Picat passes arguments S and Sout to predicate p. Note that only the global variables that occur within the loop are passed to p.

## 4   Related Work

The canonical-form language that is used in the Picat compiler is called *matching clauses* in B-Prolog [17]. This canonical form narrows the gap between the high-level constructs and the underlying virtual machine.

Functions are naturally a basic notion in functional logic languages, such as Curry [5]. Picat, like other logic programming languages, such as Mercury [9] and Ciao [7], provides functions as a syntax extension. Picat has limited support for higher-order predicates and functions, and does not support lambda expressions. The use of higher-order calls in Picat is discouraged because of the overhead.

Classic functional and logic languages rely on recursion and higher-order facilities to describe repetitions. Many modern languages, such as F#[7] and OCaml[8], provide looping constructs. Picat's `foreach` loop is similar to B-Prolog's `foreach` loop [17], which was inspired by logical loops in ECLiPSe [12]. In ECLiPSe, variables are assumed to be local to each iteration, unless they are declared global. In B-Prolog, variables are assumed to be global to all of the iterations, unless they are declared local. In contrast, Picat adopts a simple and clean scoping rule for variables, which renders the declaration of local or global variables unnecessary.

The list comprehension, which can be traced back to SETL [13], was made popular by Haskell. The optimization that computes a value instead of creating a list when a comprehension is immediately fed into an aggregate function, such as `sum`, is a special application of the idea of deforestation [14]. The same idea is employed in compiling loops whose iterators contain the range `..` and the `zip` function. The Picat compiler does not apply deforestation to user-defined functions or built-in functions in other contexts.

It is rare for declarative languages to provide assignments. An assignment of the form `S[I] := RHS` is similar to the `setarg` built-in in Prolog. An assignment of the form `X := RHS`, where X is a variable, is translated into unification at compile time. The transformation rules that eliminate assignments are employed in building the static single assignment form (SSA) for imperative programs, which simplifies program analysis and compilation [2]. The Picat compiler introduces a new predicate for every branching statement that contains assignments, even for if-then-else, which could be compiled inline. This makes it unnecessary to introduce a phi function [2] when branches merge.

There are abundant examples that demonstrate the usefulness and convenience of Picat's language constructs for modeling. In [4], several examples are given for GCJ problems.

## 5   Conclusion

This paper has presented the Picat language, and has shown how to compile Picat's high-level language constructs into canonical-form pattern-matching rules. The high-level language constructs give Picat flexibility and brevity needed for scripting. Picat provides a comprehensive box of tools for describing and solving combinatorial search problems. The high-level constructs also facilitate modeling with these tools.

**Acknowledgement.** Neng-Fa Zhou is supported in part by the NSF under the grant number CCF1618046.

---

[7] http://fsharp.org/.
[8] http://ocaml.org/.

# References

1. Colmerauer, A.: Equations and inequations on finite and infinite trees. In: Proceedings of FGCS, pp. 85–99. ICOT (1984)
2. Cytron, R., Ferrante, J., Rosen, B.K., Wegman, M.N., Zadeck, F.K.: Efficiently computing static single assignment form, the control dependence graph. ACM Trans. Program. Lang. Syst. **13**(4), 451–490 (1991)
3. Dincbas, M., Van Hentenryck, P., Simonis, H., Aggoun, A., Graf, T., Berthier, F.: The constraint logic programming language CHIP. In FGCS, pp. 693–702 (1988)
4. Dymchenko, S., Mykhailova, M.: Declaratively solving Google code jam problems with Picat. In: Pontelli, E., Son, T.C. (eds.) PADL 2015. LNCS, vol. 9131, pp. 50–57. Springer, Cham (2015). doi:10.1007/978-3-319-19686-2_4
5. Hanus, M.: Functional logic programming: from theory to curry. In: Programming Logics, pp. 123–168 (2013)
6. Van Hentenryck, P.: Constraint and integer programming in OPL. INFORMS J. Comput. **14**, 2002 (2002)
7. Hermenegildo, M.V., Bueno, F., Carro, M., López-García, P., Mera, E., Morales, J.F., Puebla, G.: An overview of Ciao and its design philosophy. Theor. Pract. Logic Program. **12**(1–2), 219–252 (2012)
8. Kowalski, R., Kuehner, D.: Linear resolution with selection function. Artif. Intell. **2**(3–4), 227–260 (1971)
9. Mercury. http://www.mercurylang.org/
10. Nethercote, N., Stuckey, P.J., Becket, R., Brand, S., Duck, G.J., Tack, G.: MiniZinc: towards a standard CP modelling language. In: Principles and Practice of Constraint Programming, pp. 529–543 (2007)
11. Schimpf, J.: Logical loops. In: Stuckey, P.J. (ed.) ICLP 2002. LNCS, vol. 2401, pp. 224–238. Springer, Heidelberg (2002). doi:10.1007/3-540-45619-8_16
12. Schimpf, J., Shen, K.: Eclipse-from LP to CLP. Theor. Pract. Logic Program. **12**(1–2), 127–156 (2012)
13. Schwartz, J.T., Dewar, R.B.K., Dubinsky, E., Schonberg, E.: Programming with Sets - An Introduction to SETL. Springer, New York (1986)
14. Wadler, P.: Deforestation: transforming programs to eliminate trees. Theor. Comput. Sci. **73**(2), 231–248 (1990)
15. Warren, D.H.D.: High-order extensions to Prolog - are they needed? Mach. Intell. **10**, 441–454 (1982)
16. Warren, D.H.D.: An abstract Prolog instruction set. Technical note 309, SRI International (1983)
17. Zhou, N.-F.: The language features and architecture of B-Prolog. Theor. Pract. Logic Program. **12**(1–2), 189–218 (2012)
18. Zhou, N.-F., Barták, R., Dovier, A.: Planning as tabled logic programming. In: Theory and Practice of Logic Programming (2015)
19. Zhou, N.-F., Kjellerstrand, H.: The Picat-SAT compiler. In: Gavanelli, M., Reppy, J. (eds.) PADL 2016. LNCS, vol. 9585, pp. 48–62. Springer, Cham (2016). doi:10.1007/978-3-319-28228-2_4
20. Zhou, N.-F., Kjellerstrand, H., Fruhman, J.: Constraint Solving and Planning with Picat. Springer, Heidelberg (2015)

# An Overview of PρLog

Besik Dundua[1], Temur Kutsia[2(✉)], and Klaus Reisenberger-Hagmayer[3]

[1] Vekua Institute of Applied Mathematics, Tbilisi State University, Tbilisi, Georgia
[2] RISC, Johannes Kepler University, Linz, Austria
kutsia@risc.jku.at
[3] Johannes Kepler University, Linz, Austria

**Abstract.** This paper describes PρLog: a tool that combines Prolog with the ρLog calculus. Such a combination brings strategy-controlled conditional transformation rules into logic programming. They operate on sequences of terms. Transformations may lead to several results, which can be explored by backtracking. Strategies provide a control on rule applications in a declarative way. They are programmable: users can construct complex strategies from simpler ones by special combinators. Different types of first- and second-order variables provide flexible control on selecting parts from sequences or terms. As a result, the obtained code is usually pretty compact and declaratively clear. In programs, PρLog-specific code can be intermixed with the standard Prolog code. The tool is implemented and tested in SWI-Prolog.

## 1 Introduction

PρLog is a tool that combines, on the one hand, the power of logic programming and, on the other hand, the flexibility of strategy-based conditional transformation systems. Its terms are built over function symbols without fixed arity, using four different kinds of variables: for individual terms, for sequences of terms, for function symbols, and for contexts. These variables help to traverse tree forms of expressions both in horizontal and vertical directions, in one or more steps. A powerful matching algorithm helps to replace several steps of recursive computations by pattern matching, which facilitates writing short and intuitively quite clear code. By the backtracking engine, nondeterministic computations are modeled naturally. Prolog's meta-programming capabilities allowed to easily write a compiler from PρLog programs (that consist of a specific Prolog code, actually) into pure Prolog programs.

PρLog program clauses either define user-constructed strategies by transformation rules or are ordinary Prolog clauses. Prolog code can be used freely within PρLog programs, which is especially convenient when some built-in primitives, arithmetic calculations, or input-output features are needed.

PρLog is based on the ρLog calculus [17] and, essentially, is its executable implementation. The inference system of the calculus is basically the SLDNF-resolution, with normal logic program semantics [15]. Therefore, Prolog was a natural choice to implement it.

© Springer International Publishing AG 2017
Y. Lierler and W. Taha (Eds.): PADL 2017, LNCS 10137, pp. 34–49, 2017.
DOI: 10.1007/978-3-319-51676-9_3

Originally, the ρLog calculus evolved from experiments with extending the language of Mathematica [24] by a package for advanced rule-based programming [16,18]. Later, these developments influenced an extension of another symbolic computation system, Maple [19], by a rule-based programming package called symbtrans (an adaptation of ρLog) used for automatic derivation of multiscale models of arrays of micro- and nanosystems, see, e.g., [2].

The ρLog calculus has been influenced by the ρ-calculus [5], which, in itself, is a foundation for the rule-based programming system ELAN [3]. There are some other languages for programming by rules, such as ASF-SDF [21], CHR [12], Claire [4], Maude [6], Stratego [22], Tom [1], just to name a few. The ρLog calculus and, consequently, PρLog differs from them, first of all, by its pattern matching capabilities. Besides, it adopts logic programming semantics (clauses are first class concepts, rules/strategies are expressed as clauses) and makes a heavy use of strategies to control transformations. In earlier papers, we showed its applicability for XML transformation and Web reasoning [7], and in modeling rewriting strategies [10]. More recently, it has been used in extraction of frequent patterns from data mining workflows [20].

The mentioned application papers, naturally, described the language and some features of PρLog, but they did not give an overview of the entire system. Moreover, there have been some new developments meanwhile: the library of built-in strategies has been modified and extended, a lighter version of PρLog has been implemented, an Emacs based development environment appeared. Therefore, we decided to describe the current status of the tool in this paper: to explain by simple examples how it works, discuss the language, architecture, built-in strategies, and the development environment.

PρLog sources, Emacs mode, and help on built-in strategies can be downloaded from its Web page

http://www.risc.jku.at/people/tkutsia/software/prholog/.

The current version has been tested for SWI-Prolog [23] version 7.2.3 or later.

## 2  Overview

PρLog atoms are supposed to transform term sequences. Transformations are labeled by what we call *strategies*. Such labels (which themselves can be compound terms, not necessarily constant symbols) help to construct more complex transformations from simpler ones.

An instance of a transformation is finding duplicated elements in a sequence and removing one of them. Let us call this process double merging. The following strategy implements the idea:

$$\text{merge\_doubles} :: (s\_X, i\_x, s\_Y, i\_x, s\_Z) \Longrightarrow (s\_X, i\_x, s\_Y, s\_Z).$$

The code, as one can see, is pretty short. merge_doubles is the strategy name. It is followed by the separator :: which separates the strategy name from the transformation. Then comes the transformation itself in the form $lhs \implies rhs$. It says that if the sequence in $lhs$ contains duplicates (expressed by two copies of the variable $i\_x$, which can match individual terms and therefore, is called an *individual variable*) somewhere, then from these two copies only the first one should be kept in $rhs$. That "somewhere" is expressed by three *sequence variables*, where $s\_X$ stands for the subsequence before the first occurrence of $i\_x$, $s\_Y$ takes the subsequence between two occurrences of $i\_x$, and $s\_Z$ matches the remaining part. These subsequences remain unchanged in the $rhs$. In P$\rho$Log, variable names start with the first letter of their kind (there are four kinds of variables: *individual, sequence, function, context*), followed by the underscore. After the underscore, there comes the actual name. For anonymous variables, we write just $i\_$, $s\_$, $f\_$, $c\_$.

Note that one does not need to code the actual search process of doubles explicitly. The matching algorithm does the job instead, looking for an appropriate instantiation of the variables. There can be several such instantiations.

Now one can ask, e.g., to merge doubles in a number sequence $(1, 2, 3, 2, 1)$:

$$?\text{- merge\_doubles} :: (1, 2, 3, 2, 1) \implies s\_Result.$$

First, P$\rho$Log returns the substitution $\{s\_Result \mapsto (1, 2, 3, 2)\}$. Like in Prolog, the user may ask for more solutions, and, via backtracking, P$\rho$Log gives the second answer $\{s\_Result \mapsto (1, 2, 3, 1)\}$. Both are obtained from $(1, 2, 3, 2, 1)$ by merging one pair of duplicates.

A double-free sequence is just a normal form of this single-step merge\_doubles transformation. P$\rho$Log has a built-in strategy for computing normal forms, denoted by **nf**, and we can use it to define a new strategy merge\_all\_doubles in the following clause (where :-, as in Prolog, stands for the inverse implication):

$$\text{merge\_all\_doubles} :: s\_X \implies s\_Y \text{ :- } \mathbf{nf}(\text{merge\_doubles}) :: s\_X \implies s\_Y, !.$$

The effect of **nf** is that it applies merge\_doubles to $s\_X$, repeating this process iteratively as long as it is possible, i.e., as long as doubles can be merged in the obtained sequences. When merge\_doubles is no more applicable, it means that the normal form of the transformation is reached. It is returned in $s\_Y$.

Note the Prolog cut at the end. It cuts the alternative ways of computing the same normal form. In fact, Prolog primitives and clauses can be used in P$\rho$Log programs. Now, for the query

$$?\text{- merge\_all\_doubles} :: (1, 2, 3, 2, 1) \implies s\_Result.$$

we get a single answer $s\_Result \mapsto (1, 2, 3)$.

Instead of the cut, we could define merge\_all\_doubles purely in P$\rho$Log terms:

$$\text{merge\_all\_doubles} :: s\_X \implies s\_Y \text{ :-}$$
$$\mathbf{first\_one}(\mathbf{nf}(\text{merge\_doubles})) :: s\_X \implies s\_Y.$$

**first_one** is another PρLog built-in strategy. It applies to a sequence of strategies, finds the first one among them, which successfully transforms the input sequence, and gives back just *one result* of the transformation. Here it has a single argument strategy **nf**(merge_doubles) and returns (by instantiating $s\_Y$) only one result of its application to $s\_X$.

In the last clause, the transformation is exactly the same in the clause head and in the (singleton) body, and both have sequence variables in the left and right hand sides ($s\_X$ and $s\_Y$). In such cases we can use more succinct notation:

$$\text{merge\_all\_doubles} := \textbf{first\_one}(\textbf{nf}(\text{merge\_doubles})).$$

This form is called the *strategy definition* form: the strategy in its left hand side (here merge_all_doubles) is defined as the strategy in its right hand side (here **first_one**(**nf**(merge_doubles))).

PρLog is good not only in selecting arbitrarily many subexpressions in "horizontal direction" (by sequence variables), but also in working in "vertical direction", selecting subterms at arbitrary depth. *Context variables* provide this flexibility, by matching the context above the subterm to be selected. A context is a term with a single "hole" in it. When it applies to a term, the latter is "plugged in" the hole, replacing it. Syntactically, the hole is denoted by a special constant. In the PρLog system it is `hole`, but here in the paper we use a more conventional notation •. There is yet another kind of variable, called *function variable*, which stands for a function symbol. With the help of these constructs and the merge_doubles strategy, it is pretty easy to define a transformation that merges double branches in a tree, represented as a term:

$$\text{merge\_double\_branches} ::$$
$$c\_Context(f\_Fun(s\_X)) \Longrightarrow c\_Context(f\_Fun(s\_Y)) \text{ :-}$$
$$\text{merge\_doubles} :: s\_X \Longrightarrow s\_Y.$$

Here $c\_Context$ is a context variable and $f\_Fun$ is a function variable. Now, we can ask to merge double branches in a given tree:

$$?\text{- merge\_double\_branches} ::$$
$$f(g(a,b,a,h(c,c)),\ h(c),\ g(a,a,b,h(c))) \Longrightarrow i\_Result.$$

PρLog returns three results, one after the other, by backtracking:

$$\{i\_Result \mapsto f(g(a,b,h(c,c)),\ h(c),\ g(a,a,b,h(c)))\},$$
$$\{i\_Result \mapsto f(g(a,b,a,h(c)),\ h(c),\ g(a,a,b,h(c)))\},$$
$$\{i\_Result \mapsto f(g(a,b,a,h(c,c)),\ h(c),\ g(a,b,h(c)))\}.$$

To obtain the first one, PρLog matched the context variable $c\_Context$ to the context $f(\bullet,\ h(c),g(a,a,b,h(c)))$, the function variable $f\_Fun$ to the function symbol $g$, and the sequence variable $s\_X$ to the sequence $(a,b,a,h(c,c))$. merge_doubles transformed $(a,b,a,h(c,c))$ to $(a,b,h(c,c))$. The other results have been obtained by taking different contexts and respective subbranches.

The right hand side of transformations in the queries need not be variables. One can have an arbitrary sequence there. For instance, we may be interested in trees that contain $h(c, c)$:

?- merge_double_branches ::
$$f(g(a, b, a, h(c, c)),\ h(c),\ g(a, a, b, h(c))) \implies c\_C(h(c, c)).$$

We get here two answers, which show instantiations of $c\_C$ by the relevant contexts:

$$\{c\_C \mapsto f(g(a, b, \bullet),\ h(c),\ g(a, a, b, h(c)))\},$$
$$\{c\_C \mapsto f(g(a, b, a, \bullet),\ h(c),\ g(a, b, h(c)))\}.$$

Similar to merging all doubles in a sequence above, we can also define a strategy that merges all identical branches in a tree repeatedly. It is not surprising that the built-in strategy for normal forms plays a role also here:

merge_all_double_branches := **first_one**(**nf**(merge_double_branches)).

For the query

?- merge_all_double_branches ::
$$f(g(a, b, a, h(c, c)),\ h(c),\ g(a, a, b, h(c))) \implies s\_Result.$$

we get a single answer $\{s\_Result \mapsto f(g(a, b, h(c)), h(c))\}$.

Finally, note that a strategy can be defined by several clauses, which are treated as alternatives.

# 3   The P$\rho$Log Language

From the brief overview above one can get a pretty clear idea about the P$\rho$Log language: Its terms and sequences are constructed from function symbols that do not have fixed arity (variadic, aka unranked, function symbols), using the four kinds of variables. The constant hole is the exception: it is always used without arguments. More precisely, terms are either individual variables, or expressions of one of the following forms: $f(\tilde{s})$, $f\_F(\tilde{s})$, or $c\_C(t)$, where $f$ is an unranked function symbol, $t$ is a term, and $\tilde{s}$ is a finite (possibly empty) sequence of terms or sequence variables. (These sequences are sometimes called hedges.) The empty sequence is denoted in the system with **eps** (for $\epsilon$), but we use more conventional notation ( ) in the paper. Two sequences can be concatenated into one, where the empty sequence plays the role of the unit element of this (meta-level) concatenation operation. Sequences are written in the parenthesis for easy parsing (when they contain more than one element) and are flat. A singleton sequence is identified with its sole element. Contexts are terms with a unique occurrence of the hole. The previous section contains several examples of terms, sequences, and contexts.

Substitutions map individual variables to terms, sequence variables to sequences, function variables to function symbols or function variables, and context variables to contexts. For example, $\{c\_Ctx \mapsto f(\bullet), i\_Term \mapsto g(s\_X), f\_Fun \mapsto g, s\_H_1 \mapsto (), s\_H_2 \mapsto (b, c)\}$ is a substitution. We can apply substitutions to sequences, which gives sequences as a result. In particular, if the sequence is a singleton term, then the result of the application is also a term. Applying the substitution above to a sequence $(c\_Ctx(i\_Term), f\_Fun(s\_H_1, a, s\_H_2))$ give the sequence $(f(g(s\_X)), g(a, b, c))$.

Note that sequence variables are not terms, and context variables always apply to terms, not to arbitrary sequences. This makes terms and contexts closed under substitution application.

The main computational mechanism for PρLog is matching. Due to sequence and context variables, it is finitary, which means that a matching problem may have finitely many solutions. For instance, the sequence $(s\_X, i\_x, s\_Y, i\_x, s\_Z)$ matches $(1, 2, 3, 2, 1)$ in two different ways:

- $\{s\_X \mapsto (), i\_x \mapsto 1, s\_Y \mapsto (2, 3, 2), s\_Z \mapsto ()\}$,
- $\{s\_X \mapsto 1, i\_x \mapsto 2, s\_Y \mapsto 3, s\_Z \mapsto 1\}$.

In the previous section, we also saw two solutions to the problem of matching $c\_C(h(c, c))$ to the result of applying the strategy merge_double_branches to the term $f(g(a, b, a, h(c, c)), h(c), g(a, a, b, h(c)))$.

A ρLog atom (ρ-atom) is a triple consisting of a strategy $st$ (which is a term) and two (hole-free) sequences $\tilde{s}_1$ and $\tilde{s}_2$, written as $st :: \tilde{s}_1 \Longrightarrow \tilde{s}_2$. Its negation is written as $st :: \tilde{s}_1 \not\Longrightarrow \tilde{s}_2$. A ρLog literal (ρ-literal) is a ρ-atom or its negation. A PρLog clause is either a Prolog clause, or a clause of the form $st :: \tilde{s}_1 \Longrightarrow \tilde{s}_2$ :- body (called a ρ-clause) where body is a (possibly empty) conjunction of ρ- and Prolog literals. Strategy definitions $str_1 := str_2$ are shortcuts for clauses of the form $str_1 :: s\_X \Longrightarrow s\_Y$ :- $str_2 :: s\_X \Longrightarrow s\_Y$.

In fact, PρLog clauses may have a more complex structure, when (some of) the literals are equipped with membership constraints, constraining possible values of sequence and context variables. Such constraints are taken into account in the matching process. For simplicity, we do not consider them in this paper.

A PρLog program is a sequence of PρLog clauses. A query is a conjunction of ρ- and Prolog literals. A restriction on variable occurrence is imposed on clauses: ρ-clauses and queries can contain only PρLog variables, while Prolog clauses and queries can contain only Prolog variables. If a ρ-clause or a query contains a Prolog literal, the only variables that can occur in that literal are PρLog individual variables. (When it comes to evaluating such Prolog literals, the individual variables are converted into Prolog variables.) A detailed description of PρLog syntax can be found in the technical report [11] and on its Web page.

We need to make sure that in the program execution process, all solving problems that arise for PρLog clauses and queries are matching problems, not unification. The reason is that matching for our language is finitary [14], while unification is infinitary [8, 13]. The latter is undesirable, because it would cause infinite branching in the program execution tree. Therefore, we would like to restrict the solving to the fragment that guarantees an existence of a terminating finitary procedure. Matching is one of such possible fragments. The restriction we impose on clauses and queries is well-modedness, extends the same notion for logic programs, introduced in [9]. It forbids uninstantiated variables to appear in one of the sides of unification problems and, hence, only matching problems arise.

More specifically, well-modedness is based on the notion of mode of a relation. A mode for the relation $\cdot :: \cdot \implies \cdot$ is a function that defines the input and output positions of the relation respectively as $in(\cdot :: \cdot \implies \cdot) = \{1,2\}$ and $out(\cdot :: \cdot \implies \cdot) = \{3\}$. A mode is defined (uniquely) for a Prolog relation as well. A clause is moded if all its predicate symbols are moded. We assume that all $\rho$-clauses are moded. As for the Prolog clauses, we require modedness only for those ones that define a predicate that occurs in the body of some $\rho$-clause. If a Prolog literal occurs in a query in conjunction with a $\rho$-clause, then its relation and the clauses that define this relation are also assumed to be moded.

Roughly, the idea of well-modedness is that the variables in the input positions should already be seen in the output positions of some earlier literals. Before defining it formally, we introduce the notation $vars(E)$ for a set of variables occurring in an expression $E$, and define $vars(E, \{p_1, ..., p_n\}) = \cup_{i=1}^{n} vars(E|_{p_i})$, where $E|_{p_i}$ is the standard notation for a subexpression of $E$ at position $p_i$. The symbol $\mathcal{V}_a$ stands for the set of anonymous variables. A ground expression contains no variables. Then well-moded queries and clauses are defined as follows:

**Definition 1.** A query $L_1, ..., L_n$ is well-moded *iff the following conditions hold for each $1 \leq i \leq n$:*

- $vars(L_i, in(L_i)) \subseteq \cup_{j=1}^{i-1} vars(L_j, out(L_j)) \setminus \mathcal{V}_a$.
- If $L_i$ is a negative literal, then $vars(L_i, out(L_i)) \subseteq \cup_{j=1}^{i-1} vars(L_j, out(L_j)) \cup \mathcal{V}_a$.
- If $L_i$ is a $\rho$-literal, then its strategy term is ground.

A clause $L_0 :- L_1, ..., L_n$ is well-moded *iff the following hold for each $1 \leq i \leq n$:*

- $vars(L_i, in(L_i)) \cup vars(L_0, out(L_0)) \subseteq \cup_{j=0}^{i-1} vars(L_j, out(L_j)) \setminus \mathcal{V}_a$.
- If $L_i$ is a negative literal, then

$$vars(L_i, out(L_i)) \subseteq \cup_{j=1}^{i-1} vars(L_j, out(L_j)) \cup \mathcal{V}_a \cup vars(L_0, in(L_0)).$$

- If $L_0$ and $L_i$ are $\rho$-literals with the strategy terms $st_0$ and $st_i$, respectively, then $vars(st_i) \subseteq vars(st_0)$.

It is easy to see that the clauses and queries in Figs. 1 and 2 are well-moded.

P$\rho$Log prologwell-moded. Well-modedness of queries is checked when they are evaluated. There is no restriction on the Prolog clauses if the predicate they define is not used in a $\rho$-clause.

P$\rho$Log execution principle is based on depth-first inference with leftmost literal selection in the goal. If the selected literal is a Prolog literal, then it is evaluated in the standard way. If it is a $\rho$-atom of the form $st :: \tilde{s}_1 \implies \tilde{s}_2$, the crucial thing is that, due to well-modedness, $st$ and $\tilde{s}_1$ do not contain variables.

Then a (renamed copy of a) program clause $st' :: \tilde{s}'_1 \implies \tilde{s}'_2 :-$ *body* is selected, such that $st'$ matches $st$ and $\tilde{s}'_1$ matches $\tilde{s}_1$ with a substitution $\sigma$. Next, the selected literal in the query is replaced with the conjunction $(body)\sigma$, $\mathbf{id} :: \tilde{s}'_2\sigma \implies \tilde{s}_2$, where $\mathbf{id}$ is the built-in strategy for identity: it succeeds iff the *rhs* matches the *lhs*. Evaluation continues further with this new query. Success and failure are defined in the standard way. Backtracking allows to explore other alternatives that may come from matching the selected query literal to the head of the same program clause in a different way, or to the head of another program clause. Negative literals are processed by the negation-as-failure rule. Well-modedness guarantees that whenever a negative $\rho$-literal is selected during the execution process, there are no variables in it except, maybe, some anonymous variables that may occur in its right-hand side.

*Example 1.* To illustrate the described PρLog inference step, consider again the example about merge_all_doubles from Sect. 2. To transform the query

$$?\text{- merge\_all\_doubles} :: (1, 2, 3, 2, 1) \implies s\_Result.$$

with the clause

$$\text{merge\_all\_doubles} :: s\_X \implies s\_Y : \ \mathbf{nf}(\text{merge\_doubles}) :: s\_X \implies s\_Y, \ !.,$$

PρLog takes the matcher $\{s\_X \mapsto (1, 2, 3, 2, 1)\}$, and produces a new query

$$?\text{- } \mathbf{nf}(\text{merge\_doubles}) :: (1, 2, 3, 2, 1) \implies s\_Y, \ !, \ \mathbf{id} :: s\_Y \implies s\_Result.$$

## 4   Implementation

PρLog is implemented in SWI-Prolog. Its programs have the extension `.rho`. In Fig. 1 one can see how exactly the program `merge.rho` for merging doubles in sequences and trees, discussed in Sect. 2, looks.

PρLog variables are, actually, Prolog constants. Therefore, one can not directly rely on Prolog unification to compute values for those variables. Consequently, the answers to the query should be computed as explicit substitutions showing what PρLog variables map to. It requires a PρLog query to be actually wrapped to a meta-query that then returns the substitutions. For the queries considered in Sect. 2, such meta-queries can be seen in Fig. 2. The predicate symbol used in them is ?.

The substitutions indicate that there is a background solving mechanism in PρLog that performs matching and computes the corresponding substitutions. Indeed, we do it by the algorithm from [14], implemented in SWI-Prolog. However, it turns out that if we do not have context variables, then we can avoid using this implementation and, instead, compute matching substitutions directly by Prolog unification, which is, naturally, a more efficient way. We have implemented this version of PρLog as well, calling it PρLog-light. To distinguish, we sometimes say PρLog-full for the version with context variables.

```
% Merging double elements in a sequence:
% If the input sequence contains a double, keep the left copy.

merge_doubles :: (s_X, i_x, s_Y, i_x, s_Z) ==> (s_X, i_x, s_Y, s_Z).

% Merging all doubles:
% Return a normal form with respect to merge_doubles.

merge_all_doubles := first_one(nf(merge_doubles)).

% Merging double branches in a tree:
% If the input tree contains a double branch, keep the left one,
% using the merge_doubles strategy.

merge_double_branches ::
    c_Context(f_Fun(s_X)) ==> c_Context(f_Fun(s_Y)) :-
    merge_doubles :: s_X ==> s_Y.

% Merging all double branches in a tree:
% Return a normal form with respect to merge_double_branches.

merge_all_double_branches := first_one(nf(merge_double_branches)).
```

**Fig. 1.** Program merge.rho for merging doubles in sequences and trees.

The PρLog distribution consists exactly of these two parts: PρLog-full and PρLog-light. Each part has the main file, called prholog.pl and prholog-l.pl, respectively. They are responsible for setting up the environments and loading the corresponding version of PρLog. The major parts of both versions are the parser, compiler, and the library of built-in strategies: parse.pl, compile.pl, library.pl files for PρLog-full, and parse-l.pl, compile-l.pl, library-l.pl files for PρLog-light, respectively.

Besides, in the full PρLog there is a solver solve.pl for matching problems and regular constraints. The light version does not require such a solver, but it still needs to check regular constraints. It is done in the file constraints-l.pl.

A typical PρLog session starts by invoking SWI-Prolog and consulting the main PρLog file. After that, the user may write/edit a .rho file in her favorite editor, and load it by executing the query ?- load('...filename.rho'), where ... stands for the full path. Next, the program can be queried as, e.g., it is shown in Fig. 2.

The parser and the compiler are invoked at the time when a .rho file is loaded. Besides syntax errors, the parser checks also for well-modedness and for occurrences of PρLog variables in Prolog literals. If no errors are detected, then the compiler compiles the filename.rho file into a Prolog file filename.pl, translating each PρLog clause into a Prolog clause. The file filename.pl is located in the same directory as filename.rho, loads immediately after the compilation, and is deleted on the exit.

```
?- ?(merge_doubles :: (1,2,3,2,1) ==> s_Result, Subst).
Subst = [s_Result---> (1, 2, 3, 2)] ;
Subst = [s_Result---> (1, 2, 3, 1)] ;
false.

?- ?(merge_all_doubles :: (1,2,3,2,1) ==> s_Result, Subst).
Subst = [s_Result---> (1, 2, 3)] ;
false.

?- ?(merge_double_branches ::
        f(g(a,b,a,h(c,c)), h(c), g(a,a,b,h(c))) ==> i_Result, Subst).
Subst = [i_Result--->f(g(a, b, h(c, c)), h(c), g(a, a, b, h(c)))] ;
Subst = [i_Result--->f(g(a, b, a, h(c)), h(c), g(a, a, b, h(c)))] ;
Subst = [i_Result--->f(g(a, b, a, h(c, c)), h(c), g(a, b, h(c)))] ;
false.

?- ?(merge_double_branches ::
        f(g(a,b,a,h(c,c)), h(c), g(a,a,b,h(c))) ==> c_C(h(c,c)), Subst).
Subst = [c_C--->f(g(a, b, hole), h(c), g(a, a, b, h(c)))] ;
Subst = [c_C--->f(g(a, b, a, hole), h(c), g(a, b, h(c)))] ;
false.

?- ?(merge_all_double_branches ::
        f(g(a,b,a,h(c,c)), h(c), g(a,a,b,h(c))) ==> i_Result, Subst)
Subst = [i_Result--->f(g(a, b, h(c)), h(c))] ;
false.
```

**Fig. 2.** Querying merge.rho.

The same parsing and compiling process is done when PρLog queries are evaluated. After compiling, the obtained Prolog query is executed. Answers are given as explicit substitutions.

# 5   Library

The library consists of definitions of built-in strategies, implemented in Prolog. They greatly simplify programming in PρLog. These strategies are protected and can not be redefined from a PρLog program. Currently there are 14 of them in the library. Except a couple of exceptions, each of them can be used both with and without regular constraints. We give a brief overview of some of those strategies, without mentioning the constraints.

*Choice.* The syntax of this strategy is

$$\mathbf{choice}(strategy_1, \ldots, strategy_n) :: sequence_1 \Longrightarrow sequence_2,$$

where $n \geq 1$. It succeeds if and only if for some $i$, $strategy_i :: sequence_1 \Longrightarrow sequence_2$ succeeds.

*Composition.* Composing strategies, making the output sequence of one the input for the other:

$$\textbf{compose}(strategy_1, \ldots, strategy_n) :: sequence_1 \implies sequence_2,$$

where $n \geq 2$. First applies $strategy_1$ to $sequence_1$. To its result, $strategy_2$ is applied and so on. $sequence_2$ is the final result. **compose** fails if one of its argument strategies fails in the process.

*Closure.* The syntax of this strategy is:

$$\textbf{closure}(strategy) :: sequence_1 \implies sequence_2,$$

It succeeds if $sequence_2$ belongs to the closure set of transforming $sequence_1$ by $strategy$. The set elements are computed one after the other, by backtracking. **closure** fails if the set is empty. An example of a query would be

$$? - \textbf{closure}(merge\_doubles) :: (1, 2, 3, 2, 1) \implies s\_Result.$$

It gives five answer substitutions via backtracking:

- $\{s\_Result \mapsto (1, 2, 3, 2, 1)\}$,
- $\{s\_Result \mapsto (1, 2, 3, 2)\}$,
- $\{s\_Result \mapsto (1, 2, 3)\}$,
- $\{s\_Result \mapsto (1, 2, 3, 1)\}$,
- $\{s\_Result \mapsto (1, 2, 3)\}$

*Identity.* The goal of this strategy is to transform a sequence to its identical one:

$$\textbf{id} :: sequence_1 \implies sequence_2.$$

It succeeds iff $sequence_2$ can match $sequence_1$.

*Returning all answers of the first applicable strategy, one by one.* Denoted by **first_all**:

$$\textbf{first\_all}(strategy_1, \ldots, strategy_n) :: sequence_1 \implies sequence_2,$$

where $n \geq 1$. Tries to apply $strategy_1$ to $sequence_1$. If this fails, it tries the next strategy and so on. When a strategy is found that succeeds, **first_all** returns *all answers* computed by it in $sequence_2$, via backtracking. If no strategy succeeds, **first_all** fails.

The strategy **first_one** mentioned earlier is similar to **first_all**, with the only difference that it returns only one answer instead of all of them.

*Returning all answers at once.* It can be seen as an analog of findall for PρLog. The syntax is

$$\textbf{all\_answers}(strategy) :: sequence_1 \Longrightarrow sequence_2.$$

It succeeds if and only if $sequence_2$ is a sequence consisting of terms of the form $ans(\tilde{s}_1), \ldots, ans(\tilde{s}_n)$, where $\tilde{s}_1, \ldots, \tilde{s}_n$ are all the sequences obtained by applying *strategy* to $sequence_1$. The symbol *ans* just plays the role of a constructor, to distinguish between different answer sequences in $sequence_2$. We could ask

$$? - \textbf{all\_answers}(merge\_doubles) :: (1, 2, 3, 2, 1) \Longrightarrow s\_Result.$$

and obtain the answer $\{s\_Result \mapsto (ans(1, 2, 3, 2), ans(1, 2, 3, 1))\}$.

*Interactive mode.* The syntax is:

$$\textbf{interactive} :: sequence_1 \Longrightarrow sequence_2.$$

It activates the interactive mode and starts dialog with the user, asking her to provide a strategy, which is then applied to $sequence_1$. The process is repeated further so that the output sequence of the previous strategy application becomes the input for the new strategy provided by the user, and so on. The interactive process stops when the user types *finish*. At that moment, the input sequence that was there is returned in $sequence_2$. **interactive** fails when the user-provided strategy fails for the current input sequence.

*n-fold iteration.* Specifies how many times a strategy can be applied repeatedly:

$$\textbf{iterate}(strategy, n) :: sequence_1 \Longrightarrow sequence_2.$$

It applies *strategy* repeatedly, $n$ times, starting from $sequence_1$. The result is returned in $sequence_2$. **iterate** fails if one of the applications fails.

The normal form strategy **nf** is similar, but instead of applying a strategy fixed number of times, it applies it until the transformation is not possible, and returns the last sequence.

*Mapping a strategy to a sequence.* Mapping is a common operation in declarative programming:

$$\textbf{map}(strategy) :: sequence_1 \Longrightarrow sequence_2.$$

It applies *strategy* to each term of $sequence_1$. For such an input term, *strategy* may, in general, return a sequence (not necessarily a single term). A sequence constructed of these results (in the same order) is then returned in $sequence_2$. **map** fails when the application of *strategy* to a term from $sequence_1$ fails. When $sequence_1$ is empty, $sequence_2$ is empty as well.

A variation of this strategy, **map_to_subhedges**, splits $sequence_1$ nondeterministically into nonempty subsequences (when $sequence_1$ is not empty) and applies *strategy* to each such subsequence. A sequence constructed from these results (in the same order) is returned in $sequence_2$. **map_to_subhedges** fails when $sequence_1$ can not split in such a way that the application of *strategy* succeeds for each split subsequence. When $sequence_1$ is empty, so is $sequence_2$.

*Rewriting.* Yet another common transformation, which transforms a term not necessarily in the top position, but by transforming its subterm, in general:

$$\mathbf{rewrite}(strategy) :: term_1 \Longrightarrow term_2.$$

It succeeds if and only if $term_2$ is obtained from $term_1$ by applying *strategy* to a subterm of it. Note that one can easily define rewriting inside full P$\rho$Log:

$$rewrite(i\_Strategy) :: c\_Context(i\_Term_1) \Longrightarrow c\_Context(i\_Term_2) :-$$
$$i\_Strategy :: i\_Term_1 \Longrightarrow i\_Term_2.$$

Nevertheless, we decided to provide the predefined strategy for rewriting in the library, because it is quite a frequently used transformation.

# 6 Development Environment

P$\rho$Log can be used in any development environment that is suitable for SWI-Prolog. We provide a special Emacs mode for P$\rho$Log, which extends the Stefan D. Bruda's Prolog mode for Emacs.[1] It supports syntax highlighting, makes it easy to load P$\rho$Log programs and anonymize variables via the menu, etc. Figure 3 can give an idea how it looks.

A tracing tool for P$\rho$Log is under development. Prolog trace is too fine-grained for this purpose, since it goes through all parsing and compilation predicates that are invoked when a P$\rho$Log query is evaluated. Instead, the P$\rho$Log-specific tracing/debugging tool should ignore (by default) all intermediate Prolog steps and show only those that are directly related to P$\rho$Log inference.

# 7 Discussion and Final Remarks

The main advantage of using P$\rho$Log is its flexibility in specifying nondeterministic computations, which allows to neatly combine conditional transformation rules with logic programming. Strategies help to separate transformation rules from the control on their application, which makes rules reusable in different transformations. It also means that, unlike Prolog, the user can apply the program clauses in different order for different queries, without rewriting the code.

Assume that we have two P$\rho$Log rules, one for the top-level transformation of a term, and the other one for transforming an argument:

$$transform\_top(i\_Strategy) :: i\_Term_1 \Longrightarrow i\_Term_2 :-$$
$$i\_Strategy :: i\_Term_1 \Longrightarrow i\_Term_2.$$
$$transform\_arg(i\_Strategy) ::$$
$$f\_Fun(s\_X, i\_Term_1, s\_Y) \Longrightarrow f\_Fun(s\_X, i\_Term_2, s\_Y) :-$$
$$i\_Strategy :: i\_Term_1 \Longrightarrow i\_Term_2.$$

---

[1] https://bruda.ca/emacs/prolog_mode_for_emacs.

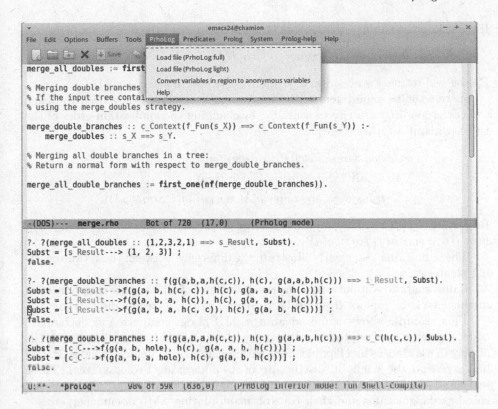

**Fig. 3.** Emacs PρLog session.

Note that the use of function and sequence variables makes the code universal (it can apply to any term, independent to their top function symbols and the number of arguments) and compact (one does not need to implement the term decomposition and traversal explicitly, the declarative specification given above is sufficient).

Now, innermost and outermost rewriting strategies can be implemented by strategy combinations only, imposing the right application order of the transformation rules.

Innermost rewriting is defined by the following recursive strategy:

$$innermost\_rewriting(i\_Strategy) :=$$
$$\textbf{first\_all}(transform\_arg(innermost\_rewriting(i\_Strategy)),$$
$$transform\_top(i\_Strategy)).$$

It gives the priority to the argument transformation by innermost rewriting (wrt the given strategy) over the top-position transformation (wrt the given strategy): If the former is applicable, **first_all** makes sure that its all possible results are returned and the latter is not tried. For instance, assume that $str$ is some concrete strategy defined by two clauses:

$$str :: f(s\_X) \Longrightarrow g(s\_X). \qquad\qquad str :: f(f(i\_X)) \Longrightarrow i\_X.$$

If we ask to rewrite $h(f(f(a)), f(a))$ by innermost rewriting:

$$? - \ innermost\_rewriting(str) :: h(f(f(a)), f(a)) \Longrightarrow i\_Result.$$

P$\rho$Log will return two results: $h(f(g(a)), f(a))$ and $h(f(f(a)), g(a))$.

If we want to experiment with outermost rewriting, we only need to define the corresponding strategy (essentially, by changing the application order of the rules, without altering them):

$$outermost\_rewriting(i\_Strategy) :=$$
$$\mathbf{first\_all}(transform\_top(i\_Strategy),$$
$$transform\_arg(outermost\_rewriting(i\_Strategy))).$$

Rewriting $h(f(f(a)), f(a))$ by this strategy gives three results: $h(g(f(a)), f(a))$, $h(a, f(a))$, and $h(f(f(a)), g(a))$.

The definitions also clearly illustrate the difference between these two rewriting strategies.

If one wants to compute only one result, instead of all, the only change needed in this case is to replace **first_all** by **first_one** in the corresponding strategy.

This example shows some advantages of P$\rho$Log: compact and declarative code; capabilities of expression traversal without explicitly programming it; the ability to use clauses in a flexible order with the help of strategies. Besides, P$\rho$Log has access to the whole infrastructure of its underlying Prolog system. These features make P$\rho$Log suitable for nondeterministic computations, implementing rule-based algorithms and their control, manipulating XML documents, etc.

As future work, one direction is finishing the implementation of P$\rho$Log trace. We also plan to improve the compiler by adding more optimization capabilities.

**Acknowledgments.** This research is partially supported by the Austrian Science Fund (FWF) under the projects P 24087-N18 and P 28789-N32, and by the Rustaveli National Science Foundation (GSRNSF) under the grants FR/508/4-120/14 and YS15 2.1.2 70.

# References

1. Balland, E., Brauner, P., Kopetz, R., Moreau, P.-E., Reilles, A.: Tom: piggybacking rewriting on Java. In: Baader, F. (ed.) RTA 2007. LNCS, vol. 4533, pp. 36–47. Springer, Berlin (2007). doi:10.1007/978-3-540-73449-9_5
2. Belkhir, W., Giorgetti, A., Lenczner, M.: A symbolic transformation language and its application to a multiscale method. J. Symb. Comput. **65**, 49–78 (2014)
3. Borovanský, P., Kirchner, C., Kirchner, H., Moreau, P.-E., Vittek, M.: Elan: a logical framework based on computational systems. ENTCS **4**, 35–50 (1996)
4. Caseau, Y., Josset, F., Laburthe, F.: CLAIRE: combining sets, search and rules to better express algorithms. TPLP **2**(6), 769–805 (2002)
5. Cirstea, H., Kirchner, C.: The rewriting calculus - parts I and II. Logic J. IGPL **9**(3), 339–410 (2001)
6. Clavel, M., Durán, F., Eker, S., Lincoln, P., Martí-Oliet, N., Meseguer, J., Quesada, J.F.: Maude: specification and programming in rewriting logic. Theor. Comput. Sci. **285**(2), 187–243 (2002)

7. Coelho, J., Dundua, B., Florido, M., Kutsia, T.: A rule-based approach to XML processing and Web reasoning. In: Hitzler, P., Lukasiewicz, T. (eds.) RR 2010. LNCS, vol. 6333, pp. 164–172. Springer, Berlin (2010). doi:10.1007/978-3-642-15918-3_13

8. Comon, H.: Completion of rewrite systems with membership constraints. Part II: constraint solving. J. Symb. Comput. **25**(4), 421–453 (1998)

9. Dembinski, P., Maluszynski, J.: And-parallelism with intelligent backtracking for annotated logic programs. In: Proceedings of 1985 Symposium on Logic Programming, pp. 29–38. IEEE-CS (1985)

10. Dundua, B., Kutsia, T., Marin, M.: Strategies in PρLog. In: Fernández, M. (ed.) 9th International Workshop on Reduction Strategies in Rewriting and Programming, WRS 2009, vol. 15 of EPTCS, pp. 32–43 (2009)

11. Dundua, B., Kutsia, T., Reisenberger-Hagmayer, K.: An overview of PρLog. RISC Report Series 16–05, RISC, University of Linz (2016)

12. Frühwirth, T.W.: Theory and practice of constraint handling rules. J. Log. Program. **37**(1–3), 95–138 (1998)

13. Kutsia, T.: Solving equations with sequence variables and sequence functions. J. Symb. Comput. **42**(3), 352–388 (2007)

14. Kutsia, T., Marin, M.: Matching with regular constraints. In: Sutcliffe, G., Voronkov, A. (eds.) LPAR 2005. LNCS (LNAI), vol. 3835, pp. 215–229. Springer, Berlin (2005). doi:10.1007/11591191_16

15. Lloyd, J.: Foundations of Logic Programming, 2nd edn. Springer, Heidelberg (1987)

16. Marin, M., Kutsia, T.: On the implementation of a rule-based programming system and some of its applications. In: Konev, B., Schmidt, R. (eds.) Proceedings of 4th International Workshop on the Implementation of Logics, WIL 2004, pp. 55–69 (2003)

17. Marin, M., Kutsia, T.: Foundations of the rule-based system ρLog. J. Appl. Non-Classical Logics **16**(1–2), 151–168 (2006)

18. Marin, M., Piroi, F.: Rule-based programming with Mathematica. In: Proceedings of the 6th International Mathematica Symposium, Alberta, Canada (2004)

19. Monagan, M.B., Geddes, K.O., Heal, K.M., Labahn, G., Vorkoetter, S.M., McCarron, J., DeMarco, P.: Maple 10 programming guide. Maplesoft (2005)

20. Nguyen, P.: Meta-mining: a meta-learning framework to support the recommendation, planning and optimization of data mining workflows. Ph.D. thesis, Department of Computer Science, University of Geneva (2015)

21. van den Brand, M., van Deursen, A., Heering, J., de Jong, H., de Jonge, M., Kuipers, T., Klint, P., Moonen, L., Olivier, P.A., Scheerder, J., Vinju, J.J., Visser, E., Visser, J.: The ASF+SDF meta-environment: a component-based language development environment. Electr. Notes Theor. Comput. Sci. **44**(2), 3–8 (2001)

22. Visser, E.: Stratego: a language for program transformation based on rewriting strategies. In: Middeldorp, A. (ed.) RTA 2001. LNCS, vol. 2051, pp. 357–361. Springer, Berlin (2001). doi:10.1007/3-540-45127-7_27

23. Wielemaker, J., Schrijvers, T., Triska, M., Lager, T.: SWI-prolog. Theor. Pract. Logic Program. **12**(1–2), 67–96 (2012)

24. Wolfram, S.: The Mathematica Book, 5th edn. Wolfram-Media, Champaign (2003)

# Integrating Answer Set Programming with Object-Oriented Languages

Jakob Rath[✉] and Christoph Redl[✉]

Institut für Informationssysteme, Technische Universität Wien,
Favoritenstraße 9-11, 1040 Vienna, Austria
jakob.rath@student.tuwien.ac.at, redl@kr.tuwien.ac.at

**Abstract.** Answer Set Programming (ASP) is a declarative programming paradigm which allows for easy modeling and solving of hard problems that are often cumbersome to implement in object-oriented programming languages. It was successfully applied to a range of applications from artificial intelligence, such as combinatorial or scheduling problems. On the other hand, real-world applications for end-users usually consist also of components which cannot be (easily) solved in ASP, such as user interaction via graphical user interfaces, presentation of results, and interfaces to data sources. Instead, realizing such components is typically in the domain of traditional (object-oriented) programming languages. To address this issue, we introduce a *language* which allows for a *formal specification of the input and output of an ASP program*, which can be exploited to easily interface the program from object-oriented languages using a dedicated library. While the language is independent from the concrete object-oriented language, we also provide and present a reference implementation as a Python library. We then discuss some applications which can be realized on top of our approach.

**Keywords:** Answer Set Programming · Nonmonotonic reasoning · Interface to object-oriented languages

## 1 Introduction

Answer Set Programming (ASP) is a declarative programming paradigm based on nonmonotonic reasoning and a multi-model semantics [7]. The problem at hand is encoded as an ASP program in such a way that its models, called *answer sets*, correspond one-to-one to the solutions of the problem. Thanks to disjunction and default negation, the formalism has a high expressiveness, and thanks to various language extensions such as aggregates, many problems from artificial intelligence such as combinatorial and scheduling problems can be encoded in ASP in an intuitive way. In contrast, solving such problems in traditional object-oriented programming languages is often cumbersome as an algorithm needs to

This research has been supported by the Austrian Science Fund (FWF) project P27730.

be specified. ASP has also been successfully applied to various real-world applications from industry, e.g. *workforce management* [12] and *automatic suggestion of holiday plans for tourists* [9]; for further examples we refer to [8].

However, typical applications for end-users also contain components which cannot be (easily) solved in ASP, but their realization is rather in the domain of traditional object-oriented languages. These components include, for instance, graphical user interfaces, presentation of results, and interfaces to data sources. As a concrete example, consider a packing problem which needs to be solved by employees of a logistics company, such as to distribute a set of goods to a minimum number of trucks under given side constraints. While the core problem is a typical use case for ASP, if it occurs as part of a real application, data needs to be imported from databases, parameters need to be entered by the user, and the results must be further processed by other system components, such as for accounting purposes. In ASP, the input is specified via facts and the output is presented as answer sets. However, since typical users of such an application are no computer scientists and are not used to read and write formal notations, more appropriate interfaces must be developed. Moreover, even if users are used to ASP programs, a manual transfer of data between the ASP program and other components is cumbersome. Instead, this should be transparent from the user. Hence, an interface between the ASP program and other components is needed.

An ad hoc solution when developing an application is to implement such an interface from scratch. To this end, facts are generated and piped to the ASP solver, which computes its answer sets that are then parsed and transformed into objects. However, while the details of generating facts and transforming the answer sets to objects depend on the application, it seems that these steps are similar in most cases. This calls for a generic interface which can be instantiated depending on the application at hand.

To address this issue, we present a language for ASP which allows the programmer to *annotate* ASP programs with *specifications of their input and output*. Based on these annotations, the ASP program can then be used from the object-oriented code similarly to modules by sending input to it and retrieving its answer sets in form of objects. We specify the language independently of the concrete object-oriented language and the ASP solver at hand. Instead, the formalism can be instantiated for arbitrary languages resp. solvers which provide a certain minimum set of features. However, we also provide an implementation of this language for Python, using the DLVHEX solver [11] as solver backend.

Unlike existing approaches such as JASP [4] and EmbASP [5], our system uses annotations of the ASP program rather than embeddings of the ASP program into the object-oriented code, and the input and output is specified in a language-independent manner. This has the advantage that the program is more independent of the remaining components of the application, which allows for easier adoption or integration into multiple applications (which might even be implemented in different programming languages), similarly to modules in software engineering. As a further difference to some existing approaches such as [10], which modifies the ASP language by providing access to objects defined in the object-oriented code, our language does *not modify* but rather *extend* ASP in a conservative way using annotations, i.e., all annotated programs in our system are still ordinary ASP programs and can also be used independently.

The structure of the remaining part of the paper is as follows:

- In Sect. 2 we recapitulate the syntax and semantics of ASP.
- In Sect. 3 we introduce the language for specifying the input and output of ASP programs and illustrate it with examples.
- In Sect. 4 we present our prototypical implementation PY-ASPIO (ASP Interface to Object-oriented programs) in Python.
- In Sect. 5 we discuss possible real-world applications in more detail.
- In Sect. 6 we discuss related work and point out differences to ours.
- In Sect. 7 we conclude and give an outlook on possible future work.

## 2   Preliminaries

We briefly recapitulate Answer Set Programming (ASP) [7], and refer to [1] for a more in-depth overview of the field of ASP. Our alphabet consists of possibly infinite sets of constant symbols $\mathscr{C}$ (including all integers), variables $\mathscr{V}$, function symbols $\mathscr{F}$, and predicate symbols $\mathscr{P}$. We assume that $\mathscr{V}$ is disjoint from all other sets, while symbols may be shared between the other sets. We let the set of terms $\mathscr{T}$ be the least set such that $\mathscr{C} \subseteq \mathscr{T}$, $\mathscr{V} \subseteq \mathscr{T}$, and $f \in \mathscr{F}$, $T_1, \ldots, T_\ell \in \mathscr{T}$ implies $f(T_1, \ldots, T_\ell) \in \mathscr{T}$. An (ordinary) atom is of form $p(t_1, \ldots, t_\ell)$ with predicate symbol $p \in \mathscr{P}$ and terms $t_1, \ldots, t_\ell \in \mathscr{T}$, abbreviated as $p(\mathbf{t})$; we write $t \in \mathbf{t}$ if $t = t_i$ for some $1 \leq i \leq \ell$. A term resp. atom is called *ground* if it does not contain variables. A (default) literal is either an atom $a$ or a default-negated atom not $a$.

**Definition 1.** *An* answer set program $P$ *consists of rules*

$$a_1 \vee \cdots \vee a_k \leftarrow b_1, \ldots, b_m, \text{not } b_{m+1}, \ldots, \text{not } b_n \ , \tag{1}$$

*where each $a_i$ and each $b_j$ is an atom. A non-disjunctive rule with empty body (i.e., $k = 1$ and $n = 0$) is called a fact.*

For such a rule $r$ we let $H(r) = \{a_1, \ldots, a_k\}$ be its *head*, $B^+(r) = \{b_1, \ldots, b_m\}$ be its *positive body* and $B^-(r) = \{b_{m+1}, \ldots, b_n\}$ be its *negative body*. A rule resp. program is ground if it contains only ground atoms.

An interpretation $I$ is a subset of the set of atoms $A(P)$ occurring in the ground program $P$ at hand, where $a \in I$, also denoted $I \models a$, expresses that $a$ is true and $a \notin I$, also denoted $I \not\models a$, that $a$ is false. Conversely, a negated literal not $a$ is satisfied under $I$, denoted $I \models \text{not } a$, if $I \not\models a$, and it is unsatisfied, denoted $I \not\models \text{not } a$, otherwise. A ground rule $r$ of form (1) is satisfied under $I$, denoted $I \models r$, if $a_i \in I$ for some $1 \leq i \leq k$, or $b_i \notin I$ for some $1 \leq i \leq m$, or $b_i \in I$ for some $m+1 \leq i \leq n$. A ground program $P$ is satisfied under $I$, denoted $I \models P$, if each $r \in P$ is satisfied under $I$. A set of literals $L$ is satisfied under $I$, denoted $I \models L$, if $I \models l$ for all $l \in S$.

The answer sets of a ground program $P$ are defined using the *(GL-)reduct* [7] $P^I = \{H(r) \leftarrow B^+(r) \mid r \in P, I \not\models b \text{ for all } b \in B^-(r)\}$ of $P$ wrt. an interpretation $I$.

**Definition 2.** *An interpretation $I$ is an answer set of a ground program $P$, if $I$ is a $\subseteq$-minimal model of $P^I$.*

*Example 1.* Consider the program $P = \{a \leftarrow \text{not } b; \ b \leftarrow \text{not } a\}$. Its answer sets are $I_1 = \{a\}$ and $I_2 = \{b\}$.                                    □

We let $AS(P)$ be the set of answer sets of $P$. The answer sets of a program $P$ with variables are given by the answer sets of its *grounding* $grnd(P)$, which results from $P$ if all variables are replaced by all terms in all possible ways. Throughout the rest of the paper we assume that suitable safety conditions on $P$ guarantee that $grnd(P)$ is finite.

# 3   Specifying the External Interface of ASP Programs

In this section we present a language which allows for specifying the interfaces of ASP programs in order to use them from object-oriented code. It comprises of the *input specification*, which declares what input arguments are expected and how they are mapped to ASP facts, and the *output specification*, which defines how the answer sets are mapped back to objects. The language is realized by conservative *annotations* added to the program, while the rules remain in ordinary ASP syntax and thus can also be used stand-alone. Each program has exactly one input and exactly one output specification.

In view of the implementation (cf. Sect. 4), such an ASP program can then be interfaced from the object-oriented program using a library, which receives the ASP program and input arguments as parameters. It then evaluates the ASP program under the given input and returns its results as objects generated from its answer sets. This is described by

$$O = eval(P, v_1, \ldots, v_n),$$

where $P$ is an ASP program, $v_1, \ldots, v_n$ are input arguments, and $O$ is a set of objects corresponding one-to-one to the answer sets (which in turn correspond to the solutions to the problem at hand). The object-oriented code can then process these objects in a loop.

Internally, the evaluation of an ASP program from object-oriented code with given input arguments consists of three steps:

1. Facts are generated from the input arguments according to the input specification.
2. These facts along with the original ASP program are passed to the ASP solver.
3. The answer sets are transformed into objects according to the output specification.

The exact transformation performed by *eval* will be described in the rest of this section. However, we first make some assumptions about the object-oriented language at hand. This is in order to allow for instantiating the approach also for arbitrary programming languages which provide the following minimum set of features (while we provide a reference implementation for Python, cf. Sect. 4).

### 3.1    The Object-Oriented Language

Most importantly, our system assumes the language to be object-oriented. Data is organized in *classes*, which, for the purposes of this paper, are definitions of structures with *named attributes* and *methods*. An *object* is an instance of a class which assigns certain values to its attributes and is accessible via a variable in the object-oriented code. For an object $x$ we let $x.\,attr$ be the value of the attribute *attr*.

The language must provide at least the classes *str* and *int* with the usual functionality for representing character strings and integers, respectively. Moreover, classes that are to be used during input mapping are required to provide a *toString* method which returns a string representation of the object at hand, that can be used as an ASP constant.

Furthermore, the following collection types are required, i.e., types that allow for storing (ordered or unordered) groups of objects. For these collection types we allow *type parameters* $T$ specified in angle brackets; that is, the type of objects which can be stored in the respective collection is constrained by this parameter.

- *Set$\langle T \rangle$*: a collection of unique objects of type $T$.
- *Dictionary$\langle K, V \rangle$*: a mapping from objects of type $K$ (the *keys*) to objects of type $V$ (the *values*).
- *Tuple$\langle T_1, \ldots, T_n \rangle$*: an ordered list of fixed length $n$, where the component at position $i$ is of type $T_i$ for $1 \leq i \leq n$.
- *Sequence$\langle T \rangle$*: a finite ordered sequence containing objects of type $T$, where elements are addressable by an integer index.

For a collection object $x$ of type *Tuple* or a *Sequence*, let $x[i]$ for $i \in \mathbb{N}$ be its $i$-th element.

### 3.2    Input Specification

We now describe our language for specifying the input of an ASP program. The input specification defines the expected arguments and how they are mapped to ASP facts. Before we introduce the language for the general case, we show an intuitive example.

*Example 2.* Assume we have a graph represented by a set of instances of the class Node. The attribute label of this class is a unique string identifying the node, and the attribute neighbors is a list containing the neighbor nodes. The following input specification takes such a set of nodes as input and maps it to the two predicates vertex and edge:

```
1 INPUT (Set<Node> nodes) {
2     vertex(n.label) for n in nodes;
3     edge(n.label, m.label) for n in nodes for m in n.neighbors; }
```

More precisely, the input of the ASP program is a set of nodes, given as an instance of class Set<Node>, where Node is a custom class defined in the object-oriented code. Given this input, line 2 defines the predicate vertex by generating a fact vertex(n.label) for every object n in the set nodes.

Similarly, line 3 defines the predicate edge from the adjacency lists of the nodes. To this end, the loop-like construct iterates over the nodes and for each node over its (attribute) neighbors. Multiple iterations are evaluated from left to right, i.e., variables bound in an iteration are available in all iterations to the right, and in the predicate arguments. The outer loop iterates over all nodes, and, for each node, the inner loop over its neighbors.                    □

**Definition of the Language.** In general, an *input specification* $\iota$ is of the form

$$\textbf{INPUT } (t_1 \; v_1, \ldots, t_n \; v_n) \; \{s_1; s_2; \ldots s_k;\}$$

where $v_1, \ldots, v_n$ are *input parameters* to the ASP program of types $t_1, \ldots, t_n$, and $s_1, \ldots, s_k$ are predicate specifications defined as follows. Each *predicate specification* $s_i$ for $1 \leq i \leq k$ is of form

$$p(x_1, \ldots, x_m) \textbf{ for } w_1 \textbf{ in } y_1 \ldots \textbf{ for } w_\ell \textbf{ in } y_\ell \qquad (2)$$

where $p \in \mathscr{P}$ is a predicate symbol, $x_1, \ldots, x_m$ are objects of any type, $w_1, \ldots, w_\ell$ are (iteration) variables, and $y_1, \ldots, y_\ell$ are collections.

The first step in the evaluation of a program $P$ with an input specification $\iota$ of the above form under parameters $v_1, \ldots, v_n$, i.e., the evaluation of $eval(P, v_1, \ldots, v_n)$, is the construction of facts $genFacts(\iota, v_1, \ldots, v_n) = \bigcup_{1 \leq i \leq k} genFacts(s_i, v_1, \ldots, v_n)$ from the given parameters. To this end, each predicate specification $s_i$ of form (2) is handled independently as follows and yields a set of input facts $genFacts(s_i, v_1, \ldots, v_n)$.

The constructs **for** $w_i$ **in** $y_i$ in a predicate specification $s$ for $1 \leq i \leq \ell$ are *iteration clauses* which are used to let $w_i$ iterate over the contents of collection $y_i$, similarly to loops in procedural languages. If $y_i$ is a Set, then $w_i$ iterates over its elements, if it is a Dictionary resp. Sequence/Tuple, then $w_i$ iterates over its *pairs* of the current key resp. index and value. Multiple iteration clauses are nested from left to right, i.e., the leftmost iteration clause defines the outermost iteration. For a predicate specification of form (2), an iteration variable $w_i$ can be accessed in all $y_j$ with $j > i$ and in $x_1, \ldots, x_n$.

Such a predicate specification $s$ generates all facts $genFacts(s, v_1, \ldots, v_n)$ of the form $p(u_1, \ldots, u_m)$, where each term $u_j \in \mathscr{T}$ for $1 \leq j \leq m$ is the string representation $x_j$.toString() of the corresponding object $x_j$. In $x_j$, all iteration variables $w_1, \ldots, w_\ell$ defined by $s$ and all input parameters $v_1, \ldots, v_n$ can be accessed.

**Language Shortcuts.** When iterating over a *Sequence* $y$ using **for** $w$ **in** $y$, the current index and element are accessed by $w[0]$ and $w[1]$, respectively. Iteration over a *Dictionary* $y$ works analogously, where $w[0]$ and $w[1]$ yield the current key and value, respectively. Towards a more readable notation, further allow to use a list of iteration variables $(w_1, \ldots, w_m)$ in place of a single iteration variable $w$. Then, $w_i$ is automatically assigned the value of $w[i]$ for all $1 \le i \le m$. For instance, an iteration **for** $w$ **in** $y$ over the key-value pairs $(w[0], w[1])$ in the *Dictionary* $y$ may be written as **for** $(k, v)$ **in** $y$. In case of iteration over nested collection types, this shortcut can be repeated recursively, i.e., an element in a list of iteration variables can itself be a list. Additionally, it is possible to use the anonymous variable _. Each occurrence of _ is viewed as a new variable that is never referenced.

*Example 3.* The following example illustrates the iteration over a sequence. The input is a series of measurements of the current *temperature* and *humidity*, respectively, which corresponds to the type Sequence<Tuple<int, int>>; the time point serves as index in this sequence.

```
1  INPUT (Sequence<Tuple<int, int>> readings) {
2     temperature(x[0], x[1][0]) for x in readings;
3     humidity(t, hum) for (t,(_,hum)) in readings; }
```

The specification of the predicate temperature uses a single iteration variable $x$. Since readings is of type *Sequence*, this iteration variable $x$ is assigned pairs of the current index and value, where the value itself is a pair of temperature and humidity. Hence, $x[0]$ refers to the current index and $x[1]$ refers to a pair of measurements, where $x[1][0]$ is the temperature and $x[1][1]$ is the humidity. In contrast, the definition of humidity uses a (nested) pair of iteration variables $(t, (\_, hum))$ which are directly assigned the time point $t$ and the humidity $hum$. Since the temperature value is not used in this definition, it is ignored by using an anonymous variable. ☐

## 3.3  Output Specification

The evaluation of an ASP program yields a collection of answer sets. The output specification enables the object-oriented program to extract information from them by assigning values to the attributes of a certain class depending on the atoms in the current answer set. Then, each answer set yields one instance of this class.

Before we introduce the language in the general case we present an intuitive example.

*Example 4.* Assume we have evaluated an ASP program that computes a graph represented by the predicates *vertex* and *edge* (cf. Example 2), and received the answer set $I$. Assume that every vertex $v$ has exactly one associated color $c$ represented by $color(v, c)$. Consider the answer set

$$I = \{vertex(a), vertex(b), vertex(c), edge(a, b), edge(a, c),$$
$$color(a, blue), color(b, red), color(c, red)\}$$

and the following output specification:

```
1 OUTPUT {
2    labels = set { query: vertex(X); content: X; };
3    red_nodes = set { query: color(X, red); content: X; }; }
```

It defines the values of the attributes labels and red_nodes of the output class, depending on the current answer set $I$. The value of the attribute
labels is a new instance of class *Set*, whose elements $x$ are extracted from
atoms $vertex(x) \in I$. To this end, the **query** specifies a set of literals which are
matched against the atoms in the answer set $I$. For every match, the argument
terms of the matched atoms are assigned to the corresponding variables in the
query, and an element to be added to the *Set* instance is constructed according
to the **content** property. In this example, for the given answer set $I$, the value
of labels will thus correspond to the set $\{a, b, c\}$. Similarly, the set red_nodes
contains the labels of all red-colored nodes, i.e., the values $\{b, c\}$.    □

**Definition of the Language.** We now explain output specifications in the general case. The basic building blocks are *(attribute) expressions* which transform
atoms, sets of atoms, and/or the results of subexpressions to attribute values
(see below). The value $mapOutput(e, I)$ of an expression $e$ is itself an object,
that is constructed relative to a fixed answer set $I$. Based on expressions, an
*output specification* $\omega$ is then of the form

$$\textbf{OUTPUT} \ \{w_1 = e_1; \ldots w_k = e_k; \}$$

where $w_1, \ldots, w_k$ are pairwise distinct attributes and $e_1, \ldots, e_k$ are expressions.
For a program $P$ with such an output specification $\omega$, each answer set $I \in AS(P)$
is then mapped to an object $mapOutput(\omega, I)$, which contains the attributes $w_i$,
whose values are given by $mapOutput(e_i, I)$, for all $1 \leq i \leq k$.

- *Basic Expressions* are integer and string constants $e$ which evaluate to themselves, i.e., $mapOutput(e, I) = e$ for all $I$. We show their usage together with
  collection expressions.
- *Collection Expressions* are of one of the following forms:
  - **set** { **query**: $q$; **content**: $e$; }
  - **sequence** { **query**: $q$; **index**: $i$; **content**: $e$; }
  - **dictionary** { **query**: $q$; **key**: $k$; **content**: $e$; }

In all cases, the **query** $q = l_1, \ldots, l_n$ specifies a set of (possibly nonground) literals, where each variable must occur in a positive literal akin to safe rules, which
are to be checked against the answer set $I$ at hand in order to find substitutions
$S(q) = \{\sigma : V(q) \to \mathscr{T} \mid I \models \sigma(q)\}$ for the variables $V(q)$ occurring in $q$, which
satisfy the query under $I$, akin to query answering. Then, for each such substitu-
tion $\sigma$, **content** $e$ specifies a (sub)expression which defines how to construct an
object from the current variable substitution. In the simplest case, this is a variable occurring in $q$ which will, after application of the substitution $\sigma$, be a basic
expression (i.e., a constant). However, the **content** can also be nested collection
or composite (see below) expressions, in which case it is recursively evaluated.

Moreover, for **sequence**, $i$ is a variable or integer constant, and for **dictionary**, $k$ is a (sub)expression.

The value $mapOutput(e, I)$ of the expression $e=$**set** $\{$ **query** :$q$; **content** :$e'$; $\}$ wrt. an answer set $I$ is a *Set* with the elements $\{mapOutput(\sigma(e'), I) \mid \sigma \in S(q)\}$, where $\sigma(e')$ results from $e'$ if all variables $X$ occurring in $e'$ are replaced by $\sigma(X)$.

Given the expression $e =$ **sequence** $\{$ **query**: $q$; **index**: $Y$; **content**: $e'$; $\}$, the value $mapOutput(e, I)$ wrt. an answer set $I$ is an instance of *Sequence* containing all elements $mapOutput(\sigma(e'), I)$ for $\sigma \in S(q)$, ordered by the index $\sigma(Y)$ (which is assumed to be an integer and yields an error otherwise).

*Example 5.* To illustrate, consider the following output specification:

```
1 OUTPUT {
2     indices = set { query: p(I, X); content: int(I); };
3     xs = sequence { query: p(I, X); index: I; content: X; }; }
```

The definition of indices gathers the first argument of all atoms of $p$ into a *Set*. Note that all constant symbols are mapped to *str* instances by default. The constructor int can be used to convert strings to *int* values. On the other hand, the definition of xs constructs an instance of *Sequence*. The positions of the elements in xs are determined by the variable given as **index**, which must occur in **query**. For instance, for the answer set $I = \{p(0, a), p(1, b), p(2, a)\}$, the value of indices is the set $\{0, 1, 2\}$ and the value of xs is the sequence $(a, b, a)$. □

Similarly, given $e =$ **dictionary** $\{$ **query**: $q$; **key**: $k$; **content**: $v$; $\}$, the value $mapOutput(e, I)$ wrt. an answer set $I$ is an instance of *Dictionary*, which maps for all $\sigma \in S(q)$ the key $mapOutput(\sigma(k), I)$ to the value $mapOutput(\sigma(v), I)$. Note that the result of applying a substitution $\sigma$ to the **key** $k$ is a general expression itself, which needs to be recursively evaluated. This is opposed to the **index** in the previous paragraph, which is, after application of $\sigma$, always a basic expression.

*Example 6.* The following output specification demonstrates how collection expressions can be nested. We assume that every node $x$ is assigned exactly one color $c$, which is represented by an atom $color(x, c)$. Suppose we want to extract a dictionary which maps each color to the set of nodes with that color. This is done as follows:

```
1 OUTPUT {
2     labels_by_color = dictionary {
3         query: color(X, C);
4         key: C;
5         content: set { query: color(L, C); content: L; }; }; }
```

Evaluating this expression under the answer set $I$ from Example 4, the dictionary labels_by_color yields the mappings *blue* $\mapsto \{a\}$ and *red* $\mapsto \{b, c\}$. Note that the variable $C$ is introduced in the **dictionary** expression and for every match $\sigma$ of its **query** color(X, C), the **set** expression is evaluated with $C$ fixed to the matched value $\sigma(C)$, thus generating a set of labels colored by color $C$. □

– *Composite Expressions* are instances of custom classes of the object-oriented language. They are created by passing appropriate parameters to their constructors, i.e., the expression $cls(e_1, \ldots, e_k)$ with (sub)expressions $e_1, \ldots, e_k$ creates an instance of the class $cls$ by calling its constructor with the arguments constructed by the (sub)expressions $e_1, \ldots, e_k$. A special case thereof is the instantiation of *Tuple*, which is written as $(e_1, \ldots, e_k)$.

*Example 7.* We continue with the answer set $I$ from Example 4.

```
1  OUTPUT {
2      graph = Graph(
3          set { query: vertex(X); content: X; },
4          set { query: edge(X, Y); content: (X, Y); });
5      colored_nodes = set {
6          query: color(X, C);
7          content: ColoredNode(X, C); }; }
```

The variable `graph` holds an instance of the custom class `Graph`, which is to be defined in the object-oriented language. To create the `Graph` instance, its constructor is called with the set of labels (cf. Example 4) and the set of edges as parameters. The set of edges is defined by a *Tuple* $(x, y)$ for each atom $edge(x, y) \in I$. This example also demonstrates nesting of expressions. The constructor call contains two **set** expressions, and the **content** of the second **set** contains a tuple expression.

The value of `colored_nodes` is a *Set* of instances of the class `ColoredNode`, which is defined in the object-oriented language. □

### 3.4 Overall Evaluation

Given an ASP program $P$ with input specification $\iota$ and output specification $\omega$, we can now describe the complete evaluation process under input arguments $v_1, \ldots, v_n$ by

$$eval(P, v_1, \ldots, v_n) = \{mapOutput(\omega, I) \mid I \in AS(P \cup genFacts(\iota, v_1, \ldots, v_n))\}.$$

That is, in the process of evaluating $P$ with input arguments $v_1, \ldots, v_n$ we first generate the set of facts $F$ from the input arguments according to the input specification of $P$. Then, the answer sets of $P \cup F$ are computed. Finally, each answer set is mapped back to an object as per the output specification of $P$, yielding a set of objects that can be processed in the object-oriented code.

## 4 Implementation in Python

We have implemented the language from the previous section in the PY-ASPIO library[1] (<u>A</u>SP <u>I</u>nterface to <u>O</u>bject-oriented programs) in the *Python*

---

[1] Available at https://github.com/hexhex/py-aspio.

programming language[2]. The library utilizes *dlvhex*[3] as the underlying answer set solver, but adaptation to other reasoners is simple.

**Object Model.** In our implementation, an object $x$ is accepted to have an attribute *attr* if getattr(x, "attr") does not raise an AttributeError[4]. Subscripts $x[i]$ can be used on any object $x$ that supports subscription, not just *Sequence* and *Tuple* instances. For the output mapping, by default, we substitute the builtin Python classes int, str, tuple, frozenset, list, and dict for the respective abstract types *int*, *str*, *Tuple*, *Set*, *Sequence*, and *Dictionary*. In Python, the contents of sets and the keys of dictionaries are required to be *hashable* objects. Since list and dict are mutable collections and thus not hashable, they cannot immediately be used as contents of sets. However, it easy to replace these types by immutable, hashable variants either by using a constructor in the output specification, or by setting configuration parameters of the PY-ASPIO library.

**Interface of** PY-ASPIO. When interfacing an ASP program using the PY-ASPIO library, it is expected to contain the input and output specifications as defined above in special comments starting with %! inside the ASP code (while normal comments in ASP begin with just %). This ensures that annotations are conservative in the sense that the program uses still valid ASP syntax and can also be used independently of the PY-ASPIO library.

The central interface to the program is then provided by the class Program. It represents an ASP program and provides methods to evaluate it under given input and access its answer sets as objects. The actual ASP code can be provided either as file or as string passed to the constructor of the class. The input and output specifications contained in the program are parsed and interpreted at the time a program is accessed for the first time. Then, once a Program instance was created, the program can be evaluated multiple times with varying input arguments.

In the following we assume that p is an instance of Program. The ASP program is evaluated by calling the method p.solve(...) with arguments as defined by the input specification. This method returns a Python iterable that contains a Result instance for every answer set that has been computed. These Result objects possess attributes corresponding to the variables defined in the output specification of p.

If custom class constructors are used in the output specification, PY-ASPIO needs to be able to resolve class names. To this end, we distinguish two types of names:

- Qualified names (e.g., package.module.Class) are automatically resolved.
- Unqualified names must be registered manually before evaluating the ASP program. The programmer can either register each name separately with method

---

[2] https://www.python.org.

[3] http://www.kr.tuwien.ac.at/research/systems/dlvhex/.

[4] Information about Python-specific terms is available at https://docs.python.org/3/.

calls of form p.register(MyClass), or import all global names in the current scope with p.register_dict(globals()).

Most settings in PY-ASPIO have global and local counterparts. For example, it is possible to register names locally for the ASP program p by calling its instance methods, e.g., p.register(...). On the other hand, simpler applications that need to set up these bindings once for all ASP programs may call the global counterparts on the PY-ASPIO module: aspio.register(...).

*Example 8.* We show now a complete example of how the PY-ASPIO library is used. The Python script in Listing 1 loads the ASP program shown in Listing 2 and demonstrates three ways of evaluating the program and accessing the output data.

**Listing 1.** Python program in the file coloring.py

```
1 from collections import namedtuple
2 import aspio
3 # Define classes and create sample data
4 Node = namedtuple('Node', ['label'])
5 ColoredNode = namedtuple('ColoredNode', ['label', 'color'])
6 Arc = namedtuple('Arc', ['start', 'end'])
7 a, b, c = Node('a'), Node('b'), Node('c')
8 nodes = {a, b, c}
9 arcs = {Arc(a, b), Arc(a, c), Arc(b, c)}
10 # Register class names with aspio
11 aspio.register_dict(globals())
12 # Load ASP program and input/output specifications from file
13 prog = aspio.Program(filename='coloring.dl')
14 # Iterate over all answer sets
15 for result in prog.solve(nodes, arcs):
16     print(result.colored_nodes)
17 # Shortcut if only one variable is needed (note prefix "each_")
18 for colored_nodes in prog.solve(nodes, arcs).each_colored_nodes:
19     print(colored_nodes)
20 # Compute a single answer set
21 result = prog.solve_one(nodes, arcs)
22 if result is not None: print(result.colored_nodes)
23 else: print('no answer set')
```

**Listing 2.** Mapping specification and ASP code in the file coloring.dl

```
1 %! INPUT (Set<Node> nodes, Set<Arc> arcs) {
2 %!     node(n.label) for n in nodes;
3 %!     edge(arc.start.label, arc.end.label) for arc in arcs; }
4 %! OUTPUT {
5 %!     colored_nodes = set {
6 %!         query: color(X, C);
7 %!         content: ColoredNode(X, C); }; }
8 color(X, red) v color(X, green) v color(X, blue) :- node(X).
9 :- edge(X, Y), color(X, C), color(Y, C).
```

The input specification defines two input parameters, nodes and arcs (cf. Listing 2, line 1). The solve method must thus be called with

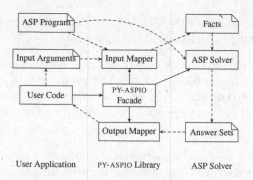

**Fig. 1.** PY-ASPIO Architecture (data flow - - →, control flow —→)

two arguments. The output specification declares a single output variable colored_nodes (cf. Listing 2, line 5), which is accessed with the same name in the Python code (cf. Listing 1, line 16). □

**Implementation Architecture.** Our system runs the ASP solver as a subprocess to compute answer sets, communicating via pipes and temporary files. Its architecture is shown in Fig. 1. Upon invoking the solver, PY-ASPIO immediately returns a wrapper object representing the set of answer sets. Iterating over this wrapper object yields each answer set as soon as it is available, i.e., the client code is not forced to wait until all answer sets have been computed. To reduce communication overhead, PY-ASPIO uses the solver's --filter option in order to capture only predicates that are needed to construct output objects, which may allow for optimizations in the solver. The output objects themselves are constructed at the time when they are first accessed by the client code, which is realized by exploiting Python's attribute access mechanism.

The exact mapping of objects to ASP terms depends on their type. Integers are passed to the solver as-is to allow use of arithmetic, and strings are passed as quoted string constants (where enclosed quotation marks have been replaced by an appropriate escape sequence). Any other objects are first converted to strings by calling Python's str function and then mapped to quoted string constants.

For more detailed information about the PY-ASPIO library, we refer to the library's documentation and example programs available at https://github.com/hexhex/py-aspio.

## 5   Applications

In this section we discuss possible applications of the PY-ASPIO library. As noted in Sect. 1, Answer Set Programming has proven well suited for solving computationally hard problems. Typical examples are planning and scheduling problems under domain-specific constraints. They are cumbersome to implement in classical languages but can be modeled easily in a declarative language.

However, a solution of the underlying computational problem in form of an ASP program is usually not enough to allow practical application. End-users are typically not trained in logic programming and thus cannot be expected to directly edit ASP files, to enter input data in form of facts or to interpret the answer sets. Moreover, even for trained personnel, manual data entry in this form would be inefficient and calls for automated interfaces to other system components which realize, e.g., user interfaces, interfaces to data sources, or other parts which cannot (easily) be solved in ASP. Such an interface is provided by the PY-ASPIO library. Since Python is suitable for developing state-of-the-art graphical user interfaces (GUI, e.g., using pyqt[5]) and Web applications (e.g., using django[6]), one can create a Python program to support data entry and presentation of results. With help of the PY-ASPIO library, it is then easy to integrate an ASP program to solve the actual underlying problem.

We now discuss some concrete possible applications.

**Creating Timetables for Schools.** The pupils of a typical school are grouped as classes and each class, depending on its grade and possibly specialization, needs to receive instruction in certain subjects for a fixed number of hours per week. Every teacher can teach certain subjects and each class should be assigned one fixed teacher per subject. The challenge is then to find a timetable where each class fulfills the teaching requirements while observing a large number of constraints, e.g., a class cannot be taught two subjects at the same time, certain subjects require special facilities which may be limited; we refer to Faber et al. [3] for a more thorough discussion.

Since the application is to be used by the administrative personnel which is in charge of the creation of timetables it should come with an easy-to-use GUI. The application further needs to connect to a database for retrieval of information about classes, such as their teaching requirements, available teachers and their subjects. The GUI may present this data and allow for specifying constraints and desired properties (e.g., that the music room is not available on Fridays). These components are typically implemented in an object-oriented language.

However, the actual creation of the timetable is more easily realized in ASP. To this end, PY-ASPIO can be used to interface the ASP program. An input specification can be used to pass the input from the GUI to the program, and an output specification is used to extract the candidate timetables into objects which can be displayed in the GUI.

Afterwards, the results can be further processed by the object-oriented components. For instance, timetables may be printed for distribution to classes and teachers. To this end, the application first needs to layout the data in a printable format and then send this layout to the printer by relying on the printing functions of the operating system, which cannot be done in ASP.

**Workforce Allocation Problem.** As part of their regular operation, companies need to assign workers to tasks under a number of (possibly weak) constraints such as necessary skills and legal restrictions. Creating these allocation

---

[5] https://www.riverbankcomputing.com/software/pyqt/intro.
[6] https://www.djangoproject.com/.

plans manually is a time-intensive and error-prone task. Ricca et al. [12] have developed an encoding in ASP, and a GUI in Java on top of the ASP program. Here, again, the object-oriented part of such an application needs to interface with other systems and the user to retrieve input data, and the output of the ASP program (allocation plans, employee statistics and/or a list of constraint violations) is used for additional processing. Besides displaying the plans, the system might generate reports about the workload statistics and forward them to the responsible managers, and automatically notify the workers of their new assignments once approved by the user.

## 6 Discussion and Related Work

The specification language has been designed to be independent from the concrete object-oriented language. While the types on the input parameters are not strictly required by our Python implementation, they allow our approach to be implemented for statically-typed languages such as C++ and Java. An implementation in C++, for example, can be realized with a separate compilation step, turning the annotated ASP program into a function that accepts the input parameters from the input specification and returns a result with a structure as defined in the output specification. The types of the expressions in the output specification can be inferred automatically to allow static declarations of the output variables, e.g. both definitions in Example 4 result in instances of $Set\langle str\rangle$.

Our system uses the DLVHEX solver as backend, which can solve HEX programs in addition to plain ASP programs. HEX is an extension of ASP that allows the incorporation of external computation sources (cf. [2] for details). Currently, external computation sources can be implemented via DLVHEX plugins written either in C++ or Python. In the latter case, PY-ASPIO allows for a seamless integration of application components, which cannot be easily realized in ASP, a declarative component, and the possibility to make callbacks to the procedural code.

We now discuss differences to existing works on bridging the gap between ASP and procedural or object-oriented languages. Oetsch et al. [10] present a system that integrates ASP with Java programs. As in our system, the ASP code resides in a separate file and is annotated with input parameters (here, the annotations show similarity to a Java function definition). However, in this system the input arguments are accessed from the rules of the ASP program using dedicated atoms, and special atoms govern the creation of output objects. Another approach is *JASP* [4], which extends Java by constructs to allow ASP code to be directly embedded in Java code, forming a hybrid language. This hybrid language is compiled to pure Java code that uses a lower-level API to interact with the ASP solver. An interesting aspect of this system is that standardized annotations of the Java Persistence API (JPA) for object-relational mapping are used to interface with ASP. In contrast to both JASP and the system presented by Oetsch et al., we do not modify the syntax of ASP itself.

Because of this, all annotated programs are still valid ASP programs that can continue to be used in existing systems. Furthermore, most ASP variations can immediately be used without adaptation of the mapping library, e.g. external atoms via existing DLVHEX plugins can already be used with PY-ASPIO.

*EmbASP* [5] is a recent work that describes the abstract architecture of an ASP framework and implements this framework as a Java library with an emphasis on support for mobile platforms. However, while EmbASP intends to provide a language-agnostic ASP framework, the definitions of the input/output mapping still depend on Java-specific features (alternatives for other languages are discussed briefly). The mapping is guided by custom annotations on Java classes, which are associated one-to-one with a predicate, where annotations on their fields define the argument positions. *asp4j*[7] is a Java library that utilizes custom class annotations to guide the mapping process, similar to EmbASP. Unlike JASP, EmbASP and asp4j, the mapping annotations in our system are in the ASP code and separate from the object-oriented code. This means the ASP program forms a self-contained component, with the input and output specifications defining an external, object-oriented interface to the declarative ASP part, while still being independent from the concrete object-oriented language. This approach enables the ASP component to be maintained separately, and allows a single ASP file to be used simultaneously by multiple applications (possibly in different programming languages, provided the custom classes have the same names). While the ASP programmer still needs certain knowledge about the object-oriented world, the object-oriented programmer can call the ASP component as-is, without requiring much accomodation on the OOP side, e.g., usually no separate data-holding objects need to be constructed by the client code when using our approach.

*Tweety* [13] is a collection of Java libraries with the goal of providing a general framework for many different approaches to knowledge representation and reasoning. Its ASP component includes a parser for ASP programs, classes to construct ASP programs in Java, and connections to several solvers. *PyASP*[8] provides a Python wrapper of the answer set solving tools gringo and clasp from the Potassco suite [6]. While both Tweety and PyASP provide an easy way to invoke an ASP solver from object-oriented code, the burden of mapping between objects and facts/answer sets is still mostly on the user because input data is passed by manually instantiating fact objects, and answer sets are returned as lists of literals which, again, must be inspected manually.

# 7   Conclusion and Outlook

We have introduced a language to provide an object-oriented interface for ASP programs. It allows for the specification of input and output data of ASP programs in terms of objects of a conventional object-oriented language. The language is flexible and can be implemented for arbitrary object-oriented

---

[7] https://github.com/hbeck/asp4j.
[8] https://pypi.python.org/pypi/pyasp.

languages which provide a minimum set of features. The approach does not depend on a specific ASP dialect or solver, which allows many ASP extensions to be used together with input/output specifications. However, we also provide a reference implementation PY-ASPIO in Python that enables programmers to easily evaluate ASP programs from Python code with the help of this language. This implementation currently supports DLVHEX as underlying ASP solver, thus offering access to the full power of HEX programs in addition to regular ASP programs.

For future work, one possible starting point concerns the language itself. More features, such as the possibility to handle errors (e.g. duplicate indices when creating sequences) may be added to increase flexibility. Also, because of the independence of the specification language from a concrete object-oriented language, implementations for other languages may be provided. In particular, for statically typed, compiled languages such as C++ and Java. While this paper focuses on interfacing with object-oriented languages, the same approach can conceivably be extended to other languages that provide appropriate data structures (e.g., in Haskell, record types might be used instead of classes). Moreover, the ASP solver is currently executed in a separate process, which incurs overhead from inter-process communication. It is worthwhile to investigate the impact of this overhead and, in case this is significant, integrate the ASP solver as a shared library in the host process to enable more efficient communication.

# References

1. Eiter, T., Ianni, G., Krennwallner, T.: Answer set programming: a primer. In: Tessaris, S., Franconi, E., Eiter, T., Gutierrez, C., Handschuh, S., Rousset, M.-C., Schmidt, R.A. (eds.) Reasoning Web 2009. LNCS, vol. 5689, pp. 40–110. Springer, Heidelberg (2009). doi:10.1007/978-3-642-03754-2_2. http://www.kr.tuwien.ac.at/staff/tkren/pub/2009/rw2009-asp.pdf
2. Eiter, T., Ianni, G., Schindlauer, R., Tompits, H.: A uniform integration of higher-order reasoning and external evaluations in answer-set programming. In: IJCAI, pp. 90–96. Professional Book Center (2005)
3. Faber, W., Leone, N., Pfeifer, G.: Representing school timetabling in a disjunctive logic programming language. In: Proceedings of the 13th Workshop on Logic Programming (WLP 1998), vol. 194 (1998)
4. Febbraro, O., Leone, N., Grasso, G., Ricca, F.: JASP: A framework for integrating answer set programming with java. In: Brewka, G., Eiter, T., McIlraith, S.A. (eds.) Proceedings of the Thirteenth International Conference Principles of Knowledge Representation and Reasoning, KR 2012, Rome, Italy, 10–14 June 2012. AAAI Press (2012). http://www.aaai.org/ocs/index.php/KR/KR12/paper/view/4520
5. Fuscà, D., Germano, S., Zangari, J., Anastasio, M., Calimeri, F., Perri, S.: A framework for easing the development of applications embedding answer set programming. In: Cheney, J., Vidal, G. (eds.) Proceedings of the 18th International Symposium on Principles and Practice of Declarative Programming, Edinburgh, United Kingdom, 5–7 September 2016, pp. 38–49. ACM (2016) http://doi.acm.org/10.1145/2967973.2968594

6. Gebser, M., Kaufmann, B., Kaminski, R., Ostrowski, M., Schaub, T., Schneider, M.: Potassco: the potsdam answer set solving collection. AI Commun. **24**(2), 107–124    (2011).    http://www.mpi-inf.mpg.de/departments/rg1/conferences/deduction10/papers/martin-gebser.pdf
7. Gelfond, M., Lifschitz, V.: Classical negation in logic programs and disjunctive databases. New Gener. Comput. **9**(3–4), 365–386 (1991)
8. Grasso, G., Leone, N., Manna, M., Ricca, F.: ASP at work: spin-off and applications of the DLV system. In: Balduccini, M., Son, T.C. (eds.) Logic Programming, Knowledge Representation, and Nonmonotonic Reasoning. LNCS, vol. 6565, pp. 432–451. Springer, Heidelberg (2011). doi:10.1007/978-3-642-20832-4_27
9. Ielpa, S.M., Iiritano, S., Leone, N., Ricca, F.: An ASP-based system for e-Tourism. In: Erdem, E., Lin, F., Schaub, T. (eds.) LPNMR 2009. LNCS, vol. 5753, pp. 368–381. Springer, Heidelberg (2009). doi:10.1007/978-3-642-04238-6_31
10. Oetsch, J., Pührer, J., Tompits, H.: Extending Object-Oriented Languages by Declarative Specifications of Complex Objects using Answer-Set Programming. CoRR abs/1112.0922 (2011). http://arxiv.org/abs/1112.0922
11. Redl, C.: The DLVHEX system for knowledge representation: recent advances (system description). In: Theory and Practice of Logic Programming
12. Ricca, F., Grasso, G., Alviano, M., Manna, M., Lio, V., Iiritano, S., Leone, N.: Team-building with answer set programming in the Gioia-Tauro seaport. TPLP **12**(3), 361–381 (2012). http://dx.doi.org/10.1017/S147106841100007X
13. Thimm, M.: Tweety: a comprehensive collection of java libraries for logical aspects of artificial intelligence and knowledge representation. In: Baral, C., Giacomo, G.D., Elter, T. (eds.) Principles of Knowledge Representation and Reasoning: Proceedings of the Fourteenth International Conference, KR 2014, Vienna, Austria, 20–24 July 2014. AAAI Press (2014). http://www.aaai.org/ocs/index.php/KR/KR14/paper/view/7811

# Extending Answer Set Programs with Interpreted Functions as First-Class Citizens

Christoph Redl$^{(\boxtimes)}$

Institut für Informationssysteme, Technische Universität Wien,
Favoritenstraße 9-11, 1040 Vienna, Austria
redl@kr.tuwien.ac.at

**Abstract.** Answer Set Programming (ASP) is a well-known problem solving approach based on nonmonotonic logic programs. Existing approaches towards integrating function terms into ASP can be organized in two classes: uninterpreted function symbols and interpreted functions; we focus on the latter. Existing approaches usually define interpreted functions in the program (e.g. using term equations), while evaluation wrt. to a *pre-existing external semantics* is neglected. However, this is useful if existing function libraries shall be accessed or if a function is more naturally implemented in procedural code. In this paper, we propose the declarative language of $\text{HEX}^{\text{IFU}}$-*programs* which extends answer set programs (ASP) with such interpreted functions. However, rather than just providing a means for evaluating functions, it further turns interpreted functions into *first-class citizens*, i.e., functions are represented by accessible objects in the program. This paves the way for *functionals (higher-order functions)*, i.e., functions that take other functions as arguments or return them. We provide then a rewriting of such programs to HEX-*programs*, an extension of ASP with external sources, and an implementation based on this rewriting. Afterwards we present applications which motivated our work, e.g. the adoption of design pattern from software engineering. Finally, we discuss properties of the formalism and differences to related work.

**Keywords:** Answer set programming · Nonmonotonic reasoning · FLP semantics · Function symbols

## 1 Introduction

Answer Set Programming (ASP) is a declarative programming paradigm based on nonmonotonic programs and a multi-model semantics [18]. For the integration of function symbols into ASP there exist basically two fairly different classes of

This research has been supported by the Austrian Science Fund (FWF) project P27730.

Y. Lierler and W. Taha (Eds.): PADL 2017, LNCS 10137, pp. 68–85, 2017.
DOI: 10.1007/978-3-319-51676-9_5

approaches: viewing them either as *uninterpreted function symbols* or as *interpreted functions*.

The former view uses them as constructors for structuring information but with no inherent semantics. It is supported by many state-of-the-art grounders such as GRINGO [15] and recent releases of DLV [22]. In this case, the term $multiply(add(4,5),3)$ might be used to represent the computation $(4 + 5) \cdot 3$, but since all function terms have a Herbrand semantics (i.e., they evaluate to themselves), there is no way to actually evaluate the term wrt. the intended semantics. The second view is followed by some existing approaches which, however, define functions *within* programs with first-order-like interpretations using e.g. term equations in rule heads. This allows for detaching from Herbrand interpretations and syntactically different function terms can be equal, which yields new modeling possibilities. For instance, $loc(redCar) = loc(blueCar)$ represents that $redCar$ and $blueCar$ have the same location, in which case the comparison evaluates to true, while the terms would never be equal under a Herbrand semantics.

However, existing approaches do not support the call of functions whose semantics is defined *outside* of the logic program. Using such *externally* defined functions is motivated by practical observations. Some types of computations are more naturally implemented in a procedural languages, e.g. because numeric computations often lead to a large grounding. Moreover, pre-existing libraries of functions for special purposes (such as mathematical computations and physics simulations) are typically provided for procedural languages and it would be cumbersome to redefine them.

In this paper we suggest a new language, called HEX$^{\text{IFU}}$-*programs*, to address this restriction. To this end, we associate function symbols with a given *external semantics*. However, rather than just adding a possibility to evaluate terms, it further turns interpreted functions into *first-class citizens* (accessible objects) that can be handled similarly as object constants and terms over uninterpreted function symbols; but at specific points, their semantics may be applied to parameters. This allows for passing them to other functions or retrieving them and paves the way for *functionals* (also known as *higher-order functions*), i.e., functions that take other functions as parameters or return them. Applications can be found in *software design patterns* such as the *factory* and the *strategy pattern*, accessing heterogeneous knowledge-bases via a generic interface, and typical usecases in functional programming such as a *mapping* function.

HEX$^{\text{IFU}}$-programs are based on (and further extend) HEX-programs, an extension of ASP with external sources such as description logic ontologies and Web resources. HEX-programs support external atoms to pass information from the logic program (given by predicate extensions and constants), to an external source, which in turn returns values to the program. For instance, the external atom $\&synonym[aircraft](X)$ might be used to find the synonyms $X$ of $aircraft$, e.g. *airplane*. However, unlike interpreted functions in HEX$^{\text{IFU}}$-programs, external atoms in standard HEX-programs are *no* first-class citizens and *cannot* be accessed as objects, which inhibits the aforementioned applications.

In more detail, after the preliminaries (Sect. 2), the organization of the paper and our contributions are as follows:

- In Sect. 3 we present HEX$^{\text{IFU}}$-*programs* as our main contribution. To this end, we first introduce a representation of interpreted functions by terms. Based on this, we introduce HEX-programs with *interpreted function (ifu-)atoms*. A special case thereof are ASP programs with interpreted functions.
- In Sect. 4 we define a rewriting of HEX$^{\text{IFU}}$-programs to standard HEX-programs. This is the basis for the implementation of a HEX$^{\text{IFU}}$-reasoner.
- In Sect. 5 we present applications of HEX$^{\text{IFU}}$-programs motivated by design patterns in software engineering, existing applications of KR-formalisms, and typical applications of functionals in functional programming. We further discuss how they benefit from the features of HEX$^{\text{IFU}}$-programs compared to standard HEX-programs.
- In Sect. 6 we discuss finiteness properties and the computational complexity of HEX$^{\text{IFU}}$-programs. We show how a pre-existing framework for deciding finite groundability of HEX-programs can also be applied to HEX$^{\text{IFU}}$-programs. Overall, we show that important properties of HEX-programs still hold for HEX$^{\text{IFU}}$-programs.
- In Sect. 7 we discuss related work, point out differences to our approach, conclude and give an outlook on future work.

## 2  Preliminaries

We recapitulate HEX-programs as follows. Our alphabet consists of possibly infinite, mutually disjoint sets of constant symbols $\mathscr{C}$ (including all integers), variables $\mathscr{V}$, function symbols $\mathscr{F}$, predicate symbols $\mathscr{P}$, and external predicates $\mathscr{X}$. We let the set of terms $\mathscr{T}$ be the least set such that $\mathscr{C} \subseteq \mathscr{T}$, $\mathscr{V} \subseteq \mathscr{T}$, and $f \in \mathscr{F}, \bar{T}_1, \ldots, \bar{T}_\ell \in \mathscr{T}$ implies $f(\bar{T}_1, \ldots, \bar{T}_\ell) \in \mathscr{T}$.[1] A term is called *ground* if it does not contain variables.

We start with basic concepts. A ground (ordinary) atom is of form $p(t_1, \ldots, t_\ell)$ with predicate symbol $p \in \mathscr{P}$ and ground terms $t_1, \ldots, t_\ell \in \mathscr{T}$, abbreviated as $p(\mathbf{t})$; we write $t \in \mathbf{t}$ if $t = t_i$ for some $1 \leq i \leq \ell$. An *assignment* over the (finite) set $\mathscr{A}$ of atoms is a set $A \subseteq \mathscr{A}$, where $a \in A$ expresses that $a$ is true and $a \notin A$ that $a$ is false. A builtin atom is of form $t_1 \circ t_2$ with terms $t_1, t_2 \in \mathscr{T}$ and comparison operator $\circ \in \{=, \neq, <, \leq, \geq, >\}$. For a ground builtin atom $t_1 \circ t_2$ and any assignment $A$ we have that $A \models t_1 = t_2$ if $t_1$ is (syntactically) equal to $t_2$ and $A \not\models t_1 = t_2$ otherwise. Conversely, $A \models t_1 \neq t_2$ if $t_1$ and $t_2$ are (syntactically) different and $A \not\models t_1 \neq t_2$ otherwise. Operators $<, \leq, \geq$ and $>$ have the standard semantics and are defined only if $t_1$ and $t_2$ are integers.

We recall HEX-programs, which generalize (disjunctive) logic programs under the answer set semantics [18]; for more details and background, see [12].

---

[1] We let $\bar{T}$ denote a *meta-variable* (not to be confused with ASP variables in the object language) which represents a constant from $\mathscr{C}$, an ASP variable from $\mathscr{V}$, or a ground or non-ground functional terms (e.g. $f(a)$, $g(X)$).

**Syntax of HEX-Programs.** HEX-programs extend ASP programs by *external atoms* to enable a bidirectional interaction between a program and external sources. A *ground external atom* is of the form $\&g[\mathbf{y}](\mathbf{t})$, where $\mathbf{y} = y_1, \dots, y_k$ is a list of input parameters (predicate names or terms), called *input list*, and $\mathbf{t} = t_1, \dots, t_l$ are output terms.

**Definition 1.** *A ground HEX-program $\Pi$ consists of rules*

$$a_1 \vee \cdots \vee a_h \leftarrow b_1, \dots, b_m, \text{not } b_{m+1}, \dots, \text{not } b_n ,$$

*where each $a_i$ is a ground ordinary atom, and each $b_j$ is a ground ordinary, builtin or external atom; for such a rule $r$ we let $H(r) = \{a_1, \dots, a_h\}$ be its head and $B(r) = \{b_1, \dots, b_m, \text{not } b_{m+1}, \dots, \text{not } b_n\}$ be its body.*

**Semantics of HEX-Programs.** In the following, assignments are over the set $\mathscr{A}$ of ordinary atoms occurring in the program $\Pi$ at hand. The semantics of a ground external atom $\&g[\mathbf{y}](\mathbf{t})$ wrt. an assignment $A$ is given by the value of a $1+k+l$-ary *Boolean oracle function* $f_{\&g}$ that is defined for all possible values of $A$, $\mathbf{y}$ and $\mathbf{t}$. We say $\&g[\mathbf{y}](\mathbf{t})$ is *true* relative to $A$ if $f_{\&g}(A, \mathbf{y}, \mathbf{t}) = \mathbf{T}$, and *false* if $f_{\&g}(A, \mathbf{y}, \mathbf{t}) = \mathbf{F}$. Satisfaction of rules and ASP programs [18] is then extended to HEX rules and programs as follows. An assignment $A$ satisfies an atom $u$, denoted $A \models u$, if $u \in A$, and it does not satisfy it, denoted $A \not\models a$, otherwise. It satisfies a default-negated atom not $a$, denoted $A \models \text{not } a$, if $A \not\models a$, and it does not satisfy it, denoted $A \not\models \text{not } a$, otherwise. A rule $r$ is satisfied under assignment $A$, denoted $A \models r$, if $A \models a$ for some $a \in H(r)$ or $A \not\models a$ for some $a \in B(r)$.

The answer sets of a HEX-program $\Pi$ are defined as follows. Let the *Faber-Leone-Pfeifer-reduct)* [13], also called FLP-reduct (unrelated to functional logic programming), of $\Pi$ wrt. an assignment $A$ be the set $f\Pi^A = \{r \in \Pi \mid A \models b \text{ for all } b \in B(r)\}$ of all rules whose body is satisfied by $A$. We define:

**Definition 2.** *An assignment $A$ is an answer set of a HEX-program $\Pi$, if $A$ is a $\subseteq$-minimal model of $f\Pi^A$.* [2]

*Example 1.* Consider the program $\Pi = \{p \leftarrow \&id[p]()\}$, where $\&id[p]()$ is true iff $p$ is true. Then $\Pi$ has the answer set $A_1 = \emptyset$ as it is a $\subseteq$-minimal model of $f\Pi^{A_1} = \emptyset$. □

We also use programs with variables and consider them as shortcuts for all ground instances. The answer sets of a program $\Pi$ with variables are defined as the answer sets of the program $grnd(\Pi)$, which results from $\Pi$ if all variables $\mathscr{V}$ are substituted by all ground terms from $\mathscr{T}$ in all possible ways. For now we assume that safety conditions guarantee the existence of a finite grounding which suffices for answer set computation and restrict our discussion to ground programs. We come back to safety in Sect. 6.

---

[2] For ordinary $\Pi$, these are Gelfond & Lifschitz's answer sets.

# 3  Interpreted Functions as First-Class Citizens

Function symbols are often uninterpreted, i.e., they are used for structuring information but have no intrinsic semantics. For instance, the term $multiply(add(4,5),3)$ might represent the expression $(4+5) \cdot 3$, but there is no way to evaluate it. Existing approaches towards interpreted functions typically define functions as part of the program, e.g. using term equations (see Sect. 7 for more details). However, the evaluation wrt. an external semantics was neglected. On the other hand, external atoms in HEX-programs and VI-programs [8], have such a semantics. But unlike terms, they are not *first-class citizens* [6], i.e., they are not objects with an own identity that can be passed as arguments to or returned from (other) external atoms.

One might support the evaluation of ground terms under a given semantics by adopting the semantics of builtin atoms such that e.g. $X = multiply(add(4,5),3)$ evaluates to true if $X$ is 27 (assuming that the semantics associated with the function symbols is as expected) and to false otherwise. However, the term $multiply(add(4,5),3)$ represents the *application* of the (unnamed) function $\cdot(p_1,p_2,p_3) = (p_1+p_2) \cdot p_3$ under the concrete parameters 4, 5 and 3, but *not* the function itself. Also the non-ground term $multiply(add(X,Y),Z)$ is only a shortcut for a number of evaluations of $\cdot(p_1,p_2,p_3)$ under lists of parameters, but the function itself is not represented by an accessible object. This prohibits the composition of new functions, passing them as parameters to other functions, or retrieving them as return values. To address these restrictions, we propose an extension of HEX-programs with interpreted functions featuring the following:

– Function symbols from $\mathscr{F}$ are associated with externally defined semantics.
– Based on $\mathscr{F}$, called *basic functions*, new functions can be composed.
– Each basic or composed function is represented by a dedicated term $t$, which can be used wherever uninterpreted terms (such as constants) can also be used.
– A term $t$ in the program, which represents a function, can be applied to a list of parameters to compute the value of the respective function under the parameters.

We first show how functions can be represented by terms and introduce then the HEX-extension of HEX$^{IFU}$-programs.

**Representing Interpreted Functions by Terms.** We assume that each *basic function* $f \in \mathscr{F}$ has an arity $\ell$ and a (total) semantics function $sem_f(\mathbf{y}) \colon \mathscr{C}^\ell \mapsto \mathscr{T}$ defined for all $\ell$-ary vectors $\mathbf{y} \in \mathscr{C}^\ell$ of constants. We let $\mathscr{C}$ contain dedicated constant symbols $\#i$ for all integers $i \geq 1$, called *placeholders*, which are used to represent function parameters.

We then use $\mathscr{T}$ as *function-representing (fr-)terms* to turn interpreted functions into accessible objects. To this end, a ground fr-term $t \in \mathscr{T}$ represents a $\gamma(t)$-ary function $\hat{t}(p_1,\ldots,p_{\gamma(t)})$, which substitutes all occurrences $\#i$ in $t$ by $p_i$, and then applies the semantics $sem_f(\mathbf{y})$ of the function symbols $f$ in $t$, where $\gamma(t)$ is the largest $i$ such that $\#i$ occurs in $t$, or 0 if no $\#i$ occurs. Intuitively, $\gamma(t)$

is the number of parameters which are expected to be passed to the function represented by $t$.

*Example 2.* The fr-term $t_1 = multiply(add(\#1, \#2), \#3)$ represents in standard mathematical notation the function $\hat{t}_1(p_1, p_2, p_3) = (p_1 + p_2) \cdot p_3$, assuming that the basic functions *multiply* and *add* have the expected semantics.

The fr-term $t_2 = add(\#1, 1)$ defines the increment function $\hat{t}_2(p_1) = p_1 + 1$ using basic function *add* by fixing the second operand to 1, while the first is the one of $\hat{t}_2$. $\square$

It is important to note that an fr-term $t = f(t_1, \ldots, t_\ell)$ with $f \in \mathscr{F}$ and $t_1, \ldots, t_\ell \in \mathscr{T}$ itself represents a (composed) function, and *not* the application of $f$ to $t_1, \ldots, t_\ell$. Instead, the subterms $t_1, \ldots, t_\ell$ define how the function $\hat{t}$ is composed of other functions, and constants $\#i$ in $t$ specify how the parameters of $\hat{t}$ are passed to these basic functions (cf. $t_1$ in the previous example). The actual parameters $p_1, \ldots, p_{\gamma(t)}$ of $\hat{t}$ are specified at the point when $\hat{t}$ is applied as described below.

The semantics of basic functions $f \in \mathscr{F}$ is directly defined by $sem_f(\cdot)$. We now formalize the evaluation of the function $\hat{t}$ given by an fr-term $t$ under parameters $p_1, \ldots, p_{\gamma(t)}$ recursively on top of functions $sem_f(\cdot)$ for all $f \in \mathscr{F}$ as follows:

**Definition 3.** *For a list of ground terms* $t, p_1, \ldots, p_{\gamma(t)}$ *we let*

$$
val(t, p_1, \ldots, p_{\gamma(t)}) = \begin{cases} val(sem_f(\mathbf{t}'), p_1, \ldots, p_{\gamma(t)}) & \text{if } t = f(\mathbf{t}) \text{ and } \mathbf{t}' \text{ is free of } \#i, \\ f(\mathbf{t}') & \text{if } t = f(\mathbf{t}) \text{ and there is a } \#i \text{ in } \mathbf{t}', \\ p_i & \text{if } t = \#i \text{ for some } 1 \leq i \leq \gamma(t), \\ t & \text{otherwise,} \end{cases}
$$

*where* $\mathbf{t}$ *and* $\mathbf{t}'$ *are* $\ell$-ary vectors with $t'_i = val(t_i, p_1, \ldots, p_{\gamma(t)})$ *for all* $1 \leq i \leq \ell$.

The idea is as follows. If the fr-term $t$ representing the function $\hat{t}$ to be evaluated is a nested term $f(\mathbf{t})$ (first two cases), then all subterms $\mathbf{t} = t_1, \ldots, t_\ell$, which represent functions that $\hat{t}$ is composed of, are first recursively evaluated. The results of these evaluations are given by $\mathbf{t}' = t'_1, \ldots, t'_\ell$. If $\mathbf{t}'$ is free of placeholders (first case), then the semantics of the outermost basic function $f$ is applied. Due to functionals (shown in more detail in Example 8), the return value of $sem_f(\mathbf{t}')$ may contain further functions that must be interpreted, which is why we recursively apply *val* to the result. Otherwise (second case), the functional term $f(\mathbf{t}')$ contains at least one placeholder and is returned as an fr-term representing a new function. For non-nested terms, placeholders are replaced by the respective parameters (third case), and all other constants are kept (fourth case).

*Example 3 (cont'd).* Reconsider the functional term $t = multiply(add(\#1, \#2), \#3)$ and suppose $\hat{t}$ is to be evaluated under parameters 4, 5 and 3, i.e., we compute $val(t, 4, 5, 3)$.

We recursively evaluate the subterms $t_1 = add(\#1, \#2)$ and $t_2 = \#3$ of $t$ under 4, 5, 3. To this end, we determine $t'_1 = val(add(\#1, \#2), 4, 5, 3)$ and $t'_2 = val(\#3, 4, 5, 3)$. The former is recursively evaluated by computing $val(\#1, 4, 5, 3) = 4$, $val(\#2, 4, 5, 3) = 5$ and evaluating $t'_1 = val(sem_{add}(4, 5)) = 9$. The latter yields $t'_2 = val(\#3, 4, 5, 3) = 3$.

Finally, since none of $t'_1, t'_2$ contains placeholders, we evaluate $val(sem_{multiply}(t'_1, t'_2)) = val(sem_{multiply}(9, 3)) = 27$, and thus we have $val(t, 4, 5, 3) = 27$. □

Beginning from the deepest nesting level, $val(\cdot)$ evaluates the functions $\hat{t}$ is composed of recursively but stops if some $\#i$ occur. Functions with a smaller nesting level than the placeholder remain uninterpreted until their parameters are specified. Although pre-existing placeholders in $t$ are replaced during evaluation, new placeholders may be introduced by $p_1, \ldots, p_\ell$.

*Example 4.* Consider $t = add(\#1, 1)$ and suppose $\hat{t}$ is evaluated under $p_1 = add(\#1, \#2)$. Then $t' = val(t, p_1) = add(add(\#1, \#2), 1)$ represents the new function $\hat{t}'(p_1, p_2) = (p_1 + p_2) + 1$ with two parameters that returns the increment of their sum. The fr-term $t'$ can then be used to apply $\hat{t}'$ to parameters, e.g. $val(t', 10, 20) = 31$. □

**Programs with Interpreted Functions.** Next, we need a means for applying functions given by fr-terms to parameters, i.e., for accessing $val(\cdot)$ from the program. To this end, we introduce *interpreted function (ifu-)atoms*, whose syntax is inspired by builtin atoms:

**Definition 4.** *An* interpreted function (ifu-)atom *is of kind* $\bar{R} =_\$ \bar{T}[\bar{P}_1, \ldots, \bar{P}_\ell]$, *where* $\bar{R} \in \mathscr{T}$ *is a comparison operand,* $\bar{T} \in \mathscr{T}$ *is an fr-term, and* $\bar{P}_1, \ldots, \bar{P}_\ell \in \mathscr{T}$ *are parameters.*

Here, the subscript $\$$ of the comparison operator is used to distinguish an ifu-atom from equality builtin atoms. While builtin atoms over $=$ compares terms syntactically, $=_\$$ evaluates the term on the right-hand side before comparison. We have that $\bar{R}, \bar{T}, \bar{P}_1, \ldots, \bar{P}_\ell$ are possibly non-ground to allow exploiting the ASP grounder.

Informally, a ground ifu-atom $r =_\$ t[p_1, \ldots, p_{\gamma(t)}]$ is intended to be true iff $r$ is equal to the value of the function represented by fr-term $t$ under parameters $p_1, \ldots, p_{\gamma(t)}$ holds. Based on Definition 3 we define:

**Definition 5.** *A ground ifu-atom $a$ of form $r =_\$ t[t_1, \ldots, t_n]$ is true wrt. assignment $A$, denoted $A \models a$, if $n = \gamma(t)$ and $r$ has the value of $val(t, t_1, \ldots, t_n)$, and false, denoted $A \not\models a$, otherwise.*

*Example 5.* The ifu-atom $X =_\$ add(\#1, 1)[Y]$ applies the increment function, represented by the fr-term $add(\#1, 1)$, to the parameter $Y$ and compares the result with $X$. □

Note that because functions are represented by terms, an ifu-atom contains a pair of parentheses (from the fr-term) followed by a pair of brackets (from the parameter list). However, as we will see in the next example, using ASP variables as fr-term conceals the parentheses, which results in a syntax similar to standard mathematical notation. We formalize HEX-programs with ifu-atoms as follows:

**Definition 6.** *A* HEX-*program with interpreted functions* (HEX$^{\text{IFU}}$*) is a* HEX-*program, where rule bodies may contain ifu-atoms.*

The notions of models of rules/programs and of answer sets carry over.

*Example 6.* Consider the fact *compInitials*(*concat*(*first*(#1), *first*(#2))) $\leftarrow$. The fr-term in the extension of *compInitials* represents a function that constructs a person's initials from given first and last names. The function is based on the basic functions *concat* and *first* for string concatenation and extracting the first character of a string, respectively. If facts of kind *person*(*F, L*) $\leftarrow$ represent persons with first name *F* and last name *L*, the rule *initials*(*F, L, I*) $\leftarrow$ *person*(*F, L*), *compInitials*(*C*), *I* $=_{\$}$ *C*[*F, L*] computes the initials of all persons by applying the function, which is accessible via *C*, to the parameters.

As the example demonstrates, terms that represent interpreted functions are accessible from the extension of predicates. That is, an fr-term *t* occurs as parameters of an atom of kind *f*(*t*) $\leftarrow$. The application of the function to a list **p** of parameters is then possible using a rule of kind *res*(*T*) $\leftarrow$ *f*(*T*), *R* $=_{\$}$ *T*[**p**].

## 4 Implementation of Interpreted Functions Using HEX-**Programs**

We realized HEX$^{\text{IFU}}$-programs on top of standard HEX-programs using a rewriting. The basic idea is to pass a ground fr-term *t* and $\gamma(t)$ parameters to a dedicated external atom &*eval*, which resembles the function *val*($\cdot$) from Definition 3 by substituting each placeholder #*i* for the *i*-th argument $p_i$ and recursively evaluating subterms.

For each integer *n*, let $f_{\&eval_n}(A, t, p_1, \ldots, p_n, r)$ be the semantics of an external predicate &*eval_n* which has as input a term *t* with $n = \gamma(t)$ and parameter values $p_1, \ldots, p_n$, and returns the value of the function term in *r*; as the number of parameters is also visible from the parameter list, we drop the subscript $n$ from &*eval* in the following.

**Definition 7.** *For an assignment A and list of ground terms* $t, p_1, \ldots, p_n$ *s.t.* $\gamma(t) = n$*, let* $f_{\&eval}(A, t, p_1, \ldots, p_n, r) = \sigma$ *where* $\sigma = \mathbf{T}$ *if* $r = val(t, p_1, \ldots, p_n)$ *and* $\sigma = \mathbf{F}$ *otherwise.*

The oracle function $f_{\&eval}$ may access semantics functions $sem_f(\cdot)$ of all basic functions $f \in \mathscr{F}$. This allows for translating HEX$^{\text{IFU}}$-programs to standard HEX-programs:

**Definition 8.** *The translation of an ifu-atom $a$ of kind $\bar{R} =_\$ \bar{T}[\bar{P}_1, \ldots, \bar{P}_\ell]$ to an external atom is given by $\tau(a) = \&eval[\bar{T}, \bar{P}_1, \ldots, \bar{P}_\ell](\bar{R})$.*

For HEX$^{\text{IFU}}$-program $\Pi$, we let $\tau(\Pi)$ be $\Pi$ after replacing each ifu-atom $a$ by $\tau(a)$.

We demonstrate the translation with the following example:

*Example 7 (cont'd).* Reconsider the fr-term $t = concat(first(\#1), first(\#2))$. Then $N =_\$ t[tom, johnson]$ is translated to $\&eval[t, tom, johnson](N)$. This external atom is true for $N = tj$ and false otherwise. $\quad\square$

This translation is sound and complete wrt. the semantics given by Definition 5.

**Proposition 1.** *An assignment $A$ is an answer set of a HEX$^{\text{IFU}}$-program $\Pi$ if an only if it is an answer set of the HEX-program $\tau(\Pi)$.*

Interpreted functions have been implemented in the DLVHEX solver, cf. http://www.kr.tuwien.ac.at/research/systems/dlvhex. The syntax is as in this paper, with $=_\$$ written as $= \$$. The system comes with several examples with interpreted functions.

# 5   Applications of HEX$^{\text{IFU}}$-Programs

We now present several applications of HEX$^{\text{IFU}}$-programs. For each of them, we show how they benefit from the features of HEX$^{\text{IFU}}$-programs compared to standard HEX-programs.

**Software Design Patterns.** Our main motivation for HEX$^{\text{IFU}}$-programs were *functionals*. They can be used to realize programming methods motivated by design patterns in software engineering, cf. e.g. [14]. An example is the *abstract factory pattern* which uses a *factory* class $F$ for creating objects of one of several concrete classes $C_1, \ldots, C_n$ which implement the same interface $C$. Instead of instantiating one of $C_1, \ldots, C_n$ directly, the decision which class to instantiate is delegated to factory $F$. The client retrieves only a reference of type $C$ and uses it abstractly without knowing (and caring) which of the concrete types $C_1, \ldots, C_n$ the reference refers to.

Similarly, functionals in HEX$^{\text{IFU}}$-programs allow for retrieving a function from an external atom that can later be used without knowing its exact type.

*Example 8.* Consider function $getHashFunction()$ that serves as a factory and returns a unary function, which is unknown to the implementer of the HEX-program but still has an associated semantics that can be applied. Then $r(H) \leftarrow F =_\$ getHashFunction()[], H =_\$ F(padl)$ evaluates $getHashFunction()$ (without parameters) to retrieve a concrete hash function $F$, which is subsequently applied to compute the hash value $H$ of $padl$. $\quad\square$

A similar example is the *strategy pattern*, where the algorithm/technique to be applied is selected at runtime based on the data at hand. For instance, a validation to be performed for incoming data usually depends on the type of the data. As a concrete example, consider matching strings against regular expressions. The regular expression for checking phone numbers is clearly different from one for checking email addresses. In such cases, the selection of an appropriate validation function can be done by a dedicated function $\&getValidator[type](V)$ which implements the logic of the decision, i.e., the construction of an appropriate regular expression, depending on the $type \in \{phone, email, url, \ldots\}$ of the given data. The concrete verification function returned by the selection function can then be applied to a *value*:

*Example 9.* Suppose $\&getValidator[type](V)$ returns a function $V$ for verifying data of the given *type*. Provided that the returned verification functions evaluate to 1 if the check is passed and to 0 otherwise, a concrete *value* is verified by the ifu-atom $1 =_\$ V(value)$.

Suppose employee data is given by facts of form $emp(id, attType, attValue)$, where *id* is a unique identifier for each employee, and *attType* and *attValue* specify the value of a certain attribute. For example, $emp(3, firstname, john)$ defines that the first name of employee 3 is *john*. In the following, $r_1$ imports a verification function for each attribute type specified for at least one employee and $r_2$ applies it to all values of this type.

$r_1 : validators(AttType, V) \leftarrow emp(Id, AttType, AttValue), \&getValidator[AttType](V).$

$r_2 : invalid(Id) \leftarrow emp(Id, AttType, AttValue), validators(AttType, V), 0 =_\$ V[AttValue].$

The program derives $invalid(id)$ for all identifiers *id* of employee with invalid entries.

Benefits: Without functionals and interpreted functions as accessible objects, one must implement separate validation rules for all attribute type, which differ only in the external atom which performs the evaluation, but be of the same structure otherwise. This would introduce redundancies which make it more cumbersome to maintain the program.                                                          □

**Integrating Heterogeneous Knowledge Bases.** Another example is the integration of multiple data sources which are possibly implemented in different formalisms, as realized e.g. by *multi-context systems* [5]. A functional can serve as a central dictionary that supports lookups of concrete knowledge-bases with a common query interface. Lookups are then answered with functions that allow for accessing the concrete knowledge-base abstractly without knowing its type and location.

*Example 10.* For instance, suppose $lookup(\#1)$ provides access to the central dictionary and is accessible via predicate *l*. Then rule $data(A) \leftarrow l(D), K =_\$ D[employee], A =_\$ K[query]$ can be used to answer queries over the *employee* knowledge-base using the access function $D$, which returns an abstract knowledge-base $K$ that can be used to answer queries without knowing its type.

Benefits: As above, without functionals separate rules of the same basic structure must be defined for each type of knowledge-based, which differ only in the external atom.                                                                   □

**Realizing Traditional Higher-order Functions.** Also typical (generic) higher-order functions known from functional programming can be realized on top of HEX$^{\mathrm{IFU}}$. These include, e.g., *map* for applying a custom function to all elements from a list, *fold* for aggregating values in a data structure, or *sort* with a custom comparison function.

*Example 11.* Consider the external atom $\&map[f, p](X)$ which applies function $f$, given as an fr-term, to all elements in the extension of predicate $p$ and the function for computing a person's initials as shown in Example 6. Then the rule $res(R) \leftarrow compInitials(C), R =_\$ \&map[C, person](X)$ can be used to compute the initials of all persons in the extension of predicate *person*.

Benefits: Without functionals as accessible objects, one may define $\&map[fn, p](X)$ where *fn* is the *name* of a function to be applied to $p$. However, all functions identified by such names must be known to the implementation of $\&map$ and are not arbitrary.                                                □

**Syntax Relaxation.** Finally, interpreted function symbols are also a more natural alternative for external atoms with functional behavior such as string functions (concatenation, substring, etc.). The syntax is lightweight and similar to builtin atoms.

**Discussion.** While it is possible to simulate functionals by standard HEX-programs if all involved external sources are provided by the implementer of the HEX-program, this is in general not the case. For instance, Example 8 can be implemented such that not the hash function but only its name $N$ is imported into the program. Consider the modified rule $r(H) \leftarrow \&getHashFunctionName[](N), \&applyHashFunction[N, padl](H)$. The name of the hash function $N$ is passed to a dedicated external atom $\&applyHashFunction$, which internally selects the function identified by $N$ and applies it to the given string. Now $N$ plays the role of $F$ from Example 8, but is instantiated with a string instead of an fr-term. The parameters of $\&applyHashFunction$ do not contain fr-terms but only object constants, i.e., $\&applyHashFunction$ is not a functional. However, now $\&applyHashFunction$ must be aware of all possible hash functions; if a new one is added, the external source $\&applyHashFunction$ must be modified. This is impractical if the function to be passed as argument and the functional itself are provided by different third parties, or if one is provided by a third party and the other one is newly developed. Then the programmer cannot modify the sources and moving functionality from one source to the other is not possible. Also if the set of possible functional parameters is unrestricted, such as for $\&map$, simulating functionals by a standard function is not possible, as it would need to be prepared for an infinite number of possible functions.

# 6   Properties of HEX$^{\text{IFU}}$-Programs

We now investigate relations to programs with uninterpreted function symbols, finiteness and computational properties of HEX$^{\text{IFU}}$-programs.

**Relations to Uninterpreted Function Symbols.** One can show that ASP- or HEX-programs with *uninterpreted* functions amount to a special case of HEX$^{\text{IFU}}$-programs, where each function term is interpreted by itself.

**Proposition 2.** *Let $\Pi$ be a* HEX-*program and let $\Pi'$ be the* HEX$^{\text{IFU}}$-*program resulting from $\Pi$ if each builtin atom $x \circ y$ is replaced by $x =_\$ y$ and $sem_f(\mathbf{y}) = f(\mathbf{y})$ for all function symbols $f$ and $\mathbf{y} \in \mathscr{C}^{\gamma(f)}$. Then the answer sets of $\Pi$ and $\Pi'$ coincide.*

**Finite Groundability.** We call a program $\Pi$ *finitely groundable* if there is a finite $\Pi' \subseteq grnd(\Pi)$ s.t. $\Pi$ and $\Pi'$ have the same answer sets. In this case, it is implied that all answer sets are also finite. For uninterpreted function symbols, several safety concepts have been introduced which allow for deciding finite groundability. For instance, the notion of $\omega$-*restricted logic programs*, which hinges on predicate dependencies, allows function symbols under a level mapping to control the introduction of new terms with function symbols to ensure decidability [29]. More expressive variants thereof are $\lambda$-*restricted* [17], *argument-restricted programs* [23] and *bounded programs* [19]. For an overview of classes of programs with uninterpreted function symbols, cf. e.g. [1].

However, since we consider interpreted functions, these notions are not directly applicable. A HEX$^{\text{IFU}}$-program might be finitely groundable, while it is not finitely groundable if functions are left uninterpreted, or vice versa.

*Example 12.* Consider the HEX$^{\text{IFU}}$ program $\Pi = \{p(a); \; p(Y) \leftarrow p(X), Y =_\$ id(X)\}$ where $id$ is an interpreted function s.t. $sem_{id}(t) = t$ for all terms $t \in \mathscr{T}$. Its only answer set is $A = \{p(a)\}$. In contrast, if $id$ is considered as an uninterpreted function symbol as in $\Pi' = \{p(a); \; p(Y) \leftarrow p(X), Y = id(X)\}$, then there is no finite grounding as the rule derives infinitely many atoms of form $p(id^n(a))$ for all $n \geq 0$.                    □

Conversely, it can also happen that a HEX-program with uninterpreted function symbols is finitely groundable, but after assigning a semantics to the functions it is not.

*Example 13.* Consider the HEX-program $\Pi = \{a \leftarrow 2 = inc(1); \; int(X) \leftarrow a, X > 0\}$. Then its only answer set is $A = \emptyset$ because $2 = inc(1)$ is false, thus $a$ is unsupported and the rule $int(X) \leftarrow a, X > 0$ is never applicable. However, if function $inc$ is interpreted with $sem_{inc}(n) = n + 1$ for all $n \geq 0$, as in the HEX$^{\text{IFU}}$-program $\Pi' = \{a \leftarrow 2 =_\$ inc(1); \; int(X) \leftarrow a, X > 0\}$, then $2 =_\$ inc(1)$ is always true, $a$ is derived and $int(X) \leftarrow a, X > 0$ derives infinitely many atoms, i.e., $\Pi'$ is not finitely groundable.                    □

Because interpreted functions are closely related to external atoms, as evidenced by our rewriting, it is appropriate to reuse concepts for HEX-programs. The *liberal safety framework* [11] is defined for HEX-programs and derives finite groundability of programs based on its syntactic structure *and* semantic properties of external atoms, where the latter are asserted by the provider of an external source. Such properties are, e.g., the existence of a well-ordering (the output of an external source is no greater than its input according to some ordering), monotonicity/antimonotonicity, and finite domains of external atoms.

*Example 14.* $\Pi = \{reachable(s); \; reachable(Y) \leftarrow reachable(X), \&edge[X](Y)\}$. Without any knowledge about the semantics of the external atom $e = \&edge[X](Y)$, the program potentially introduces infinitely many new values because $e$ is involved in a cycle, finitely groundability is not guaranteed. However, if the output domain of $e$ is known to be finite[3], then the framework identifies the program as finitely groundable. ☐

For a HEX[IFU]-program $\Pi$, the basic idea is to apply the framework to the HEX-program $\tau(\Pi)$. Known properties of basic functions are exploited similarly as for external atoms. Equivalence of $\Pi$ and $\tau(\Pi)$ wrt. answer sets establishes then the following result.

**Proposition 3.** *A* HEX[IFU]-*program* $\Pi$ *is finitely groundable iff* $\tau(\Pi)$ *is finitely groundable.*

Due to the result, convenient finiteness properties of HEX-programs carry over to HEX[IFU]-programs.

**Computational Complexity.** For the computational aspect, one can first observe that unlike external atoms, ifu-atoms can only have input terms but no input predicates. Therefore, ifu-atoms can be evaluated once the program's grounding is available, but there is no need for interleaving this process with model building.

In the following, we assume that the program at hand is finitely groundable and analyze the complexity wrt. the program's grounding. This is because the grounding size depends on the semantics of the involved basic functions and, unlike ordinary ASP, one cannot specify an upper bound for the size of the grounding in terms of the size of the original program. For example, consider the rule $p(Y) \leftarrow inc(I), p(X), Y =_\$ I(X)$, where $inc(min(add(\#1, 1), lim(c))) \leftarrow$ defines a bounded increment function. That is, the function increments parameter $\#1$ up to a certain limit, which is given by the unary basic function $lim(c)$. Obviously, the limit for the increment function, and thus the size of the grounding of $\Pi$, depends on the value of $lim(c)$.

In contrast to complexity results for HEX-programs [12], we cannot reasonably restrict the Herbrand universe to be finite as this contradicts the idea of

---

[3]  The external atom $\&edge[X](Y)$ is intended to return the neighbors $Y$ of $X$ in a fixed finite graph, thus $\Pi$ computes the nodes which are reachable from a given start node $s$.

functionals which may introduce new functions. Instead, we can only rely on safety conditions (see above) which ensure that the grounding has a finite, but otherwise arbitrary size.

Then, if we assume that all functions have complexities in $C$, one can then show that complexity results of ordinary ASP [9] carry over to HEX$^{\text{IFU}}$-programs:

**Proposition 4.** *Deciding if a ground* HEX$^{\text{IFU}}$*-program* $\Pi$ *has an answer set is in* $C \circ \Sigma_2^P$ *in general and in* $C \circ NP$ *if* $\Pi$ *is disjunction-free.*

Here, $C \circ \Sigma_2^P$ denote that the problem is decidable using the power of classes $C$ and $\Sigma_2^P$ in sequence. Note that either of the two classes might dominate the overall complexity. For instance, $C \circ \Sigma_2^P$ reduces to $\Sigma_2^P$ if $C = P$. Similarily for $C \circ NP$.

Since deciding consistency of a ground HEX-program is $(\Sigma_2^P)^C$-complete where $C$ is the complexity of the external atoms [12], we conclude that HEX$^{\text{IFU}}$-programs are potentially even easier but not harder, i.e., positive properties of HEX-programs carry over.

# 7   Related Work and Conclusion

**Related Work.** We give an overview of existing approaches towards function terms with non-Herbrand semantics. They all have in common that the semantics is not given by an external theory but rather defined as part of the program and that none of the following approaches allows for accessing functions as first-class citizens.

The idea of integrating functions and logic programs is related to the field of *functional logic programming (FLP)*, cf. [20,21] for an overview. However, this integration aims at a tighter coupling of the two declarative paradigms, for instance by defining functions as equality clauses within the logic program. For example, the facts $append([], L) = L \leftarrow$ and $append([E|R], L) = [E|append(R, L)] \leftarrow$ might be used to define a list concatenation function. Arithmetic operators are allowed in some approaches such as [2]. This allows for identifying syntactically different terms as semantically equivalent. Functions defined in this way are then applied similarly as in term rewriting systems (cf. *narrowing*). However, FLP integrates features of functional programming directly into logic programs, while our approach aims at using externally defined functions within the program. Although our approach also supports the construction of new functions in the logic program, this works by composition of existing functions rather than equality clauses (cf. Example 4).

Intensional function symbols detach from Herbrand interpretations and use rules to define functions by other functions or predicates, cf. [3,7,24]. For instance, $loc(X) = garage \leftarrow car(X)$, not $loc(X) \neq garage$ expresses that cars are in the garage by default. Although relations to ASP modulo theories and to SMT are identified, cf. [4], this analysis is limited to specific theories (e.g., arithmetics).

A different kind of approaches define functions as part of the program's first-order-like interpretations, cf. e.g. [25,26]. For instance, if $color(n)$ represents the color of node $n$, the constraint $\leftarrow edge(X,Y), color(X) \neq color(Y)$ represents that adjacent nodes have different colors. When computing the reduct of the program wrt. an interpretation, function terms are evaluated and replaced by the value of the function. As a consequence, the evaluation is a strictly non-recursive process. However, the possibility to evaluate a function term to a constant is similar as in our approach. The approach corresponds to the previously developed one by [26], as proven in [7]. The definition of the function $color(\cdot)$ is part of the program's answer.

*HiLog-programs* have a second-order syntax which allow arbitrary terms to occur as predicate names [27]. For instance, the program $P =$ $\{closure(R)(X,Y) \leftarrow R(X,Y); closure(R)(X,Z) \leftarrow R(X,Y), closure(R)(Y,Z)\}$ defines the transitive closure of arbitrary relations $R$. In another rule, the closure of a concrete relation *edge* can be accessed using a HiLog literal of for $closure(edge)(X,Y)$. However, the semantics of HiLog is actually first-order, as evidenced by a translation of HiLog-programs to normal programs. To this end, general terms which are used as predicates are represented by standard predicates and function symbols. For instance, $closure(R)(X,Y)$ is represented by $call(u_3(u_2(closure, R), X, Y))$. The idea of using terms such as $closure(R)$ to represent functions which depend on other functions is similar to our fr-terms, but relations and functions are defined within the program rather than externally.

The grounder GRINGO provides an interface which supports calls to functions written in the scripting language Lua[4] before grounding, after a model has been found, and after termination [16]. However, unlike in HEX$^{\text{IFU}}$-programs, calls to such functions are constrained to happen only at specific evaluation phases and is not interleaved with model building. Also the use of functions as first-class citizens is not possible.

Last but not least, some reasoners such as DLV support pre-defined interpreted functions, e.g. for list processing (appending elements, retrieving the head element, etc.). However, the set of supported functions is fixed and hard-wired within the reasoner, while custom external functions are not supported. The same is true for well-known aggregate functions.

Uninterpreted function symbols are supported by ASP systems such as the grounder GRINGO [15] and recent releases of DLV [22]. Previous research often focused on the identification of classes of programs for which reasoning tasks, such as answer set computation or query answering, are decidable, cf. e.g. [1]. External sources as in HEX-programs were exploited in context of uninterpreted function symbols for the composition and decomposition of nested function terms, cf. [8,10]. However, the function symbols themselves do not have an externally defined semantics. In terms of our notation, the external predicates $\&compose_k$ with $k$ input and 1 output parameter, and $\&decompose_k$ with 1 input and $k$ output parameters for each $k \geq 0$ are used for composing

---

[4] http://www.lua.org.

and decomposing function terms. To this end, $f_{\&compose_k}(A, f, t_1, \ldots, t_k, x) = f_{\&decompose_k}(A, x, f, t_1, \ldots, t_k) = v$ with $v = \mathbf{T}$ if $x = f(t_1, \ldots, t_k)$ and $v = \mathbf{F}$ otherwise. However, all external predicates had fixed purposes and function symbols where not given a semantics.

**Discussion.** While having externally defined functions is central to our approach and motivated by practical observations (need for accessing pre-existing libraries, more natural or efficient implementation of some types of computations which invonve numeric computations, etc.), our approach can in principle also be instantiated in such a way that functions can be defined within the program, similarily to other approaches. To this end, one can pre-define a fixed set of basic functions which suffice to construct arbitrary functions (or at least arbitrary functions from a certain domain) by composition.[5]

**Conclusion.** We introduced HEX$^{\text{IFU}}$-programs, i.e., logic programs with interpreted functions. In contrast to existing approaches towards interpreted functions and also in contrast to HEX-programs, the new approach paves the way for functionals, i.e., functions that take other functions as parameters or return them.

However, rather than functional logic programming (cf. e.g. [20,21]), we do not aim at a tight integration of the two paradigms which allows for defining functions as part of the program, but rather at evaluating externally defined functions. Our approach is in particular flexible as it turns functions into objects that are accessible in the program.

Currently, interpreted functions are either externally defined basic functions or compositions thereof. Future work may include the support for additional means for defining new functions such as *currying* [28], i.e., the translation of a function $f \colon D_1 \times \cdots \times D_n \to R$ with $n$ parameters into a function $f' \colon D_1 \to (D_2 \to (\cdots (D_n \to R)))$ with one parameter that returns another function in the remaining $n - 1$ parameters. Also the support for functions with predicate parameters, such as supported by external atoms, is an interesting starting point. Finally, while we focused on functions in this work, also external atoms with non-functional behavior might be turned into first-class citizens. Both of the last two ideas might be realized based on parameters resp. return values whose domain consists of sets of elements.

# References

1. Alviano, M., Calimeri, F., Ianni, G., Faber, W., Leone, N.: Function symbols in ASP: overview and perspectives 31 (2011)
2. Balduccini, M.: ASP with non-herbrand partial functions: a language and system for practical use. TPLP **13**(4–5), 547–561 (2013)

---

[5] To see that this is always possible, let $runTM(m, i)$ be a function which maps the definition of a turing machine $m$ and an input string $i$ to the tape content after the machine encoded by $m$ under input $i$ terminates. Then any function $f(\mathbf{x})$ can be defined as $runTM(m_f, i)$, where $i$ encodes arguments $\mathbf{x}$ and $m_f$ is a turing machine which computes $f$.

3. Bartholomew, M., Lee, J.: Stable models of formulas with intensional functions. In: Proceedings of International Conference on Principles of Knowledge Representation and Reasoning KR, pp. 2–12 (2012)
4. Bartholomew, M., Lee, J.: Functional stable model semantics and answer set programming modulo theories. In: Proceedings of the Twenty-Third International Joint Conference on Artificial Intelligence, IJCAI 2013, pp. 718–724. AAAI Press (2013)
5. Brewka, G., Roelofsen, F., Serafini, L.: Contextual default reasoning. In: Proceedings of the Twentieth International Joint Conference on Artificial Intelligence (IJCAI 2007), January 6–12, 2007, Hyderabad, India (2007)
6. Burstall, R.: Christopher strachey-understanding programming languages. Higher-Order Symbolic Comput. **13**(1), 51–55 (2000)
7. Cabalar, P.: Functional answer set programming. CoRR abs/1006.3678. http://arxiv.org/abs/1006.3678(2010)
8. Calimeri, F., Cozza, S., Ianni, G.: External sources of knowledge and value invention in logic programming. Ann. Math. Artif. Intell. **50**(3–4), 333–361 (2007)
9. Dantsin, E., Eiter, T., Gottlob, G., Voronkov, A.: Complexity and expressive power of logic programming. ACM Comput. Surv. **33**(3), 374–425 (2001)
10. Eiter, Thomas, Fink, Michael, Krennwallner, Thomas, Redl, Christoph: HEX-programs with existential quantification. In: Hanus, Michael, Rocha, Ricardo (eds.) WLP 2013. LNCS (LNAI), vol. 8439, pp. 99–117. Springer, Cham (2014). doi:10.1007/978-3-319-08909-6_7
11. Eiter, T., Fink, M., Krennwallner, T., Redl, C.: Domain expansion for ASP-programs with external sources. Artif. Intell. **233**, 84–121 (2016)
12. Eiter, T., Ianni, G., Schindlauer, R., Tompits, H.: A uniform integration of higher-order reasoning and external evaluations in answer-set programming. In: IJCAI, pp. 90–96. Professional Book Center (2005)
13. Faber, W., Leone, N., Pfeifer, G.: Semantics and complexity of recursive aggregates in answer set programming. Artif. Intell. **175**(1), 278–298 (2011)
14. Gamma, E., Helm, R., Johnson, R., Vlissides, J.: Design Patterns: Elements of Reusable Object-oriented Software. Addison-Wesley Longman Publishing Co. Inc., Boston (1995)
15. Gebser, M., Kaminski, R., König, A., Schaub, T.: Advances in *gringo* series 3. In: Delgrande, J.P., Faber, W. (eds.) LPNMR 2011. LNCS (LNAI), vol. 6645, pp. 345–351. Springer, Heidelberg (2011). doi:10.1007/978-3-642-20895-9_39
16. Gebser, M., Kaufmann, B., Kaminski, R., Ostrowski, M., Schaub, T., Schneider, M.: Potassco: the potsdam answer set solving collection. AI Commun. **24**(2), 107–124 (2011)
17. Gebser, M., Schaub, T., Thiele, S.: GrinGo: a new grounder for answer set programming. In: Baral, C., Brewka, G., Schlipf, J. (eds.) LPNMR 2007. LNCS (LNAI), vol. 4483, pp. 266–271. Springer, Heidelberg (2007). doi:10.1007/978-3-540-72200-7_24
18. Gelfond, M., Lifschitz, V.: Classical negation in logic programs and disjunctive databases. New Gener. Comput. **9**(3–4), 365–386 (1991)
19. Greco, S., Molinaro, C., Trubitsyna, I.: Bounded programs: A new decidable class of logic programs with function symbols. In: Proceedings of the Twenty-Third International Joint Conference on Artificial Intelligence (IJCAI 2013), pp. 926–931. AAAI Press (2013)
20. Hanus, M.: Multi-paradigm declarative languages. In: Dahl, V., Niemelä, I. (eds.) ICLP 2007. LNCS, vol. 4670, pp. 45–75. Springer, Berlin (2007). doi:10.1007/978-3-540-74610-2_5

21. Hanus, M.: The integration of functions into logic programming: From theory to practice. J. Logic Program. 1920, Supplement 1, 583–628 , special Issue: Ten Years of Logic Programming (1994)
22. Leone, N., Pfeifer, G., Faber, W., Eiter, T., Gottlob, G., Perri, S., Scarcello, F.: The DLV system for knowledge representation and reasoning. ACM TOCL **7**(3), 499–562 (2006)
23. Lierler, Y., Lifschitz, V.: One more decidable class of finitely ground programs. In: Hill, P.M., Warren, D.S. (eds.) ICLP 2009. LNCS, vol. 5649, pp. 489–493. Springer, Heidelberg (2009). doi:10.1007/978-3-642-02846-5_40
24. Lifschitz, V.: Logic programs with intensional functions. In: Proceedings of International Conference on Principles of Knowledge Representation and Reasoning (KR) (2012)
25. Lin, F., Wang, Y.: Answer set programming with functions. In: Brewka, G., Lang, J. (eds.) Proceedings of the Eleventh International Conference on Principles of Knowledge Representation and Reasoning, KR 2008, Sydney, Australia, September 16–19, 2008, pp. 454–465. AAAI Press (2008)
26. Pearce, D., Valverde, A.: Towards a first order equilibrium logic for nonmonotonic reasoning. In: Alferes, J.J., Leite, J. (eds.) JELIA 2004. LNCS (LNAI), vol. 3229, pp. 147–160. Springer, Berlin (2004). doi:10.1007/978-3-540-30227-8_15
27. Ross, K.A.: On negation in HiLog. J. Logic Program. **18**(1), 206–215 (1994)
28. Schönfinkel, M.: Über die bausteine der mathematischen logik. Math. Ann. **92**, 305–316 (1924)
29. Syrjänen, T.: Omega-restricted logic programs. In: Eiter, T., Faber, W., Truszczyński, M. (eds.) LPNMR 2001. LNCS (LNAI), vol. 2173, pp. 267–280. Springer, Berlin (2001). doi:10.1007/3-540-45402-0_20

# Lowering the Learning Curve for Declarative Programming: A Python API for the IDP System

Joost Vennekens[✉]

Department Computerscience @ Technology Campus De Nayer,
KU Leuven, J.-P. De Nayerlaan 5, 2860 Sint-katelijne-waver, Belgium
joost.vennekens@kuleuven.be

**Abstract.** Programmers may be hesitant to use declarative systems, because of the associated learning curve. In this paper, we present an API that integrates the IDP Knowledge Base system into the Python programming language. IDP is a state-of-the-art logical system, which uses SAT, SMT, Logic Programming and Answer Set Programming technology. Python is currently one of the most widely used (teaching) languages for programming. The first goal of our API is to allow a Python programmer to use the declarative power of IDP, without needing to learn any new syntax or semantics. The second goal is allow IDP to be added to/removed from an existing code base with minimal changes.

## 1 Introduction

In many contexts where software is currently developed, programmer time is more valuable than computer time. In other words, it is more important to quickly and reliably produce working code, than to optimize the code's runtime. In addition to standard software engineering practices, declarative methods could play an important role in reducing development time. Indeed, a declarative specification of the end result that should be produced contains, in a sense, the minimum of information that must somehow be made available to the computer in order for it to be able to produce the desired output. Moreover, in addition to writing a program from scratch, maintaining and updating a program are typically also quite time consuming tasks. Here too, declarative methods may offer significant advantages, due to their inherent modularity.

In light of these observations, we may expect that recent years would have shown a significant increase in the use of declarative methods throughout industrial software engineering practice. However, evidence to this effect seems to lacking. There may be many reasons for this. Perhaps companies *are* frequently using declarative methods, but prefer to keep this information hidden. Or, perhaps declarative methods are not being widely used because the majority of software engineers work on simple "CRUD" (create-read-update-delete) applications, for which these methods are overkill.

© Springer International Publishing AG 2017
Y. Lierler and W. Taha (Eds.): PADL 2017, LNCS 10137, pp. 86–102, 2017.
DOI: 10.1007/978-3-319-51676-9_6

In this paper, we posit the hypothesis that there does exist a larger potential for declarative methods in software engineering than is currently being exploited, and that this potential is not being realised because of the following two contributing factors:

- Many programmers are not familiar with state-of-the-art declarative systems. While their education may have contained, say, an introductory course on Prolog programming, there would still be a substantial learning effort required before they could, e.g., solve real-world problems by means of, e.g., a modern Answer Set Programming (ASP) [10] or SMT [4] solver.
- Programming typically takes place in a larger context, where there are coworkers to be collaborated with, external systems to be interfaced with, users that need visualisations, etc. If a declarative solution cannot be easily integrated with existing code, it might be practically impossible to adopt it.

In this paper, we investigate how we might integrate a state-of-the-art declarative system within a well-known and widely-used host language, such that:

- There is essentially no learning curve for programmers who already know the host language.
- The interface between the declarative system and the imperative host language uses the existing syntax and semantics of host-language objects, so that the declarative system may easily be replaced by a piece of host-language code, should this ever prove necessary.

In this way, the resulting API fixes the two problems mentioned above and may therefore contribute to a wider adoption of declarative methods in industry. This may prove especially useful for fast prototyping, where declarative systems may offer a substantial benefit. In addition, our API may also offer a convenient way for teachers to introduce students to declarative methods.

In Sect. 2, we first discuss why we have chosen our particular combination of declarative system and host language. Section 3 then examines to what extent the host language offers objects and expressions that correspond to the inputs needed by the declarative system. Based on this analysis, Sect. 4 then presents the API that we have developed. Section 5 briefly discusses some notes on its current implementation. In Sect. 6, we present several use cases that demonstrate how the API may be used. Section 7 discusses related work. We conclude in Sect. 8.

Part of this work has been presented to a Logic Programming audience at the *International Workshop on User-Oriented Logic Programming (2015)* of the *International Conference on Logic Programming (ICLP) 2015*. The present paper extends this work by a more thorough discussion of the approach, a better comparison to related work and more illustrative examples.

## 2   Choice of Languages

There exists an important distinction between declarative *programming* languages (such as Prolog) and declarative *specification* languages (such as Answer Set Programming). The first kind of languages has an associated operational semantics, which allows algorithms to be specified in the language. By contrast, the second kind lack such an operational semantics, which makes these languages "purely" declarative: a user can specify knowledge about a problem domain, but he cannot express computations.

Both kinds of languages have their own advantages. Because this paper considers the integration of a declarative system with an imperative host language, it makes the most sense to use a declarative specification language. In this way, we obtain a clean separation between imperative and declarative aspects, which allows us to benefit to the fullest from the advantages of the declarative approach.

There exist many declarative specification languages: ASP [10], SAT/SMT [4], ProB [2], etc. In order to achieve our stated goals, we choose a language that is based as much as possible on classical first-order logic. This will allow us to use the boolean connectives and quantifiers that are part of the host language, without changing their semantics. In this paper, we have selected to use the IDP system [3]. The input language of this system, denoted as FO(·), is a conservative extension of classical first-order logic, with features such as aggregates, a type system, arithmetic and inductive definitions. As we will show in the next section, this input language can be seamlessly integrated into our chosen host language.

As our host language, we choose Python. On the one hand, this is a suitable choice because we need a somewhat flexible host language in order to be able to achieve an elegant integration. On the other hand, we also want to use a language that is wide-spread and well-known. Python is reported to be the most popular teaching language for introductory computer science courses[1] and the third most popular programming language overall[2]. We have chosen to use version 2.7 (instead of 3.x), because most of the teaching material currently in use still seems to make use of this version.

In the next section, we explore how the FO(·) input language of the IDP system can be represented in Python.

## 3   Finite First-Order Logic in Python

A vocabulary $\Sigma$ of first-order logic (FO) consists of a set of function symbols and a set of predicate symbols. The FO(·) language uses a typed variant of FO, which allows formulas to be written in a more compact way, while also helping to avoid errors. In this variant, a number of the unary predicate symbols are designated as *types*, and each other predicate symbol $P$ with arity $n$ (as well as each function symbol $F$ with arity $n$) is given a typing $P(T_1, \ldots, T_n)$ (respectively, $F(T_1, \ldots, T_n) : T_0$), which defines the types of its arguments (and its range, in case of a function symbol).

A finite structure $S$ for a vocabulary $\Sigma$ consists of a finite domain $D$ and an assignment to each symbol $\sigma \in \Sigma$ of an interpretation $\sigma^S$. If $P$ is a predicate

---

[1]  http://cacm.acm.org/blogs/blog-cacm/176450-python-is-now-the-most-popular-introductory-teaching-language-at-top-us-universities/fulltext.

[2]  http://spectrum.ieee.org/computing/software/the-2016-top-programming-languages.

symbol of arity $n$, then $P^S$ is an $n$-ary relation on $D$. The interpretations $T_i^S$ of all the types $T_i \in \Sigma$ must form a partition of the domain $D$ of $S$. In addition, the interpretation $P^S$ of each predicate $P(T_1, \ldots, T_n)$ must be well-typed, i.e., $P^S \subseteq T_1^S \times \cdots \times T_n^S$. Similarly, the interpretation $F^S$ of a function symbol $F(T_1, \ldots, T_n) : T_0$ is a function $F^S : T_1^S \times \cdots \times T_n^S \to T_0^S$.

In Python, we can use sets of tuples to represent the interpretation of a predicate symbols and dictionaries to represent the interpretation of a function symbol. To illustrate, we consider the example of representing and solving a sudoku puzzle. The puzzle grid consists of 81 cells, which are subdivided into 9 rows, 9 columns and 9 smaller $3 \times 3$ squares. The layout of this grid can be represented by a type $Cell$ and binary predicates $SameRow$, $SameCol$ and $SameSqu$, each with typing $(Cell, Cell)$. In Python:

```
Cell = range(81)
SameRow = [ (i, j) for i in Cell for j in Cell
               if i % 9 == j % 9 ]
SameCol = [ (i, j) for i in Cell for j in Cell
               if i / 9 == j / 9 ]
SameSqu = [(i, j) for i in Cell for j in Cell
           if i/3 == j/3 and (i%9)/3 == (j%9)/3]
```

To represent the numbers that are given in the sudoku grid, we use a (total) function $Given(Cell): Number$, with the type $Number$ ranging over 0 to 9, where 0 is assigned to the empty cells.

```
Number = range(9)
Given = { 0: 8, 1: 5, 3: 0, 4: 0, 5: 0 ... }
```

The task of solving a sudoku puzzle is that of finding a solution, represented by e.g. a function $Sol(Cell): Number$, that satisfies all the necessary constraints.

```
Sol = { 0: 8, 1: 5, 3: 2, 4: 3, 5: 6 ... }
```

The constraints that must be satisfied by $Sol$ can be expressed by first-order formulas over the vocabulary $\Sigma$. For instance:

$$\forall x[Cell], y[Cell] \ (SameRow(x, y) \vee SameCol(x, y) \vee SameSqu(x, y) \tag{1}$$
$$\Rightarrow Sol(x) \neq Sol(y) \vee x = y).$$

Here, the notation $x[Type]$ is used to indicate the type of the quantified variables. Obviously, this information can also be derived automatically from the typing of the predicates.

The following table shows how we can translate the logical connectives into Python expressions:

| Formula $\phi$ | Python expression $\phi^{py}$ |
|---|---|
| $P(t_1,\ldots,t_n)$ | `(t1,...,tn) in P` |
| $\neg\phi$ | `not` $\phi^{py}$ |
| $\phi \vee \psi$ | $\phi^{py}$ `or` $\psi^{py}$ |
| $\phi \wedge \psi$ | $\phi^{py}$ `and` $\psi^{py}$ |
| $\forall x[Type] : \psi \Rightarrow \phi$ | `all(`$\phi^{py}$ `for x in Type if ` $\psi^{py}$`)` |
| $\exists x[Type] : \psi \wedge \phi$ | `any(`$\phi^{py}$ `for x in Type if ` $\psi^{py}$`)` |

For instance, formula (1) corresponds to:

```
all(Sol[x] != Sol[y] or x == y for x in Cell for y in Cell
    if (x,y) in SameRow or (x,y) in SameCol or (x,y) in SameSqu)
```

In addition to satisfying this property, *Sol* also has to coincide with *Given* for all cells where the latter function is not 0:

```
not any(Sol[x] != Given[x] for x in Cell if Given[x] != 0)
```

Moreover, *Sol* should not leave any cells empty (i.e., 0 should not occur in its range):

```
all(Sol[x] != 0 for x in Cell)
```

If the above three Python expressions all evaluate to `true`, then *Sol* is a correct solution to the sudoku instance described by *Given*.

The input language FO($\cdot$) of the IDP system extends classical first-order logic with a number of additional features. Most of the *aggregates* it supports are also part of Python, e.g., `min, max` and `sum`. Another interesting feature of FO($\cdot$) are its *inductive definitions*. An example is the definition of the transitive closure $T$ of a graph $G$:

$$\left\{ \begin{array}{ll} \forall x[Node], y[Node] & T(x,y) \leftarrow \exists z\; T(x,z) \wedge T(z,y). \\ \forall x[Node], y[Node] & T(x,y) \leftarrow G(x,y). \end{array} \right\}$$

In FO($\cdot$), this definition expresses that $T$ is the least fixpoint of the operator induced by the two rules. A similar construct is not readily available in Python, but we can explicitly compute the least fixpoint, using a $\lambda$-expression that corresponds to the disjunction of the two rules of the definition.

```
def lfp(f, x=[]):
    y = f(x)
    return y if y == x else lfp(f,y)

node_pairs = [(x,y) for x in Node for y in Node]

d = lambda T: (lambda (x,y): ((x,y) in G or
              any((x,z) in G and (z,y) in T for z in Node)))

TC = lfp(lambda T: filter(d(T), node_pairs))
```

In addition to such monotone inductive definitions, IDP also allows non-monotone inductive definitions, such as definitions over a well-founded order. The IDP system interprets such non-monotone definitions by, essentially, the well-founded model semantics [17]. As shown in [5], this coincides with how such definitions are interpreted in mathematical texts. Again, also this computation could be done explicitly in Python, using a λ-expression that corresponds to the disjunction of the rules of the definition.

Having examined how we can express various parts of FO(·) in Python, we now present our Python API to the IDP system.

## 4   Python Interface to the IDP System

The central concept in the API is that of a *knowledge base* (KB). A new KB can be created as follows.

```
from pyidp.typedIDP import IDP
kb = IDP()
```

A KB consists of a vocabulary, a structure for (part of) this vocabulary and a number of constraints that must be satisfied. For instance, the vocabulary and structure for the sudoku example can be added to the KB as follows:

```
kb.Type("Cell", range(81))
kb.Type("Number", range(10))
kb.Predicate("SameRow(Cell,Cell)", [ (x,y) for ... ] )
kb.Predicate("SameCol(Cell,Cell)", [ (x,y) for ... ] )
kb.Predicate("SameSqu(Cell,Cell)", [ (x,y) for ... ] )
kb.Function("Given(Cell): Number", { 0: 8, ... })
kb.Function("Sol(Cell): Number", { 0: 8, ... })
```

Each of these statements adds a symbol to the vocabulary of the KB and assigns an interpretation to it (using the same Python expressions as in Sect. 3). The API also allows to first declare the symbol and later use the assignment operator = to assign it a value. Once a symbol $\sigma$ has been added to a KB kb, it can be referred to as kb.$\sigma$. Predicates implement the *MutableSet* interface, while functions implement *Mapping*. This allows these logical object to behave as Python programmers would expect, e.g.:

```
kb.SameRow.add((0,1))
kb.Given[0] = 7
```

This also allows us to evaluate the boolean Python expressions that correspond to the rules of sudoku:

```
all(kb.Sol[x] != kb.Sol[y] or x == y
    for x in kb.Cell for y in kb.Cell if (x,y) in kb.SameRow
        or (x,y) in kb.SameCol or (x,y) in kb.SameSqu)
```

Instead of immediately evaluating this expression, we can also add it as a *constraint* to the knowledge base:

```
kb.Constraint(
  """all(Sol[x] != Sol[y] or x == y
    for x in Cell for y in Cell if (x,y) in SameRow
        or (x,y) in SameCol or (x,y) in SameSqu)""")
```

Each KB has a boolean property `satisfiable` that can be checked to find out if all constraints that have been added to it are in fact satisfied by the KB's current interpretation of the vocabulary.

```
if kb.satisfiable:
    print "Sudoku is solved."
```

From a logical perspective, inspecting the value of this property triggers IDP's inference task of *model checking*: for the finite structure $S$ that is represented by the KB and for the constraints $\phi_1, \ldots, \phi_n$ that belong to the KB, it is checked whether $S \models \bigwedge_{1 \le i \le n} \phi_i$.

In addition to this inference task, IDP also supports *model expansion*: given a structure $S_0$ for a subvocabulary $\Sigma_0 \subseteq \Sigma$ of the vocabulary of the formulas $\phi_1, \ldots, \phi_n$, compute a structure $S$ for the vocabulary $\Sigma \setminus \Sigma_0$ such that $(S_0 \cup S) \models \phi_1 \wedge \cdots \wedge \phi_n$. This task is known to capture the complexity class NP [13].

Our API supports this inference task in a very simple way: if the programmer declares a vocabulary symbol but does not assign an interpretation to it, then any attempt to inspect the value of this symbol will trigger a call to IDP's model expansion algorithm. This will then automatically fill in the interpretation of this symbol in accordance with the constraints. If multiple different interpretations are possible, one is arbitrarily selected (but, if there are multiple such symbols, then the same model is used to generate the interpretation for all of them, so that the interpretations for different symbols are always mutually consistent). In case of the sudoku example, if we had only declared the symbol *Sol*, without assigning it a value:

```
kb.Function("Sol(Cell): Number")
```

then the following code would compute and print a solution to the given sudoku instance:

```
for x in kb.Cell:
    print kb.Sol[x]
```

A final feature of our API is that it also supports the *inductive definitions* of FO($\cdot$). The method `Define` may be used to at once declare a symbol and define it by means of a $\lambda$-expression. In the context of the sudoku example, we may use this to define the following auxiliary concept:

```
kb.Define("Diff(Cell,Cell)",
    """lambda x,y: (x,y) in SameRow
            or (x,y) in SameCol or (x,y) in SameSqu""")
```

In words, this statement defines that `Diff` is the set of all pairs of cells $(x, y)$ for which the given $\lambda$-expression holds. Once this concept has been defined, it can be used to simplify the main sudoku constraint.

```
kb.Constraint("""all(Sol[x] != Sol[y]
                for (x,y) in Diff if x != y)""")
```

Even though the above example does not demonstrate this, in general, these definitions may be inductive. For instance, the definition of transitive closure can be given as:

```
kb.Define("T(Node,Node)",
  """lambda x,y: (x,y) in G
     or any((x,z) in G and (z,y) in T for z in Node)""")
```

*Discussion.* The above API allows the IDP system to be used from Python without requiring any knowledge that a Python programmer does not already possess: semantical objects (i.e., interpretations of predicate and function symbols) take the form of standard Python sets and dictionaries, while constraints take the form of standard Python boolean expressions, and definitions make use of standard Python λ-expressions. All of these Python objects and expressions can be used in all of the normal ways and retain their normal semantics. Moreover, even those arguments that are passed as strings (e.g., to the `Constraint` method) are handled by the Python parser within the API, so standard syntactical rules apply and standard messages are generated for syntax errors.

In order to make effective use of this API, a Python programmer therefore only has to know two things:

- The property `satisfiable` of a KB is `true` if and only if all Python expressions that were added as constraints would normally (i.e., under their Python semantics) evaluate to `true`;
- If some symbol of a KB is not assigned a value, then a value will be automatically computed in such a way that all of the constraints would evaluate to `true`.

A small exception to the above discussion is that our API of course also requires the programmer to declare a typed vocabulary. This is something which has no counterpart in the dynamically typed Python language, and which therefore also requires some additional explanation. However, given the simplicity of the type system, this should be trivial to understand for any programmer.

In summary, we may therefore conclude that the API should be immediately usable with minimal learning effort.

## 5   Notes on Implementation

The implementation of our API is available for download from the following URL:

https://bitbucket.org/joostv/pyidp

Also the examples presented in this paper can be found here.

Interfacing with the IDP system is currently done in a decoupled way: when the API detects that the IDP system needs to be called, it prepares a text file with the appropriate vocabulary, structure and theory; it then calls IDP as an external process and parses its output. The results of this call are cached, so that IDP is not invoked again, as long as the KB does not change. Obviously, a tighter integration, which avoids calling IDP as an external process and communicating through text files, would improve the efficiency of the API. Moreover, a tight integration might be developed which would allow us to keep an instance of the IDP system running, such that only the differences with the previous invokation need to be communicated when a new invokation is needed.

The IDP system offers various options which can be used to speed up certain computations. For instance, it can make use of the XSB Prolog system[3] [14] to handle inductive definitions. The KB objects offered by our API have a method set_idp_option that can be used to set such options. For instance, XSB is enabled by:

```
kb.set_idp_option("xsb", "true")
```

## 6  Use Cases

In this section, we examine several ways in which the API can be used. We pay particular attention to the ease with which our API can be integrated into existing Python code and the functionality that it can deliver. Because we specifically aim at reducing the programming effort in situations where efficiency is of secondary importance (such as prototyping), we do not investigate computational complexity. In general, however, solutions using our API will of course be significantly slower than purpose-built algorithms in the host language (but comparable to using IDP as a stand-alone system).

### 6.1  Solving Combinatorial Problems

A typical use case for declarative systems is the solving of combinatorial problems. As an example, we consider the problem of solving Hidato puzzles. The goal of such puzzles is to fill in the numbers 1 to $n$ in a grid of $n$ cells, such that each $i$ and $i+1$ are in adjoining cells (horizontally, vertically or diagonally), taking into account the fact that the position of certain numbers is fixed up-front. We have taken a Python solver for such puzzles that is available online[4] and adapted it to our API.

As a vocabulary, we use types to represent the rows (R), columns (C) and numbers (Nb) that need to be entered in the cells. The predicate Cell(R,C) describes which combinations of row and column numbers corresponds to cells, while Given(R,C,Nb) gives the numbers that are already filled in. We will describe the solution to the puzzle by means of functions Row and Col that map each number to the row/column in which this number is filled in.

---

[3] http://xsb.sourceforge.net/.
[4] http://rosettacode.org/wiki/Solve_a_Hidato_puzzle#Python.

```
hid = IDP()
hid.Type("R", [1])
hid.Type("C", [1])
hid.Type("Nb", [1])
hid.Predicate("Cell(R,C)", [])
hid.Predicate("Given(R,C,Nb)", [])
hid.Function("Row(Nb): R")
hid.Function("Col(Nb): C")
```

As constraints, we first need to express that the solution must coincide with the numbers that are given.

```
hid.Constraint("all(Row(v) == r and Col(v) == c for (r,c,v) in Given)")
```

Next, each cell may only contain one number and numbers may only appear in the cells:

```
hid.Constraint(
    """all(c == d for c in Nb for d in Nb
           if Row(c) == Row(d) and Col(c) == Col(d))""")
hid.Constraint("all(Cell(Row(n),Col(n)) for n in Nb)")
```

Finally, there is the constraint that each number must be in the Moore neighbourhood of its successor.

```
hid.Constraint(
    """all(abs(Row(c) - Row(c+1)) < 2
           and abs(Col(c) - Col(c+1)) < 2
           for c in Nb if c < max(Nb))""")
```

The Python solution from which we start defines three functions: setup initialises the data structure representing the puzzle, solve computes the solution and printboard visualises it. By making a few small changes to setup and printboard, we can make these functions use the KB hid constructed above. We thereby replace the entire solve function, as the solution will now be computed by the IDP system as soon as printboard tries to visualise it.

```
def setup(s):
    lines = s.splitlines()
    hid.C = range(len(lines[0].split()))
    hid.R = range(len(lines))
    cellcount = 1
    for r, row in enumerate(lines):
        for c, cell in enumerate(row.split()):
            if cell == ".": # not a cell
                continue
            hid.Nb.add(cellcount)
            hid.Cell.add((r,c))
            if cell != "__": # cell not empty
```

```
                    hid.Given.add((r,c,int(cell)))
            cellcount += 1

def print_board():
    d = {-1: "", 0: "__"}
    bmax = max(hid.Nb)
    form = "%" + str(len(str(bmax)) + 1) + "s"
    matrix = [[' ' for i in hid.C]
                            for i in hid.R]
    for c in hid.Nb:
        matrix[hid.Row[c]][hid.Col[c]] = c
    for r in matrix:
        print "".join(map(lambda x:form%x,r))
```

We can now solve a Hidato puzzle as follows:

```
hi = """\
__ 33 35 __ __  .   .   .
__ __ 24 22 __  .   .   .
__ __ __ 21 __ __   .   .
__ 26 __ 13 40 11   .   .
27 __ __ __  9 __   1   .
 .   .  __ __ 18 __ __   .
 .   .   .   .  __  7 __ __
 .   .   .   .   .   .  5 __"""
```

```
setup(hi)
print_board()
```

## 6.2  Working with Graphs

The following class GraphKB extends the generic IDP Knowledge Base class with some specific functionality for working with undirected graphs. When constructing such a GraphKB, the nodes of the graph can be initialised by means of a given set and the edges by means of an adjacency list. The predicate Edge is defined as the symmetric closure of the adjacency list. This class also offers a convenience method to define the transitive closure of a given relation.

```
class GraphKB(IDP):

    def __init__(self, nodes=[0], adj_list=[]):
        super(GraphKB, self).__init__()
        self.Type("Node", nodes)
        self.Predicate("Adj(Node,Node)", adj_list)
        self.Define("Edge(Node,Node)",
            "lambda x,y: Adj(x,y) or Adj(y,x)")
```

```
def def_TC(self, original, tc_name):
    formula = """lambda x,y: {0}(x,y) or
    any({1}(x,z) and {1}(z,y)
        for z in Node)""".format(original, tc_name)
    self.Define(tc_name+"(Node, Node)", formula)
```

We can now check if a given adjacency list describes a fully connected graph:

```
conn = GraphKB(nodes, adj)
conn.def_TC("Edge", "Path")
conn.Constraint("all(Path(x,y) for x in Node for y in Node)")
if conn.satisfiable:
    print "Graph is fully connected"
```

We can use a similar KB to count the number of connected components in the graph. We do this by selecting a single representative from each component (its "Root") and then counting the number of these representatives.

```
cc = GraphKB(nodes, adj)
cc.def_TC("Edge", "Path")
cc.Predicate("Root(Node)")
cc.Constraint("""all(any(Path(r,x) for r in Root)
                for x in Node if not Root(x))""")
cc.Constraint("""not any(Path(x,y)
                for x in Root for y in Root if x != y)""")
print "Components: {0}".format(len(comp.Root))
```

In graph theory, an undirected graph is called a *tree* if it is connected and does not contain cycles. When checking for a cycle in an undirected graph, we of course have to exclude the trivial two-node cycles that would result from traversing the same undirected edge in both directions. This in fact makes it easier to use IDP to check that there *is* a cycle, than to check that there *is not* one. The following knowledge base tries to guess the direction in which to traverse each edge in order to produce a cycle. If it is unsatisfiable, there are no cycles.

```
cyclic = GraphKB()
cyclic.Predicate("Traverse(Node,Node)")
cyclic.Constraint("all(Edge(x,y) for (x,y) in Traverse)")
cyclic.Constraint(
  "not any(Traverse(y,x) for (x,y) in Traverse)")
cyclic.def_TC("Traverse", "TravTC")
cyclic.Constraint("any(TravTC(x,x) for x in Node)")
```

We can now combine the two knowledge bases to check whether a given adjacency list indeed describes a tree.

```
def is_tree(adj_list):
    cyclic.Adjacent = adj_list
    conn.Adjacent = adj_list
    return (bool(conn.satisfiable)
            and not bool(cyclic.satisfiable))
```

This example illustrates how additional functionality can be built on top of the KB objects of our API. In addition, the ability to combine the results of calls to different KBs also allows us to implement functionality that would be harder to implement in a single IDP KB.

## 6.3  Flexible Input/output

Bio-informatics applications may need to translate between strings of bases and strings of amino acids. In this translation, a *codon* (i.e., a sequence of three bases) corresponds to a single amino acid, according to a fixed and well-known table. For instance, the following nine bases correspond to the following three amino acids:

$$\underbrace{a\,c\,t}_{T}\,\underbrace{g\,a\,g}_{E}\,\underbrace{t\,c\,a}_{S}$$

The following knowledge base declaratively defines the relation between the two different kinds of sequence. Here, the sequences are represented by mappings of indices to, respectively, bases and amino acids.

```
k = IDP()
k.Type("Base", ['t', 'c', 'a', 'g'])
codons = [(a,b,c) for a in k.Base
          for b in k.Base for c in k.Base]
amino_acids = ('FFLLSSSSYY**CC*WLLLLPPPPHHQQRRRR' +
               'IIIMTTTTNNKKSSRRVVVVAAAADDEEGGGG')
k.Type("AmAcid", set(amino_acids))
k.Type("AIndex")
k.Type("BIndex")

k.Function("Codon(Base, Base, Base): AmAcid",
           dict(zip(codons, amino_acids)))
k.Function("BaseAt(BIndex): Base")
k.Function("AmAcidAt(AIndex): AmAcid")
k.Constraint(
  """all(Codon(BaseAt(3*i), BaseAt(3*i+1), BaseAt(3*i+2))
       == AmAcidAt(i) for i in PIndex)""")
```

The following function translates a regular Python list into a dictionary that maps list indices to values. It will be convenient to construct an interpretation for the `BaseAt` and/or `AmAcidAt` functions.

```
def sequence(list_):
    return dict(enumerate(list))
```

Using the above knowledge base, we can translate bases to amino acids as follows:

```
bases = 'actgagtca'
k.BaseAt = sequence(bases)
k.BIndex = range(len(bases))
k.AIndex = range(len(seq) / 3)
print k.AmAcidAt
```

Because of its purely declarative nature, the same knowledge base can also be used to perform the translation in the other direction.

```
amino_acids = 'TES'
k.AmAcidAt = sequence(amino_acids)
k.PAndex = range(len(seq))
k.BIndex = range(len(seq) * 3)
print k.BaseAt
```

### 6.4  Self-maintaining Data-Structures

Whenever the interpretation of one or more symbols in the vocabulary of a knowledge base changes, the API will automatically recompute the interpretation of the other symbols as soon as this is needed. To illustrate, we implement the following simple method of constructing a random fully connected directed acyclic graph:

- While there are still unconnected nodes:
    - Randomly select a pair $(x, y)$ of unconnected nodes
    - Add an edge from $x$ to $y$

Using the GraphKB class of Sect. 6.2, we can implement this as follows:

```
kb = GraphKB(["a","b","c","d"])
kb.def_TC("Edge", "TC")
kb.Define("Unconnected(Node,Node)",
  """lambda x,y: x != y and not (TC(x,y) or TC(y,x))""")

import random
while len(kb.Unconnected) > 0:
    kb.Edge.add(random.choice(list(kb.Unconnected)))
print kb.Edge
```

Each time the *Edge* relation is updated in the while-loop, the knowledge base is automatically invoked to keep the *Unconnected* relation up-to-date.

## 7  Related Work

There is already a long history of work attempting to close the gap between imperative and declarative programming [1]. We briefly compare our approach to some recent work in this area.

Several such approaches exist in the domain of Answer Set Programming. In [9], Python is used a layer on top of the ASP solver Claps, in order invoke this solver in this different ways. In [7], Python and ASP are more tightly coupled: the ASP solver cannot only be invoked from Python, but various pieces of Python code can also be called during the solving process. In contrast to our system, both these approaches expect the Python programs to be written by a knowledgable ASP programmer. The approach of [8] is most similar to ours: it embeds ASP in Java, allowing information contained in standard Java data structures to be completed or checked by means of ASP programs. However, while standard Java data standard structures are used, the ASP programs are still written in their standard syntax, again requiring a knowledgable ASP programmer.

In [16], an approach is presented in which a constraint solver is not added to a single host language, but can be used in the development of a domain-specific language in Racket. Like ours, the motivation behind this work is to allow the power of declarative systems to be more widely used. However, their approach differs, because they count on an intermediary—the designer of the domain-specific language—to hide the complexity of the declarative system, whereas our approach focuses on creating an interface that is natural enough to offer KB functionality directly.

In [11], a constraint solver is integrated into the Scala language. As ours does, their approach reuses the syntax of the host language to interface with the declarative system. A key difference is that, in their approach, the programmer is explicitly manipulating, combining and solving constraints, which makes the constraint solver more present in the eventual source code. A second difference is of course that Scala currently appears to be less widely known than Python.

In [12], a reasoner for FO extended with transitive closure is integrated into Java. Their KB language is therefore very similar to (but more restricted than) that of IDP. When it comes to the integration in Java, there are two main differences to our approach. First, the declarative knowledge is not written in expressions of the host language, but in a separate language (the Alloy-like JFSL [18]). Second, the integration into Java is done in an object-oriented way: the programmer defines classes in which formulas are added as, among others, class invariants, method pre-/postconditions and frame conditions. In comparison, our Python API seems more lightweight, since it does not require an object-oriented approach. When it comes to computational performance, [12] reports good results, which our implementation is not able to match.

In summary, we believe that our approach fills a niche as an easy-to-learn rapid prototyping API, that, due to Python's current popularity, may speak to a large audience.

# 8    Conclusions and Future Work

Developing an algorithm to solve a particular computational problem may require a substantial effort. Moreover, it may be time-consuming to adapt such an algorithm to even small changes in the problem specification. The use of a declarative system may therefore provide an interesting alternative, especially in situations were flexibility and development speed are of prime importance (and computational efficiency is not). Typically, this occurs in the prototyping stages of an application.

Programmers may nevertheless be reluctant to use a declarative system for a number of reasons:

- the system may be hard to learn for themselves or for their coworkers;
- generating input for the system in the appropriate format may require a large effort, as may parsing the output of the system and extracting the necessary information from it.

In this paper, we have presented a Python API for the IDP system that avoids these problems. It uses only standard Python objects and expressions, which has two main benefits:

- there is essentially no learning curve: the programmer needs to know nothing about the IDP system or its input syntax in order to make successful use of the API;
- it is easy to incorporate the API into existing Python code, or to replace an existing use of the API by native Python code.

We have presented several use cases of this API, illustrating its use to solve computational problems, to perform various graph computations, to implement flexible input/output behaviour and self-maintaining data structures.

One problem with the current implementation of our API is that there is no support for debugging the declarative specification, which may be especially problematic if the specification contains a bug that makes it inconsistent. In future work, we will address this issue. This will enable us to conduct experiments in which the API is used by programmers who are not familiar with the IDP system.

# References

1. Apt, K.R., Schaerf, A.: Programming in alma-0, or imperative and declarative programming reconciled. In: FroCos (1998)
2. Bendisposto, J., Clark, J., Dobrikov, I., Karner, P., Krings, S., Ladenberger, L., Leuschel, M. and Plagge, D.: ProB 2.0 tutorial. In: Proceedings of the 4th Rodin User and Developer Workshop, TUCS Lecture Notes (2013)
3. Bruynooghe, M., Blockeel, H., Bogaerts, B., De Cat, B., De Pooter, S., Jansen, J., Labarre, A., Ramon, J., Denecker, M., Verwer, S.: Predicate logic as a modeling language: modeling and solving some machine learning and data mining problems with IDP3. Theor. Pract. Logic Program. **15**(06), 783–817 (2014). Accepted
4. Moura, L., Bjørner, N.: Z3: an efficient SMT solver. In: Ramakrishnan, C.R., Rehof, J. (eds.) TACAS 2008. LNCS, vol. 4963, pp. 337–340. Springer, Heidelberg (2008). doi:10.1007/978-3-540-78800-3_24
5. Denecker, M.: The well-founded semantics is the principle of inductive definition. In: Dix, J., Cerro, L.F., Furbach, U. (eds.) JELIA 1998. LNCS (LNAI), vol. 1489, pp. 1–16. Springer, Heidelberg (1998). doi:10.1007/3-540-49545-2_1

6. Denecker, M., Ternovska, E.: A logic of nonmonotone inductive definitions. ACM Trans. Comput. Logic **9**(2), 14 (2008)
7. Eiter, T., Fink, M., Ianni, G., Krennwallner, T., Redl, C., Schüller, P.: A model building framework for answer set programming with external computations. Theor. Pract. Logic Program. **16**(4), 418–464 (2016)
8. Febbraro, O., Grasso, G., Ricca, F., Leone, N., JASP: A framework for integrating answer set programming with Java. In: KR (2012)
9. Gebser, M., Kaminski, R., Obermeier, P., Schaub, T.: Ricochet robots reloaded: a case-study in multi-shot ASP solving. In: Eiter, T., Strass, H., Truszczyński, M., Woltran, S. (eds.) Advances in Knowledge Representation, Logic Programming, and Abstract Argumentation. LNCS (LNAI), vol. 9060, pp. 17–32. Springer, Heidelberg (2015). doi:10.1007/978-3-319-14726-0_2
10. Gebser, M., Kaufmann, B., Neumann, A., Schaub, T.: *clasp*: a conflict-driven answer set solver. In: Baral, C., Brewka, G., Schlipf, J. (eds.) LPNMR 2007. LNCS (LNAI), vol. 4483, pp. 260–265. Springer, Heidelberg (2007). doi:10.1007/978-3-540-72200-7_23
11. Köksal, A., Kuncak, V., Suter, P.: Constraints as control. In: POPL2012 (2012)
12. Milicevic, A., Rayside, D., Yessenov, K., Jackson, D.: Unifying execution of imperative and declarative code. In: Proceedings of 33rd International Conference on Software Engineering (ICSE) (2011)
13. Mitchell, D.G, Ternovska, E.: A framework for representing and solving NP search problems. In: AAAI, pp. 430–435 (2005)
14. Swift, T., Warren, D.S.: XSB: extending prolog with tabled logic programming. Theor. Pract. Logic Program. **12**(1–2), 157–187 (2012)
15. Tasharrofi, S., Ternovska, E.: A semantic account for modularity in multi-language modelling of search problems. In: Tinelli, C., Sofronie-Stokkermans, V. (eds.) FroCoS 2011. LNCS (LNAI), vol. 6989, pp. 259–274. Springer, Heidelberg (2011). doi:10.1007/978-3-642-24364-6_18
16. Torlak, E., Bodik, R.: Growing solver aided languages with ROSETTA. In: Proceedings of ACM International Symposium on New Ideas, New Paradigms, and Reflections on Programming and Software (2013)
17. Van Gelder, A., Ross, K.A., Schlipf, J.S.: The well-founded semantics for general logic programs. J. ACM **38**(3), 620–650 (1991)
18. Yessenov, K.: A lightweight specification language for bounded program verification. Master's thesis, MIT (2009)

# Failing Faster: Overlapping Patterns for Property-Based Testing

Jonathan Fowler[✉] and Graham Hutton

School of Computer Science, University of Nottingham, Nottingham, UK
psxjf@nottingham.ac.uk

**Abstract.** In property-based testing, a key problem is generating input data that satisfies the precondition of a property. One approach is to attempt to do so automatically, from the definition of the precondition itself. This idea has been realised using the technique of needed narrowing, as in the Lazy SmallCheck system, however in practice this method often leads to excessive backtracking resulting in poor efficiency. To reduce the amount of backtracking, we develop an extension to needed narrowing that allows preconditions to fail faster based on the use of overlapping patterns. We formalise our extension, show how it can be implemented, and demonstrate that it improves efficiency in many cases.

## 1 Introduction

Property-based testing, popularised by systems such as QuickCheck [4], is an automated approach to testing in which a program is validated against a specification. In most tools, the specification consists of properties written as programs outputting Boolean values. Input data is generated randomly or systematically, and the program is executed in an attempt to find a counterexample. In order to generate the input data, it is often required to write a custom generator. For example, consider the following simple property of a sorting function:

$$propSort\ n\ l = perm\ n\ l \implies sort\ l \equiv [0\mathinner{.\,.}(n-1)]$$

This property has two arguments, given by a number $n$ and a list of numbers $l$. The property itself states that if the list $l$ is a permutation of the numbers from 0 to $n-1$, then sorting this list will give the expected result. However, while the above definition captures a valid property, it suffers from a practical problem. In particular, if we use a standard generator for a list of numbers, then the precondition $perm\ n\ l$ will rarely be met, making it difficult to generate enough test cases to adequately test the $sort$ function.

To overcome this problem, a custom generator is often used. For example, the QuickCheck system [4] provides a range of type-classes and combinators for building custom generators, using which we can define a generator for properties such as $propSort$. Nevertheless, writing custom generators is time consuming and for more complex examples, such as generating well-typed terms, is the subject of ongoing research [12,17]. Furthermore, it is difficult to combine such generators,

© Springer International Publishing AG 2017
Y. Lierler and W. Taha (Eds.): PADL 2017, LNCS 10137, pp. 103–119, 2017.
DOI: 10.1007/978-3-319-51676-9_7

in the sense that two generators that are efficient in isolation may no longer be efficient when they are combined together in some way.

Another approach is to attempt to derive an efficient generator from the definition of the precondition, in our example the property *perm*. One realisation of this approach is to use the technique of *needed narrowing* [1,10] from functional logic programming. For example, Lazy Smallcheck [19] adopts a narrowing strategy and EasyCheck [2] directly uses the needed narrowing language Curry. Using this approach, a program is evaluated in a speculative manner. Beginning with a free input variable, the variable is refined by choosing a constructor when the value is required to proceed with evaluation. If evaluation ends negatively then the process backtracks, while if it ends positively then we have generated a value satisfying the condition. However, a naturally written property often does not make an efficient generator. In particular, the generator may be forced to backtrack excessively if it finds itself in a branch of the program for which the constraints are never satisfied, as we shall see in the next section.

In this paper, we explore a new technique to help reduce the amount of backtracking that is required in a needed-narrowing approach to property-based testing. The technique, which is a generalisation of the parallel conjunction approach used in several tools [3,13,19], allows evaluation of multiple branches of the program simultaneously, potentially allowing a result to be derived at an earlier stage of refinement. Particularly for commonly-used operators such as conjunction, disjunction and addition, both arguments can be evaluated in tandem. To achieve this, we use a form of *overlapping pattern matching*. The pattern matching is resolved in an order-independent fashion and overlapping patterns are allowed. More precisely, in this paper we:

- Motivate and introduce the use of overlapping patterns for needed narrowing property-based testing using our permutation example (Sect. 2).
- Define our source language and formalise the notion of overlapping patterns within this language using a needed narrowing semantics (Sect. 3).
- Give an overview of our prototype implementation (Sect. 4), and explore the benefits of overlapping patterns in two case studies (Sect. 5).
- Compare with related work (Sect. 6) and conclude (Sect. 7).

The paper is aimed at a general functional programming audience with some experience of property-based testing systems such as QuickCheck, but no specialist knowledge of needed narrowing is assumed. For the purposes of examples, we use a Haskell-like syntax and semantics. Although we only apply our technique to property-based testing, we believe it could also be used to improve the efficiency of other tools and languages based on needed narrowing.

## 2    Motivation and Basic Idea

To motivate the need for overlapping pattern matching we take a deeper look at the example from the introduction. We show that naively evaluating the *perm* precondition with a needed narrowing strategy results in excessive backtracking, and how the use of an overlapping conjunction operator mitigates the problem. We begin by defining the *perm* condition as follows:

$$perm \quad :: Nat \rightarrow [Nat] \rightarrow Bool$$
$$perm \; n \; l = length \; l \equiv n \; \wedge \; all \; (<n) \; l \; \wedge \; allDiff \; l$$

That is, a list $l$ is a permutation of the natural numbers below a given limit $n$ if three conditions are satisfied: the list has the correct length, all the numbers in the list are below the limit, and all the numbers in the list are different. Pre-conditions defined as a conjunction of constraints in this manner are a common pattern in properties. Because needed narrowing is more effective on algebraic data types than on primitive data types [16], we assume an inductive type *Nat* of natural numbers built up from basic constructors *Zero* and *Suc*.

By running a needed narrowing evaluation on the above definition for *perm*, we can generate values satisfying the constraints. Needed narrowing is based upon the idea of extending normal evaluation to include *free variables*, with the values of such variables being refined as evaluation proceeds. We give a brief overview to the technique below; for a more in-depth introduction, see [9,15].

At the start of evaluation, a free variable is chosen for each argument of the program and the program is reduced until the value of a variable is required to continue. The program is then *suspended* on the variable. To allow further progress, a constructor is chosen for the suspended variable and the program is then reduced further in the same way. If evaluation fails to succeed we backtrack, choosing alternative constructors for each variable.

For example, if we consider the first constraint $length \; l \equiv n$ in *perm* for the case when $n = 4$, needed narrowing will yield the following solution:

$$l = [x_0, x_1, x_2, x_3]$$

Along the way we would discard lists such as $[x_0, x_1, x_2]$ which fail to satisfy the constraint. The variables $x_0$–$x_3$ are free in the solution, in the sense they can be substituted for any value while still satisfying the constraint. Continuing with evaluation of the second constraint, $all \; (<4) \; l$, we further refine the variables. We consider a *partial* solution, in which the constraint is not yet satisfied, to illustrate a situation in which excessive backtracking will occur:

$$l = [1, 1, x_2, x_3]$$

This list begins with two ones and according to the current constraint, $all \; (<4) \; l$, we have neither failed nor succeeded and as such we should carry on refining $x_2$ and $x_3$. However, when we arrive at the final constraint, $allDiff \; l$, this partial solution will fail, and we have to backtrack over all combinations of $x_2$ and $x_3$ before we can continue again. Moreover, as we consider generating longer permutations, the amount of backtracking increases exponentially.

Note that the problem is not resolved by reordering the constraints. For example, suppose that we swapped the order of the last two constraints:

$$perm \; n \; l = length \; l \equiv n \; \wedge \; allDiff \; l \; \wedge \; all \; (<n) \; l$$

Then we quickly run into a similar issue. For example, the partial solution, $l = [4, x_1, x_2, x_3]$ does not fail the *allDiff* $l$ constraint, however it will fail the *all* $(<4)$ $l$ constraint but only after the remaining variables $x_1$–$x_3$ are refined while evaluating *allDiff*. In both cases, the backtracking is caused because a partial solution fails to satisfy a later constraint but this is not evident at the time due to the evaluation order. A natural way to avoid this problem is to evaluate all the constraints simultaneously, rather than sequentially.

To realise this behaviour, we replace traditional pattern matching in our language with *overlapping* pattern matching. Pattern matching in the language is then order-independent, and in each iteration of needed narrowing all relevant arguments to a pattern match are normalised. By way of example, consider the logical conjunction operator, which is traditionally defined as follows:

$$False \land \_ = False$$
$$True \land x = x$$

Using this definition, progress can only be made by evaluating the first argument of a conjunction, because each clause of the definition depends on the value of the first argument. Instead, we re-define the operator using overlapping patterns, using a special-purpose pragma to indicate the change in intended semantics:

```
{-# OVERLAP (∧) #-}
False  ∧  _      = False
_      ∧  False  = False
True   ∧  x      = x
x      ∧  True   = x
```

The definition has two new clauses, given by simply commuting the order of the arguments in the original definition. The idea is that a pattern match can succeed on any of the four clauses, independent of the order that they are stated in. Using this definition, progress can be made by evaluating either argument of the conjunction as the new clauses are no longer dependent on the first argument. For example, we can now reduce $x \land False$ to *False* for any expression $x$, which is not the case with the original definition. To take advantage of this additional power, the underlying needed narrowing mechanism must be modified to evaluate both arguments of the pattern match before it refines variables.

In *perm* example above, we considered the list $l = [1, 1, x_2, x_3]$ and found that it required a large amount of backtracking. In particular, the constraint *allDiff* $l$ only failed once we had considered all combinations of $x_2$ and $x_3$. The new overlapping conjunction operator avoids this problem because it is not biased to the left-argument, allowing *allDiff* $l$ to fail immediately for this example list without the need to further refine the remaining variables.

This additional efficiency is also borne out in practice. For example, using the implementation that we describe in Sect. 4, in the time it takes to generate one hundred valid permutations of length eight for the *perm* constraint defined using the traditional conjunction operator, we can generate one hundred valid permutations of length thirty using the overlapping version.

However, we have to be careful when using overlapping pattern matching not to introduce non-determinism. Consider the following dangerous function:

```
{-# OVERLAP danger #-}
danger False _    = False
danger _     False = True
danger True  True = True
```

Using this definition, *danger False False* can reduce to either *False* or *True*, depending on whether the first or second clause is used, and is therefore non-deterministic. To counter this, we require confluence laws which guarantee that evaluation is deterministic if all expressions are terminating.

Other logical operators such as disjunction and implication can be defined using overlapping patterns in a similar manner to conjunction, and will benefit from similar improvements in efficiency. The mechanism can also be used with other data types. For example it is straightfoward to define overlapping versions of the addition and maximum operators on natural numbers, and for the applicative operator <*> on the *Maybe* type [14]. As illustrated by the latter example, overlapping definitions are not restricted to commutative operators. The *maximum* function is defined and used in Sect. 5, and a range of other useful overlapping definitions are provided in our implementation [8].

## 3   Generalizing and Formalizing

In this section we define the syntax and semantics of our language of overlapping patterns. We consider the normalising subset of the language and show that a confluence restriction on definitions is sufficient to guarantee that the language is deterministic. We then extend the semantics with needed narrowing, and show that the new semantics is sound and complete with respect to the original.

We use a simple functional programming core language with definitions, constructors, variables, lambda expressions and application. To simplify the theory, the language only allows one form of pattern matching: at the top-level of a function definition, interpreted in an overlapping, order-independent manner. However, other forms of pattern matching, such as **case** expressions and non-overlapping patterns, can readily be rewritten in this form.

The syntax of the language is formally defined as follows:

$$Defn_X ::= \overline{Var\ \overline{Patt} = Expr_X}$$
$$Expr_X ::= Con \mid Var \mid X \mid Expr_X\ Expr_X \mid \lambda Var\ .\ Expr_X$$
$$Patt ::= Con\ \overline{Patt} \mid Var$$

That is, a definition is made up of a list of clauses, with a pattern for each argument on the left and an expression on the right. We use an overline to represent a list of elements, e.g. $\overline{Patt}$ is a potentially empty list of patterns. Expressions and definitions are parameterised by a set of free variables $X$, which is only used in the needed narrowing semantics. The language has standard set of typing rules, which we omit for brevity. Each type has a set of constructors and the patterns used in definitions should form a covering of these constructors. Each variable should only appear once in a pattern, and the only free variables in an expression should be those that appear in the set $X$.

We often use $f$ for definitions, $e$ for expressions, $c$ for constructors, $u$ and $v$ for closed variables, $x$ and $y$ for free variables, and $p$ and $q$ for patterns.

## 3.1　Semantics

We give a standard small-step operational semantics to the language in a contextual style. We start by defining a full reduction semantics, in which any reducible term in an expression can be reduced. This allows us to define notions of equivalence and establish confluence properties. We then define a call-by-name evaluation strategy by limiting the form of contexts that can be used, which is then used to define the needed narrowing strategy.

First we define a *local* semantics $\to_R \subseteq Expr_X \times Expr_X$ that performs basic reduction steps on expressions, which is then lifted into an evaluation context. As usual, a *substitution* is a mapping from variables to expressions, and we write $e[s]$ for the application of a substitution to each variable in an expression, $\emptyset$ for the identity substitution that maps each variable to itself, and $s;t$ for the composition of substitutions. The first local rule is the standard $\beta$-rule:

$$\frac{}{(\lambda v.e)\ e' \to_R e[v \mapsto e']}\ \text{SUB}$$

The second rule states that we can reduce a definition if the pattern of any of its clauses matches the arguments, where $f\ \overline{p} = e \in \text{defn}(f)$ means that the clause $f\ \overline{p} = e$ is part of the definition for the function $f$. In contrast to traditional pattern matching, the clauses of a definition may be applied in any order.

$$\frac{f\ \overline{p} = e' \in \text{defn}(f) \qquad \text{Matches}(\overline{p},\ \overline{e},\ s)}{f\ \overline{e} \to_R e'[s]}\ \text{MATCH}$$

The predicate **Matches** used above captures the idea of a successful match of expressions against patterns, where **Match** gives the definition for a single pattern, **Matches** for a list of patterns, and $s$ is the resulting substitution:

$$\frac{}{\text{Match}(v,\ e,\ \{v \mapsto e\})} \qquad \frac{\text{Matches}(\overline{p},\ \overline{e},\ s)}{\text{Match}(c\ \overline{p},\ c\ \overline{e},\ s)}$$

$$\frac{}{\text{Matches}(\epsilon,\ \epsilon,\ \emptyset)} \qquad \frac{\text{Match}(p,\ e,\ s) \qquad \text{Matches}(\overline{p},\ \overline{e},\ t)}{\text{Matches}(p\ \overline{p},\ e\ \overline{e},\ s;t)}$$

In turn, a *context* is an expression with a singular hole in any location, as defined by the following set of inference rules:

$$\frac{}{[]\ \text{context}}\ \text{HOLE} \qquad \frac{\mathbf{C}\ \text{context}}{(\lambda v.\mathbf{C})\ \text{context}}\ \text{LAM}$$

$$\frac{\mathbf{C}\ \text{context}}{(\mathbf{C}\ e)\ \text{context}}\ \text{APP-L} \qquad \frac{\mathbf{C}\ \text{context}}{(e\ \mathbf{C})\ \text{context}}\ \text{APP-R}$$

We use inference rules above rather than a grammer because the extra generality of this notation is used when contexts are revised later on. As usual, we write $\mathbf{C}[e]$ for the result of replacing the hole in $\mathbf{C}$ with the expression $e$.

Using the local semantics and the notion of contexts we can now define the full reduction semantics for expressions in our language.

**Definition 1.** The *full reduction* semantics, $\to \subseteq Expr_X \times Expr_X$, is given by:

$$\frac{e \to_R e' \qquad \mathbf{C}\ \text{context}}{\mathbf{C}[e] \to \mathbf{C}[e']}$$

**Definition 2.** $\to^*$ is the reflexive/transitive closure of $\to$.

To ensure that our language is deterministic and avoid examples such as *danger False False* from Sect. 2 that have more than one normal form, we require all definitions to satisfy a confluence property. To formalise this property we first define the notions of definitional equivalence and unification.

**Definition 3.** Two expressions are *definitionally equivalent*, written $e \equiv e'$, if there exists reduction sequences from $e$ and $e'$ to the same expression:

$$e \equiv e' \iff \exists e''.\ e \to^* e'' \wedge e' \to^* e''$$

Informally, two patterns are unifiable if there exists an expression which matches both the patterns. We can formalise this by giving a pair of substitutions which when applied to each pattern yield the common expression.

**Definition 4.** The *most general unifier* is defined by the inference rules below. $\text{Unify}(p,\ q,\ s_1,\ s_2)$ denotes the unification of patterns $p$ and $q$ by substitutions $s_1$ and $s_2$, and similarly for a list of patterns with $\text{Unifies}$. Note we are using the assumption that every variable appears only once in each pattern here.

$$\frac{\text{Unifies}(\overline{p},\ \overline{q},\ s_1,\ s_2)}{\text{Unify}(c\ \overline{p},\ c\ \overline{q},\ s_1,\ s_2)} \qquad \frac{}{\text{Unify}(v,\ p,\ \{v \mapsto p\},\ \emptyset)}$$

$$\frac{}{\text{Unify}(p,\ v,\ \emptyset,\ \{v \mapsto p\})}$$

$$\frac{}{\text{Unifies}(\epsilon,\ \epsilon,\ \emptyset,\ \emptyset)} \qquad \frac{\text{Unify}(p,\ q,\ s_1,\ s_2) \qquad \text{Unifies}(\overline{p},\ \overline{q},\ s_1',\ s_2')}{\text{Unifies}(p\ \overline{p},\ q\ \overline{q},\ s_1;s_1',\ s_2;s_2')}$$

This definition has the expected behaviour, that is:

$$\texttt{Unify}(p,\ q,\ s_1,\ s_2) \implies p[s_1] = q[s_2] \qquad \text{(unifier)}$$
$$\wedge\ \forall t_1 t_2.\ p[t_1] = q[t_2].\ \exists r.\ s_1; r = t_1 \wedge s_2; r = t_2 \quad \text{(most general)}$$

If the patterns of two clauses of a definition are unifiable then, given a suitable context, it is possible for two different MATCH reductions in our semantics to be applied. In order to maintain determinism for such clauses a confluence restriction is required. The confluence restriction states that the right-hand sides of each pair of clauses must be definitionally equivalent under their unifying substitution if one exists. For the terminating subset of the language we can check whether a definition satisfies the confluence property automatically by generating the unifiers pairwise and normalising each clause.

**Definition 5.** A definition satisfies the *confluence restriction* if for any pair of clauses, $f\ \overline{p} = e$ and $f\ \overline{q} = e'$, we have the following property:

$$\texttt{Unifies}(\overline{p},\ \overline{q},\ s_1,\ s_2) \implies e[s_1] \equiv e'[s_2]$$

**Theorem 1.** *The relation $\to^*$ is confluent if all the definitions satisfy the confluence restriction, i.e. for any reductions $e \to^* e_1$, $e \to^* e_2$, there exists an expression $e'$ such that $e_1 \to^* e'$ and $e_2 \to^* e'$.*

*Proof.* By parallel reduction with special consideration for overlapping patterns. □

It follows in the standard way from the above confluence property that any expression that only has finite reduction sequences has precisely one normal form. Hence, our semantics is deterministic for such expressions. We return to the issue of expressions with infinite reduction sequences in the concluding section.

## 3.2   Evaluation Order

Our current semantics allows reduction rules to be applied in any context and in any order. This is convenient for defining the behavioural properties of the semantics, but in order to define the needed narrowing semantics and give an efficient implementation, we need to restrict where reduction rules are applied. To do this we define a subset of contexts called *evaluation contexts*.

Our notion of evaluation context is call-by-name, and hence only evaluates the left-hand side of an application. When the left-most expression is a definition, we evaluate the arguments until a pattern match is possible. For efficiency, we only reduce arguments that could lead to a pattern match. Sometimes more than one argument needs to be reduced to allow a pattern match, in which case we reduce the arguments in a left-biased order. The rules are defined formally below, where $\overline{\mathbf{C}}$ is a list of expressions with one context.

$$\frac{}{\bullet\ \text{evalcxt}}\ \text{HOLE} \qquad \frac{\mathbf{C}\ \text{evalcxt}}{(\mathbf{C}\ e)\ \text{evalcxt}}\ \text{APP-L} \qquad \frac{\texttt{Subjects}(\overline{\mathbf{C}},\ f)}{(f\ \overline{\mathbf{C}})\ \text{evalcxt}}\ \text{ARGS}$$

The `Subject` predicates specify the parts of the arguments that should be reduced. The contexts which form the subjects have a clause of the definition for which they are the first sub-expression blocking the pattern match. All expressions to the left of the subject should already match their respective patterns in the clause. The predicates are defined by the following rules:

$$\frac{\texttt{Subject}(\mathbf{C},\ p) \qquad \texttt{Matches}(\overline{p},\ \overline{e_0},\ \_) \qquad f\ \overline{p_0}\ p\ \overline{p_1} = \_ \in \text{defn}(f)}{\texttt{Subjects}(\overline{e_0}\ \mathbf{C}\ \overline{e_1},\ f)}$$

$$\frac{\mathbf{C}\ \text{evalcxt}}{\texttt{Subject}(\mathbf{C},\ c\ \overline{p})} \qquad\qquad \frac{\texttt{Subject}(\mathbf{C},\ p) \qquad \texttt{Matches}(\overline{p_0},\ \overline{e_0},\ \_)}{\texttt{Subject}(c\ \overline{e_0}\ \mathbf{C}\ \overline{e_1},\ c\ \overline{p_0}\ p\ \overline{p_1})}$$

**Definition 6.** The *evaluation reduction* semantics, $\rightarrow_E$, is now defined by:

$$\frac{\mathbf{C}\ \text{evalcxt} \qquad e \rightarrow_R e'}{\mathbf{C}[e] \rightarrow_E \mathbf{C}[e']}$$

## 3.3  Needed Narrowing

The needed narrowing semantics reduces an expression until all the evaluation contexts are suspended on a free variable. At this point we refine the left-most suspending variable to a new value, with the resulting refinements to the free variables being stored in an accompanying substitution. We call this type of substitution a *refinement* to disambiguate it from the general notion.

Formally, a refinement $\sigma$ of type $X \mapsto Y$ is a function from the free variable set $X$ to *partial values* with free variables $Y$, where a partial value is a term build up from constructors and variables. Composition of refinements, which we denote by $\ggg$, is defined in the standard way. The null refinement, $return \in X \mapsto X$, corresponds to the trivial substitution that maps each free variable to itself.

**Definition 7.** The *narrowing set* of a expression, $narrowing(e)$, is the set of refinements that replace the left-most suspended variable with a constructor of the correct type with new free variables for the fields. The narrowing set should be complete, in the sense that it contains every constructor of the type.

For example, the narrowing set for an expression suspended on a variable $x$ of type *Nat* is (where $x/c$ is the point refinement replacing $x$ with $c$):

$$\{x/\,\texttt{Zero}, x/\,\texttt{Suc}\,y\} \qquad\qquad (y \text{ is a fresh variable})$$

We can now define the needed narrowing reduction as follows:

**Definition 8.** The *needed narrowing* reduction, $\leadsto\ \subseteq Expr_X \times (Expr_Y \times X \mapsto Y)$, is defined by the following two inference rules:

$$\frac{e \rightarrow_E e'}{e \leadsto \langle e',\ return \rangle} \qquad\qquad \frac{e \nrightarrow_E \qquad \sigma \in narrowing(e)}{e \leadsto \langle e[\sigma],\ \sigma \rangle}$$

The first rule states that any evaluation reduction is also a needed narrowing reduction, with no refinement necessary. The second states that if no such reduction is possible then a refinement from the narrowing set should be used.

**Definition 9.** The natural extension to the reflexive/transitive closure of the needed narrowing reduction is given by composing the resulting refinements:

$$\frac{}{e \leadsto^* \langle e[\sigma], \sigma \rangle} \qquad \frac{e \leadsto \langle e, \sigma \rangle \qquad e' \leadsto^* \langle e'', \sigma' \rangle}{e \leadsto^* \langle e'', \sigma \ggg \sigma' \rangle}$$

Note that in the reflexive case we use an arbitrary substituton $\sigma$ rather than the null refinement *return*, as this simplifies the formulation of the completeness result for our new semantics, which we now present along with soundness.

**Theorem 2.** *(Needed narrowing is sound.) For every needed narrowing reduction sequence there exists a corresponding reduction in the original semantics:*

$$e \leadsto^* \langle e', \sigma \rangle \implies e[\sigma] \to_E^* e'$$

*Proof.* By induction on the needed narrowing reduction chain.    □

To ensure that the corresponding completeness theorem is valid, we restrict our attention to expressions that strongly normalise under any refinement, which we denote using the predicate `Norm`.

**Theorem 3.** *(Needed narrowing is complete.) For every reduction of a normalising expression there is a corresponding needed narrowing reduction:*

$$\text{Norm}(e_0) \wedge e_0[\sigma] \to_E^* e_1 \implies \exists \, e_1'. \, e_0 \leadsto^* \langle e_1', \sigma \rangle \wedge e_1 \equiv e_1'$$

*Proof.* By induction on the length of reduction sequences, which are guaranteed to be finite by the normalisation precondition. In order to complete the proof, we require a slightly generalised induction hypothesis:

$$\text{Norm}(e_0) \wedge \text{Norm}(e_0') \wedge e_0[\sigma] \to_E^* e_1 \wedge e_0 \equiv e_0'$$
$$\implies \exists \, e_1'. \, e_{0'} \leadsto^* \langle e_1', \sigma \rangle \wedge e_1 \equiv e_1'    □$$

## 4    Implementation

In this section we give an overview of our prototype implementation of a property-based testing system based upon the ideas that we have introduced in the previous sections. The system itself is freely available on GitHub [8].

The source language used in the implementation is a core functional language with a Haskell-like syntax. The language includes algebraic data types and supports definitions with both overlapping and traditional pattern matching. Definitions are not currently checked for confluence, but as noted earlier this would be possible in a more mature implementation. For the purposes of the case studies in the next section we use Haskell syntax, which is translated into caseless monomorphic code in our implementation.

The implementation realises the needed-narrowing evaluation in a virtual machine encoded in Haskell. The result of evaluation is given by a lazy search tree, where each node comprises a free variable and sub-trees that provide constructor bindings for the variable, and the leaves are normal-form results. Different search strategies correspond to different methods of traversing the tree.

Properties in our system are functions with return type *Result*, which represents three possible outcomes: a failed precondition, in which case the test case is invalid; a successful result, where the test case satisfies the property; and a failure, where the test case is a counterexample. Properties are typically defined using a specialised implication operator ( $\implies$ ) :: $Bool \to Bool \to Result$.

Our system implements a random search strategy. At each node we select a random constructor according to a defined distribution, until we arrive at a result. If the precondition failed, we backtrack to try and find a valid result. It is sensible to limit the amount of backtracking as sometimes we might arrive at a state with no nearby solutions. We do this by limiting how many variables we can reverse, randomly enumerating all possible constructors at each variable in an attempt to find a continuation. For example, if the backtrack limit is set to three, and a failure occurs at a node which is twelve deep in the tree, we will backtrack to a minimum of depth nine in search of a solution.

## 5 Case Studies

In this section we consider two examples of using our system in practice. The first example involves the generation of ordered trees and demonstrates how overlapping patterns can be used to encode bespoke size constraints. The second generates typed expressions for a simple language and demonstrates a useful technique for writing efficient narrowing generators. In both examples we focus on the generation of data satisfying a constraint.

Our aim in each case is to find a definition of the constraint that eliminates the need for backtracking (apart from rebinding of a single constructor). We say that such a constraint *fails fast*. Formally, a constraint fails fast if when testing any partial value against the constraint it either directly fails or there is a refinement of the value that succeeds. The needed narrowing generator formed by a constraint which fails fast is generally efficient. All our examples, together with more detailed performance results, are available on GitHub [8].

### 5.1 Ordered Trees

Consider a type of binary trees with natural numbers stored in the nodes, with the additional constraint that numbers within the tree are ordered:

```
data Tree = Leaf | Node Tree Nat Tree
ordered                  :: Tree → Bool
ordered Leaf             = True
ordered (Node t0 a t1) = allTree (≤ a) t0 ∧ allTree (≥ a) t1
                       ∧ ordered t0 ∧ ordered t1
```

Note that *ordered* uses the overlapping version of conjunction to ensure that it can be tested in an efficient manner, and is defined using an auxiliary function *allTree* that checks if every element in a tree satisfies a given condition.

Now consider a function to delete a number from a tree while still maintaining the ordering invariant, as captured by the following property [15,16]:

```
propDelete     :: Nat → Tree → Bool
propDelete a t = ordered t ⟹ ordered (delete a t)
```

Unfortunately, if we test this property in its current form it will often fail to halt, because randomly generated values of recursively defined types such as trees are often infinite. To resolve this problem, narrowing-based testers usually limit the size of the solution by depth or by the number of constructors [15,16,19]. However, these metrics are often too simple to avoid backtracking.

To avoid bactracking in our example we need to limit only the depth of the tree and not the depth of elements (limiting the depth of elements limits their value but they have a minimum value dictated by the preceding elements.) Overlapping patterns allow us to limit the size with bespoke constraints. A function to calculate the *depth* of a tree can be defined as follows:

```
depthTree :: Tree → Nat
depthTree Leaf = Zero
depthTree (Node t1 _ t2) = Suc (max (depthTree t1) (depthTree t2))
```

In turn, our property can then be refined to include a depth limit:

```
propDelete n a t = ordered t ∧ depthTree t ≤ n ⟹ ordered (delete a t)
```

The use of overlapping patterns is crucial in two ways for this kind of example. Firstly, in the new definition of *propDelete*, the sizing constraint relies on overlapping conjunction to be visible while the ordering constraint is being tested. Secondly, and more interestingly, the definition for *depthTree* relies on an overlapping version of the maximum function for natural numbers:

```
{-# OVERLAP max #-}
max :: Nat → Nat → Nat
max Zero   Zero   = Zero
max (Suc x) y     = Suc (max x (pred y))
max x     (Suc y) = Suc (max (pred x) y)
```

The auxiliary function *pred* decrements a natural number, stopping at zero. A traditional maximum function would be left-biased and so the right branch of the tree could become arbitrarily large without triggering the size limit.

The constraint *ordered t* $\wedge$ *depthTree t* $\leqslant n$ fails fast for any *n*. Although on initial testing overlapping patterns may not seem to give a performance benefit, analysis of the results show that without overlapping patterns the distribution is heavily skewed towards trivial small trees. If the shape of the tree is given, overlapping patterns offer a significant performance improvement.

## 5.2 Well-Typed Expressions

In this example we generate typed expressions for a simple language. We use this example to demonstrate a technique for building constraints that fail fast which combines well with the use of overlapping patterns. The language has addition, conditional expressions, natural numbers, and logical values:

**data** *Expr* = *Add Expr Expr* | *If Expr Expr Expr* | *N Nat* | *B Bool*

A useful property for this language states that for any well-typed expression up to a given depth, evaluating the expression will not produce an error:

*propEval n e* = *typed e* $\wedge$ *depthExpr e* $\leqslant n$ $\implies$ *notError* (*eval e*)

We will focus on the *typed* condition. This condition has a simple definition in terms of a more general function *typeof* that attempts to determine the type of an expression, which may be either *Nat* or *Bool*, with the *Maybe* mechanism being used handle the possibility that an expression may be ill-typed:

$$
\begin{aligned}
&\textbf{data } \textit{Type} = \textit{Nat} \mid \textit{Bool} \\
&\textit{typeof} \qquad\qquad :: \textit{Expr} \rightarrow \textit{Maybe Type} \\
&\textit{typeof} \ (\textit{Add } e \ e') \ = \textbf{case} \ (\textit{typeof } e, \textit{typeof } e') \ \textbf{of} \\
&\qquad\qquad\qquad\quad (\textit{Just Nat}, \textit{Just Nat}) \rightarrow \textit{Just Nat} \\
&\qquad\qquad\qquad\quad \_ \qquad\qquad\qquad \rightarrow \textit{Nothing} \\
&\textit{typeof} \ (\textit{If } e \ e' \ e'') = \textbf{case} \ (\textit{typeof } e, \textit{typeof } e', \textit{typeof } e'') \ \textbf{of} \\
&\qquad\qquad\qquad\quad (\textit{Just Bool}, \textit{Just } t', \textit{Just } t'') \mid t' \equiv t'' \rightarrow \textit{Just } t' \\
&\qquad\qquad\qquad\qquad\qquad\qquad\qquad\qquad\qquad \rightarrow \textit{Nothing} \\
&\qquad\qquad\qquad\quad \_ \\
&\textit{typeof} \ (N \ \_) \qquad = \textit{Just Nat} \\
&\textit{typeof} \ (B \ \_) \qquad = \textit{Just Bool}
\end{aligned}
$$

However, the function *typeof* has an inefficient narrowing semantics. For example, an expression of the form *If* (*Add u v*) *w*·*x* is ill-typed for any *u, v, w, x*, because it is already evident that the first argument is not a logical value, but a version of *typed* defined using the function *typeof* would not be able to deduce this until specific expressions had been filled in for the variables *u* and *v*. In other words, the *typed* condition does not fail fast.

To solve this problem we define an alternative constraint, *hastype* :: *Expr* $\rightarrow$ *Type* $\rightarrow$ *Bool*, in which the type of the expression is taken as an argument rather then returned as a result. In this manner, the type is refined during the narrowing process alongside the expression itself.

$$hastype\ (Add\ e\ e')\ Nat\ = hastype\ e\ Nat\ \wedge\ hastype\ e'\ Nat$$
$$hastype\ (If\ e\ e'\ e'')\ t\ \ = hastype\ e\ Bool\ \wedge\ hastype\ e'\ t\ \wedge\ hastype\ e''\ t$$
$$hastype\ (N\ \_)\ Nat\ \ \ \ = True$$
$$hastype\ (B\ \_)\ Bool\ \ \ = True$$
$$hastype\ \_\ \_\ \ \ \ \ \ \ \ \ \ \ = False$$

If we reconsider our example expression, $If\ (Add\ u\ v)\ w\ x$, then we can see our new typing constraint identifies this as being ill-typed:

$$hastype\ (If\ (Add\ u\ v)\ w\ x)\ t$$
$$= hastype\ (Add\ u\ v)\ Bool\ \wedge\ hastype\ w\ t\ \wedge\ hastype\ x\ t$$
$$= False\ \wedge\ hastype\ w\ t\ \wedge\ hastype\ x\ t$$
$$= False$$

The *hastype* program does not fail fast but satisfies a similar weaker condition: any partial value formed by evaluating the constraint with free arguments either directly fails when applied to the constraint, or there is a refinement of the value that succeeds. Using the *hastype* constraint, our original property concerning well-typed expressions up to a given depth can now be reformulated to include the type of the expression as an additional narrowing variable:

$$propEval\ n\ t\ e = hastype\ e\ t\ \wedge\ depthExpr\ t \leqslant n\ \implies\ noError\ (eval\ e)$$

Note that the typing variable has no effect on the validity of the property, and is only used to make the narrowing process more efficient. Without the use of overlapping conjunction, attempting to generate expressions that satisfy both of these constraints simultaneously would typically fail to terminate, whereas the above definition can generate such expressions in an efficient manner.

## 5.3    Other Examples

We have also considered two more sophisticated examples, in the form of red-black trees and simply-typed lambda expressions. In both cases we were able to create generators that are both practical in terms of efficiency and modular in terms of how they are writen. For example, in the case of red-black trees, the required constraint is obtained simply by combining separate constraints for red nodes, black nodes, the ordering of elements, and the depth of the tree. Our final red-black tree implementation is similar to that used the Reach system [15], except that the additional efficiency that arises from using overlapping patterns results in the consistent finding of a bug which this system struggles to find.

## 6    Related Work

The functional logic language Curry [11] implements needed narrowing, and supports the use of overlapping patterns in definitions. However, the semantics is different to our system. In particular, our overlapping patterns are deterministic, with evaluation proceeding along a single branch, whereas in Curry such patterns are non-determistic, with evaluation considering every matching branch.

The form of overlapping patterns that we use in our system is similar to that proposed by Cockx [5,6], who develops the idea in the context of dependent type theory and the Agda programming language. However, the intended purpose is different, with our aim being to improve the performance of property-based testing under a needed-narrowing semantics, and Cockx seeking to simply the development of proofs in a dependently-typed setting.

A number of narrowing-based testing tools use the notion of parallel conjunction. The idea originates in Lindblad's work on data generation [13] and Lazy Smallcheck [19], both of which use an enumerative style of testing. Subsequently, parallel conjunction has been used by Claessen et al. [3] to randomly generate data with a uniform distribution. Parallel conjunction is equivalent to overlapping conjunction, but whereas previous testing work using this operator has been more practically focused, we have given a precise narrowing semantics for a general form of overlapping definitions. The research of Claessen et al. is the most similar to our work, in that they also use a narrowing-style for random testing. However, their aim of producing a uniform distribution, via the use of Feat [7], makes backtracking hard to avoid for many problems.

## 7   Conclusion and Future Work

In this article we have motivated and formalised an extension to needed narrowing to allow overlapping patterns in definitions. We use the needed narrowing evaluation to generate data satisfying a constraint from a program specifying a constraint. Overlapping patterns allow us to achieve this in an efficient manner using composable constraints. Below we discuss some limitations of our approach, and suggest some possible directions for further work.

While overlapping patterns can improve the performance of property-based testing, the use of narrowing can lead to subtle performance issues, as we saw in Sect. 5 with the *typeof* constraint. To avoid performance issues close attention must be paid to possible sources of backtracking. Overlapping patterns help by making it easier to define constraints with limited backtracking, but they are no silver bullet, and further research is required to establish appropriate methodologies for identifying and limiting sources of backtracking.

The use of an overlapping conjunction operator is ubiquitous and performance critical in our examples, but it is not yet clear whether the more general notion of overlapping patterns is necessary. For example, in the case studies that we have considered the use of other overlapping functions, such as *max*, can be replaced by additional narrowing variables. However, the resulting function will usually be less general than its overlapping counterpart.

The interaction between other language features, narrowing and overlapping patterns is also an interesting topic for further work. Adding the capability to refine and narrow first and higher-order functions is one area for which the trie representation of partial functions used in the extended Lazy Smallcheck [18] offers a starting direction. We are also keen to explore how our approach can be extended to handle coinductive types and dependent types.

To demonstrate the practicality of our approach, we developed a prototype implementation in Haskell. It would be interesting to add overlapping patterns to a more established tool, either a property based testing library such Lazy Smallcheck [19], or a functional logic language such as Curry [11]. An alternative approach to enable practical use would be to extend the implementation to automatically translate a precondition into a QuickCheck generator [4].

# References

1. Antoy, S., Echahed, R., Hanus, M.: A needed narrowing strategy. J. ACM **47**(4), 776–822 (2000)
2. Christiansen, J., Fischer, S.: EasyCheck — test data for free. In: Garrigue, J., Hermenegildo, M.V. (eds.) FLOPS 2008. LNCS, vol. 4989, pp. 322–336. Springer, Heidelberg (2008). doi:10.1007/978-3-540-78969-7_23
3. Claessen, K., Duregård, J., Pałka, M.H.: Generating constrained random data with uniform distribution. In: Codish, M., Sumii, E. (eds.) FLOPS 2014. LNCS, vol. 8475, pp. 18–34. Springer, Heidelberg (2014). doi:10.1007/978-3-319-07151-0_2
4. Claessen, K., Hughes, J.: QuickCheck: a lightweight tool for random testing of Haskell programs. In: International Conference on Functional Programming (2000)
5. Cockx, J.: Overlapping and Order-Independent Patterns in Type Theory. Ph.D. thesis, Master thesis, KU Leuven (2013)
6. Cockx, J., Piessens, F., Devriese, D.: Overlapping and order-independent patterns. In: Shao, Z. (ed.) ESOP 2014. LNCS, vol. 8410, pp. 87–106. Springer, Heidelberg (2014). doi:10.1007/978-3-642-54833-8_6
7. Duregård, J., Jansson, P., Wang, M.: Feat: functional enumeration of algebraic types. In: Haskell Symposium, vol. 47, no. 12 (2012)
8. Fowler, J.: The overlap check system for property-based testing (2016). https://github.com/JonFowler/OverlapCheck
9. Fowler, J., Huttom, G.: Towards a theory of reach. In: Serrano, M., Hage, J. (eds.) TFP 2015. LNCS, vol. 9547, pp. 22–39. Springer, Heidelberg (2016). doi:10.1007/978-3-319-39110-6_2
10. Hanus, M.: A unified computation model for functional and logic programming. In: Symposium on Principles of Programming Languages (1997)
11. Hanus, M.: Curry - An Integrated Functional Logic Language. Technical report (2016)
12. Hritcu, C., Hughes, J., Pierce, B.C., Spector-Zabusky, A., Vytiniotis, D., Azevedo de Amorim, A., Lampropoulos, L.: Testing noninterference, quickly. In: ACM SIGPLAN Notices, vol. 48 (2013)
13. Lindblad, F.: Property directed generation of first-order test data. In: Symposium on the Trends in Functional Programming (2007)
14. McBride, C., Paterson, R.: Applicative programming with effects. J. Funct. Program. **18**(1), 1–13 (2008)
15. Naylor, M., Runciman, C.: Finding inputs that reach a target expression. In: International Conference on Source Code Analysis and Manipulation (2007)
16. Naylor, M.F.: Hardware-Assisted and Target-Directed Evaluation of Functional Programs. Ph.D. thesis. University of York (2008)

17. Pałka, M.H., Claessen, K., Russo, A., Hughes, J.: Testing an optimising compiler by generating random lambda terms. In: International Workshop on Automation of Software Test (2011)

18. Reich, J.S., Naylor, M., Runciman, C.: Advances in lazy smallcheck. In: Hinze, R. (ed.) IFL 2012. LNCS, vol. 8241, pp. 53–70. Springer, Heidelberg (2013). doi:10. 1007/978-3-642-41582-1_4

19. Runciman, C., Naylor, M., Lindblad, F.: SmallCheck and lazy smallcheck automatic exhaustive testing for small values. In: Symposium on Haskell (2008)

# Boltzmann Samplers for Closed Simply-Typed Lambda Terms

Maciej Bendkowski[1], Katarzyna Grygiel[1], and Paul Tarau[2(✉)]

[1] Theoretical Computer Science Department, Faculty of Mathematics and Computer Science Jagiellonian University, ul. Prof. Łojasiewicza 6, 30-348 Kraków, Poland
{bendkowski,grygiel}@tcs.uj.edu.pl
[2] Department of Computer Science and Engineering,
University of North Texas, Denton, TX, USA
paul.tarau@unt.edu

**Abstract.** Simply-typed lambda terms are often used in the internal language of compilers and proof assistants, for which generation of large, uniformly distributed random terms is instrumental for testing correctness and scalability. Recently, Boltzmann samplers have enabled uniform random generation of large terms belonging to several families of combinatorial objects that have a regular structure, amenable to methods from analytic combinatorics. Unfortunately, no closed formula or generating function facilitating such methods is known for closed simply-typed lambda terms. Moreover, given their asymptotic sparsity in the family of closed lambda terms, filtering simply-typed terms in the much larger set of terms generated by a Boltzmann sampler becomes quickly intractable. By taking advantage of the synergy between logic variables, unification with occurs check and efficient backtracking in today's Prolog systems we advance this technique to term sizes interesting not only for correctness but also for scalability tests, by deriving Boltzmann samplers returning in a few seconds simply-typed random lambda terms of size 120 and above. We also apply our techniques to the generation of uniformly random closed simply-typed normal forms and give some hints on pushing them further via parallel execution algorithms.

**Keywords:** Boltzmann samplers · Random generation of simply-typed lambda terms · Type inference · Combinatorics of lambda terms · Random generation of simply-typed normal forms

## 1 Introduction

Simply-typed lambda terms [1,2] enjoy a number of nice properties, such as strong normalization, i.e., termination for all evaluation-orders, a Cartesian closed category mapping and a set-theoretical semantics. More importantly, via

The first two authors have been partially supported by the Polish National Science Center grant 2013/11/B/ST6/00975. The third author has been supported by NSF grant 1423324.

© Springer International Publishing AG 2017
Y. Lierler and W. Taha (Eds.): PADL 2017, LNCS 10137, pp. 120–135, 2017.
DOI: 10.1007/978-3-319-51676-9_8

the Curry-Howard isomorphism, closed lambda terms that are *inhabitants* of simple types can be seen as proofs for tautologies in the implicational fragment of *minimal logic* which, in turn, correspond to the simple types. Extended with a fix-point operator, simply-typed lambda terms can be used as the intermediate language for compiling Turing-complete functional languages. Recent work on the combinatorics of lambda terms [3–5], relying on generating functions and techniques from analytic combinatorics [6], has provided counts for several families of lambda terms and clarified important quantitative properties of interesting subclasses of lambda terms. With the techniques provided by generating functions [6], it was possible to separate the *counting* of the terms of a given size for several families of lambda terms from their more computation intensive *generation*, resulting in several additions (e.g., **A220894, A224345, A114851**) to the On-Line Encyclopedia of Integer Sequences [7].

On the other hand, the combinatorics of simply-typed lambda terms, given the absence of closed formulas or context-free grammar-based generators, due to the intricate interaction between type inference and the applicative structure of lambda terms, has left important problems open, including the very basic one of counting the number of closed simply-typed lambda terms of a given size. At this point, obtaining counts for simply-typed lambda terms requires going through the more computation-intensive generation process.

Fortunately, by taking advantage of the synergy between logic variables, unification with occurs check and efficient backtracking it is possible to significantly accelerate the generation of simply-typed lambda terms [8] by interleaving it with type inference steps.

While the generators described in the afore-mentioned paper can push the size of the simply-typed lambda terms by a few steps higher, one may want to obtain uniformly sampled random terms of significantly larger size, especially if one is concerned not only about correctness but also about scalability of compilers and program transformation tools used in the implementation of functional programming languages and proof assistants.

This brings us to the main contribution of this paper. We will first build efficient generators for simply-typed lambda terms that work by interleaving term building and type inference steps. From them, we will derive Boltzmann samplers returning random simply-typed lambda terms [9] of sizes between 120 and 150, assuming a slight variation of the "natural size" introduced in [10], assigning to each constructor a size given by its arity. We will also extend this technique to the random generation of simply-typed closed normal forms, based on the same definition of size.

The paper is organized as follows. Section 2 describes generators for plain, closed and simply-typed terms of a given size. Section 3 derives Boltzmann samplers for random generation of simply-typed closed lambda terms. Section 4 describes generators for lambda terms in normal form as well as their closed and simply-typed subsets. Section 5 derives Boltzmann samplers for random generation of simply-typed closed lambda terms in normal form. Section 6 discusses techniques for possibly pushing higher the sizes of generated random terms. Section 7 overviews related work and Sect. 8 concludes the paper.

The paper is structured as a literate Prolog program. The code has been tested with SWI-Prolog 7.3.8 and YAP 6.3.4. It is also available as a separate file at http://www.cse.unt.edu/~tarau/research/2016/ngen.pro.

# 2  Generators for Lambda Terms of a Given Natural Size

We start by generating all lambda terms of a given size, in the de Bruijn notation.

## 2.1  De Bruijn notation

De Bruijn indices [11] provide a robust *name-free* representation of lambda term variables. Closed terms[1] that are identical up to renaming of variables, i.e., are $\alpha$-convertible, share a unique representation. This allows each variable occurrence to be replaced by a non-negative integer marking the number of lambda abstractions between the variable and its binder. Following [10] we assume a unary notation of integers using the constant 0 and the constructor s/1 for the successor. Lambda abstraction and application constructors are represented using l/1 and a/2, respectively. And so, the set $\mathcal{L}$ of *plain lambda terms* is given by the following grammar:

$$\mathcal{L} = \mathcal{L}\mathcal{L} \mid \lambda\mathcal{L} \mid \mathcal{D},$$

where $\mathcal{D}$ denotes the set $\{0, \ s(0), \ s(s(0)), \ldots\}$ of de Bruijn indices.

Throughout the paper we assume that each constructor is of *weight* equal to its arity and the *size* of a lambda term is the sum of the weights of its building constructors.

## 2.2  Generating Plain Lambda Terms

Generation of plain lambda terms of a given size proceeds by consuming at each step a size unit, represented by the constructor s/1. This ensures that, for a size definition allocating a number of size units to each of the constructors of a term, generation is constrained to terms of a given size. As there are $n+1$ leaves (labeled 0) in a tree with $n$ a/2 constructors, we implement our generator to consume as many size-units as the arity of each constructor, in particular 0 for 0 and 2 for the constructor a/2. This means that we will obtain the counts for terms of natural size $n+1$ when consuming $n$ size-units.

```
genLambda(s(S),X):-genLambda(X,S,0).

genLambda(X,N1,N2):-nth_elem(X,N1,N2).
genLambda(l(A),s(N1),N2):-genLambda(A,N1,N2).
genLambda(a(A,B),s(s(N1)),N3):-
  genLambda(A,N1,N2),
  genLambda(B,N2,N3).
```

---

[1] A lambda term is called *closed* if it has no free variables and *open* otherwise. A term is called *plain* if it is either closed or open.

Note that `nth_elem/3` consumes progressively larger size-units for variables of a higher de Bruijn index, a property that conveniently mimics the fact that, in practical programs, variables located farther from their binders are likely to occur less frequently than those closer to their binders.

```
nth_elem(0,N,N).
nth_elem(s(X),s(N1),N2):-nth_elem(X,N1,N2).
```

**Example 1.** *Plain lambda terms of size 2 (with size of each constructor given by its arity).*

```
?- genLambda(s(s(s(0))),X).
X = s(s(0)) ; X = l(s(0)) ; X = l(l(0)) ; X = a(0, 0) .
```

Counts for plain lambda terms are given by the sequence **A105633** in [7].

### 2.3  Generating Closed Lambda Terms

We derive a generator for closed lambda terms by counting with help of a list of logic variables. At each lambda binder 1/1 step, a new variable is added to the list associated with a path from the root. For now, we simply use the length of the list as a counter for 1/1 nodes on the path.

The predicate `genClosed/2` builds this list of logic variables as it generates binders. When generating a leaf variable, it picks "non-deterministically" one of the variables among the list of variables corresponding to binders encountered on a given path from the root Vs. In fact, this list of variables will be ready to be used later to store the types inferred for a given binder.

```
genClosed(s(S),X):-genClosed(X,[],S,0).

genClosed(X,Vs,N1,N2):-nth_elem_on(X,Vs,N1,N2).
genClosed(l(A),Vs,s(N1),N2):-genClosed(A,[_|Vs],N1,N2).
genClosed(a(A,B),Vs,s(s(N1)),N3):-
  genClosed(A,Vs,N1,N2),
  genClosed(B,Vs,N2,N3).
```

Like `nth_elem` in the case of plain lambda terms, the predicate `nth_elem_on` assigns larger and larger s/1 weights as the de Bruijn indices, computed in successor arithmetic.

```
nth_elem_on(0,[_|_],N,N).
nth_elem_on(s(X),[_|Vs],s(N1),N2):-nth_elem_on(X,Vs,N1,N2).
```

**Example 2.** *Closed lambda terms of natural size 5.*

```
?- genClosed(s(s(s(s(s(0))))),X).
X = l(l(l(l(s(0))))) ; X = l(l(l(l(l(0))))) ; X = l(l(a(0, 0))) ;
X = l(a(0, l(0))) ; X = l(a(l(0), 0)) ; X = a(l(0), l(0)) .
```

Counts for closed lambda terms are given by the sequence **A275057** in [7].

## 2.4    Generating Simply-Typed Lambda Terms

We will derive a generator for simply-typed lambda terms with help from the logic variables used simply as counters in the case of closed terms, to contain the types on which de Bruijn indices pointing to the same binder should agree.

```
genTypable(X,V,Vs,N1,N2):-genIndex(X,Vs,V,N1,N2).
genTypable(l(A),(X->Xs),Vs,s(N1),N2):-genTypable(A,Xs,[X|Vs],N1,N2).
genTypable(a(A,B),Xs,Vs,s(s(N1)),N3):-
  genTypable(A,(X->Xs),Vs,N1,N2),
  genTypable(B,X,Vs,N2,N3).

genIndex(0,[V|_],V0,N,N):-unify_with_occurs_check(V0,V).
genIndex(s(X),[_|Vs],V,s(N1),N2):-genIndex(X,Vs,V,N1,N2).
```

We expose this algorithm via two interfaces: one for plain terms and one for closed terms.

```
genPlainTypable(S,X,T):-genTypable(S,_,X,T).

genClosedTypable(S,X,T):-genTypable(S,[],X,T).

genTypable(s(S),Vs,X,T):-genTypable(X,T,Vs,S,0).
```

For convenience, we shift the sequence by one to match the size definition where both application nodes and 0 leaves have size 1 as originally given in [10]. As there are $n+1$ leaf nodes for $n$ application nodes, consuming two units for an application rather than one for an application and one for a leaf as done in [10], speeds up the generation process as we are able to apply the size constraints at application nodes, earlier in the recursive descent.

**Example 3.** *Plain simply-typed lambda terms of natural size 3.*

```
?- genPlainTypable(s(s(s(s(0)))),X,T).
X = s(s(s(0))),T = A ;
X = l(s(s(0))),T =  (A->B) ;
X = l(l(s(0))),T =  (A->B->A) ;
X = l(l(l(0))),T =  (A->B->C->C) ;
X = a(0, s(0)),T = A ;
X = a(0, l(0)),T = A ;
X = a(s(0), 0),T = A ;
X = a(l(0), 0),T = A .
```

Counts for plain simply-typed lambda terms, up to size 16, are given by the sequence:

$$0, 1, 2, 3, 8, 17, 42, 106, 287, 747, 2069, 5732, 16012, 45283, 129232, 370761, 1069972.$$

Counts for closed simply-typed lambda terms are given by the sequence **A272794** in [7]. The first 16 entries are:

$$0, 0, 1, 1, 2, 5, 13, 27, 74, 198, 508, 1371, 3809, 10477, 29116, 82419, 233748.$$

# 3    A Boltzmann Sampler for Simply-Typed Terms

A naive way of sampling uniformly random lambda terms is to generate all terms of a given size and extract a random one out of them. Unfortunately, given the fact that the number of lambda terms grows exponentially with $n$, this technique quickly becomes intractable.

## 3.1    Designing Boltzmann Samplers

In their breakthrough paper [12], Duchon et al. introduced a powerful framework of *Boltzmann samplers* meant for random generation of combinatorial objects. Exploiting the analytic nature of the formal power series (see, e.g. [6]) related to the counts of objects in question, as well as their intrinsic recursive structure, it is possible to develop an efficient sampling algorithm.

The key idea behind Boltzmann samplers consists in setting a proper probability space defined on the set of combinatorial objects in such a way that any two objects of the same size are equally likely to be sampled. The price we pay for the efficiency and uniformity is the lack of control over the exact outcome size.

The process of sampling lambda terms follows their top-down recursive structure. At each step, the algorithm decides which constructor to use next, according to pre-computed *branching probabilities*. Depending on the type of the chosen constructor, the sampler either terminates, if 0 was chosen, or proceeds to construct the arguments recursively.

Although the size of the outcome is not deterministic, it is possible to control its *expected* size by adjusting the branching probabilities used in the sampling process. As in [9], the desired branching probabilities can be calibrated to set the expected size to a given finite value.

Such an approach allows us to rapidly sample random plain lambda terms of sizes of order 500,000. Given the asymptotic sparsity of closed simply-typed lambda terms in the set of plain ones [10], the sampling process has to be interleaved with a *rejection* phase where undesired terms are discarded as soon as possible and the whole process is restarted. Due to the immense number of expected retrials, the power of Boltzmann samplers is therefore significantly constrained. Following our empirical experiments, we calibrated the branching probabilities so to set the expected outcome size to 120 – the currently biggest practical size achievable.

## 3.2    Deriving a Boltzmann Sampler from an Exhaustive Generator

When generating all terms of a given size, the Prolog system explores all possibilities via backtracking. For a random generator, deterministic steps will be used instead, guided by the probabilities determined by the Boltzmann sampler.

Our code is parameterized by the size interval for the generated random terms as well as the maximum number of steps until the *being closed* and *being simply-typed* constraints are both met. Moreover, the code relies on precomputed constants corresponding to branching probabilities. Their values are obtained according to the recursive combinatorial specification of lambda terms by determining the appropriate complex function and evaluating it in the vicinity of its dominant singularity. The detailed process of computing the desired values is described in [9]. In our case, it turns out that in order to construct a plain term of expected size 120 the probabilities in question are as follows:

- the probability of constructing a de Bruijn index is 0.35700035696434995
- the probability of a lambda abstraction is 0.29558095907
- the probability of an application is 0.34741868396.

Furthermore, whenever we decide to create a de Bruijn index the probability of constructing zero is equal to 0.7044190409261122, while a successor is chosen with probability 0.29558095907. Hence, at each step of the construction process we draw uniformly at random a real from the interval $[0, 1]$ and on its basis we decide which constructor to add.

```
min_size(120).
max_size(150).
max_steps(10000000).
boltzmann_index(R):-R<0.35700035696434995.
boltzmann_lambda(R):-R<0.6525813160382378.
boltzmann_leaf(R):-R<0.7044190409261122.
```

The very high value of retries, max_steps, is coming from the discussed sparsity of simply-typed terms among all plain terms. The Boltzmann sampler can be fine-tuned via min_size and max_size to search for terms in an interval for which the probabilities of the sampler have been calibrated.

The predicate ranTypable returns a term X, its type T as well as the size of the term and the number of trial steps it took to find the term.

```
ranTypable(X,T,Size,Steps):-
  max_size(Max),
  min_size(Min),
  max_steps(MaxSteps),
  between(1,MaxSteps,Steps),
    random(R),
    ranTypable(Max,R,X,T,[],0,Size0),
  Size0>=Min,
  !,
  Size is Size0+1.
```

Note that it calls the predicate random/1, returning a random value between 0 and 1, with the convention that each predicate provides such a value for the next one(s) it calls, convention that will be consistently followed in the code.

The predicate ranTypable/7 follows the outline of the corresponding non-deterministic generator, except that it is driven by deterministic choices provided by the Boltzmann branching probabilities that decide which branch is taken.

Note that the parameter Max preempts growing a term above the specified size interval as early as that happens. Like in the generator, on which it is based, type inference is interleaved with term building. As a result, we prevent building terms with subterms that are not simply-typed, as soon as such a subterm is found.

```
ranTypable(Max,R,X,V,Vs,N1,N2):-boltzmann_index(R),!,
  random(NewR),
  pickIndex(Max,NewR,X,Vs,V,N1,N2).
ranTypable(Max,R,l(A),(X->Xs),Vs,N1,N3):-boltzmann_lambda(R),!,
  next(Max,NewR,N1,N2),
  ranTypable(Max,NewR,A,Xs,[X|Vs],N2,N3).
ranTypable(Max,_R,a(A,B),Xs,Vs,N1,N5):-
  next(Max,R1,N1,N2),
  ranTypable(Max,R1,A,(X->Xs),Vs,N2,N3),
  next(Max,R2,N3,N4),
  ranTypable(Max,R2,B,X,Vs,N4,N5).
```

Besides ensuring that types assigned to a leaf are consistent with the type acquired so far by their binder, the predicate `pickIndex/7` also enforces the property of being a closed term by picking variables from the list of possible binders above it, on the path to the root.

```
pickIndex(_,R,0,[V|_],V0,N,N):-boltzmann_leaf(R),!,
  unify_with_occurs_check(V0,V).
pickIndex(Max,_,s(X),[_|Vs],V,N1,N3):-
  next(Max,NewR,N1,N2),
  pickIndex(Max,NewR,X,Vs,V,N2,N3).
```

Finally, the helper predicate `next/4` ensures that the size count accumulated so far is not above the required interval, while providing a random value to be used by the next call.

```
next(Max,R,N1,N2):-N1<Max,N2 is N1+1,random(R).
```

**Example 4.** *A uniformly random simply-typed lambda term of size* 137 *and its type, obtained after* 1070126 *trial steps in* 4.388 *s.*

```
l(a(l(l(l(l(l(l(a(s(s(0)),a(l(a(l(l(1(0)))),l(a(0,a(0,a(s(s(0)),
  a(l(a(l(0),a(a(l(l(l(l(s(s(s(0))))))),s(s(0))),a(0,a(0,a(l(1(0)),
  l(a(l(l(l(s(s(s(0)))))),s(0))))))))))),1(0)))))))),a(0,a(s(s(0)),
  a(a(s(0),0),0)))))))))),l(a(l(a(0,a(l(l(s(0))),1(l(1(0)))))),
  l(a(l(a(0,a(l(a(l(l(l(l(s(0)))),l(s(s(0))))),l(s(0))))),a(l(l(a(l(0),
  l(a(l(l(l(a(0,a(0,l(1(0)))))),l(s(0))))))),s(s(0)))))))))
```

```
(A->B->((C->D->D)->E->F->G)->(((E->F->G)->G)->
  ((E->F->G)->G)->C->D->D)->((E->F->G)->G)->E->F->G)
```

## 4    Generating Simply-Typed Normal Forms

Normal forms are lambda terms that cannot be further $\beta$-reduced. In other words, they avoid *redexes* as subterms, i.e., applications with lambda abstractions on their left branches.

## 4.1 Generating Normal Forms of Given Size

To generate normal forms we simply add to `genLambda` the constraint `notLambda/1` ensuring that the left branch of an application node is anything except an `l/1` lambda node.

```
genNF(s(S),X):-genNF(X,S,0).


genNF(X,N1,N2):-nth_elem(X,N1,N2).
genNF(l(A),s(N1),N2):-genNF(A,N1,N2).
genNF(a(A,B),s(s(N1)),N3):-notLambda(A),genNF(A,N1,N2),genNF(B,N2,N3).


notLambda(0).
notLambda(s(_)).
notLambda(a(_,_)).
```

**Example 5.** *Plain normal forms of natural size 5.*

```
?- genNF(s(s(s(s(s(0))))),X).
X = s(s(s(0))) ;
X = l(s(s(0))) ;
X = l(l(s(0))) ;
X = l(l(l(0))) ;
X = l(a(0, 0)) ;
X = a(0, s(0)) ;
X = a(0, l(0)) ;
X = a(s(0), 0) .
```

Counts for plain (untyped) normal forms, up to size 16, are given by the sequence:

$$0, 1, 2, 4, 8, 17, 38, 89, 216, 539, 1374, 3562, 9360, 24871, 66706, 180340, 490912.$$

## 4.2 Interleaving Generation and Type Inference

Like in the case of the set of simply-typed lambda terms, we can define the more efficient combined generator and type inferrer predicate `genTypableNF/5`.

```
genPlainTypableNF(S,X,T):-genTypableNF(S,_,X,T).

genClosedTypableNF(S,X,T):-genTypableNF(S,[],X,T).

genTypableNF(s(S),Vs,X,T):-genTypableNF(X,T,Vs,S,0).

genTypableNF(X,V,Vs,N1,N2):-genIndex(X,Vs,V,N1,N2).
genTypableNF(l(A),(X->Xs),Vs,s(N1),N2):-genTypableNF(A,Xs,[X|Vs],N1,N2).
genTypableNF(a(A,B),Xs,Vs,s(s(N1)),N3):-notLambda(A),
  genTypableNF(A,(X->Xs),Vs,N1,N2),
  genTypableNF(B,X,Vs,N2,N3).
```

**Example 6.** *Simply-typed normal forms of size 6 and their types.*

```
?- genClosedTypableNF(s(s(s(s(s(0)))))),X,T).
X = l(l(l(s(0)))),T =  (A->B->C->B) ;
X = l(l(l(l(0)))),T =  (A->B->C->D->D) ;
X = l(a(0, l(0))),T =  (((A->A)->B)->B) ;
```

We are now able to efficiently generate counts for simply-typed normal forms of a given size.

**Example 7.** *Counts for closed simply-typed normal forms up to size 18.*

$0, 0, 1, 1, 2, 3, 7, 11, 25, 52, 110, 241, 537, 1219, 2767, 6439, 14945, 35253, 83214.$

## 5  Boltzmann Sampler for Simply-Typed Normal Forms

When restricted to normal forms, the Boltzmann sampler is derived in a similar way from the corresponding exhaustive generator. In order to find the appropriate branching probabilities, we exploit the following combinatorial system defining the set $\mathcal{N}$ of *normal forms* using the set $\mathcal{M}$ of so called *neutral forms*.

$$\mathcal{N} = \mathcal{M} \mid \lambda \mathcal{N}$$
$$\mathcal{M} = \mathcal{M} \mathcal{N} \mid \mathcal{D}$$

A normal form is either a neutral term, or an abstraction followed with a normal form. A neutral term, in turn, is either an application of a neutral term to a normal form, or a de Bruijn index.

With this description of normal forms, we are ready to recompute the branching probabilities (see [12] for details) for a Boltzmann sampler generating normal forms. Similarly as in the case of plain terms, we calibrated the branching probabilities so to set the expected outcome size to 120.

The resulting probabilities are given by the following predicates:

```
boltzmann_nf_lambda(R):-R<0.3333158264186935. % an 1/1, otherwise neutral
boltzmann_nf_index(R):-R<0.5062759837493023.  % neutral: index, not a/2
boltzmann_nf_leaf(R):-R<0.6666841735813065.   % neutral: 0, otherwise s/1
```

The predicate **ranTypableNF** generates a simply-typed term X in normal form and its type T, while computing the size of the term and the number of trial steps used to find it. Note the use of Prolog's CUT ! operation to stop the search once the right size is reached.

```
ranTypableNF(X,T,Size,Steps):-
  max_nf_size(Max),
  min_nf_size(Min),
  max_nf_steps(MaxSteps),
  between(1,MaxSteps,Steps),
    random(R),
    ranTypableNF(Max,R,X,T,[],0,Size0),
  Size0>=Min,
  !,
  Size is Size0+1.
```

First, a probabilistic choice is made between a normal form wrapped up by a lambda binder and a *neutral term*.

```
ranTypableNF(Max,R,l(A),(X->Xs),Vs,N1,N3):-
  boltzmann_nf_lambda(R),!, %lambda
  next(Max,NewR,N1,N2),
  ranTypableNF(Max,NewR,A,Xs,[X|Vs],N2,N3).
```

The choice between the next two clauses is decided by the guard `boltzmann_nf_index`. If satisfied, the recursive path towards a de Bruijn index is chosen. Otherwise, an application is generated. Note the use of the CUT operation (! to commit to the first clause when its guard succeeds.

```
ranTypableNF(Max,R,X,V,Vs,N1,N2):-boltzmann_nf_index(R),!,
  random(NewR),
  pickIndexNF(Max,NewR,X,Vs,V,N1,N2). % an index
ranTypableNF(Max,_R,a(A,B),Xs,Vs,N1,N5):- % an application
  next(Max,R1,N1,N2),
  ranTypableNF(Max,R1,A,(X->Xs),Vs,N2,N3),
  next(Max,R2,N3,N4),
  ranTypableNF(Max,R2,B,X,Vs,N4,N5).
```

Finally, the choice is made between the two alternatives deciding how many successor steps are taken until a 0 leaf is reached.

```
pickIndexNF(_,R,0,[V|_],V0,N,N):-boltzmann_nf_leaf(R),!, % zero
  unify_with_occurs_check(V0,V).
pickIndexNF(Max,_,s(X),[_|Vs],V,N1,N3):- % successor
  next(Max,NewR,N1,N2),
  pickIndexNF(Max,NewR,X,Vs,V,N2,N3).
```

**Example 8.** *A random simply-typed term of size 63 in normal form and its type, generated after 1312485 trial steps in less than a second.*

```
l(l(l(l(l(a(a(s(s(0)),l(a(0,a(l(l(s(0))),l(l(l(l(l(a(s(0),l(l(a(s(0),
l(s(0))))))))))))))))),l(a(a(l(l(a(l(s(0)),a(a(a(l(s(0)),a(l(0),0)),
l(s(s(0)))),l(l(l(0)))))))),0),l(0))))))))
```

```
(A->((((B->C->D->E->((((F->G)->H)->G->H)->I)->J->I)->K)->K)->
(L->((M->N->0->0)->L)->(M->N->0->0)->L)->P)->Q->R->P)
```

As there are fewer lambda terms of a given size in normal form, one may wonder why we are not reaching comparable or larger sizes to plain lambda terms, where our sampler was able to generate terms over size 120. An investigation of the relative densities of simply-typed terms in the two sets provides the explanation.

The table in Fig. 1 compares the changes in density for simply-typed terms and simply-typed normal forms. The first column lists the sizes of the terms. Column **A** lists the number of closed simply-typed terms of a given size. Column **B** lists the ratio between plain terms and simply-typed terms. Column **C** lists counts for closed simply-typed normal forms. Column **D** lists the ratio between

| Size | A: simpl.-typed | B: plain/simpl.-typed | C: TNF | D: NF/TNF | E: Dens. ratios |
|------|-----------------|-----------------------|--------|-----------|-----------------|
| 5    | 5               | 4.400                 | 3      | 5.666     | 0.776           |
| 10   | 508             | 6.988                 | 110    | 12.490    | 0.559           |
| 15   | 82,419          | 10.568                | 6,439  | 28.007    | 0.377           |
| 20   | 16,019,330      | 15.800                | 473,628| 60.040    | 0.263           |

**Fig. 1.** Comparison of the ratios of simply-typed terms and simply-typed normal forms

terms in normal form and closed simply-typed terms in normal form. Finally, column **E** computes the ratio of the two densities given in columns **B** and **D**.

The plot in Fig. 2 shows the much faster growing sparsity of simply-typed normal forms, measured as the ratio between plain terms and their simply-typed subset and respectively the ratio between normal forms and their simply-typed subset, i.e., the results shown in columns **B** and **D**, for sizes up to 20.

Finally, the plot in Fig. 3 shows the ratio between these two quantities, i.e., those listed in column **E**, for sizes up to 20. In both charts the horizontal axis stands for the size, while the vertical one for the number of terms.

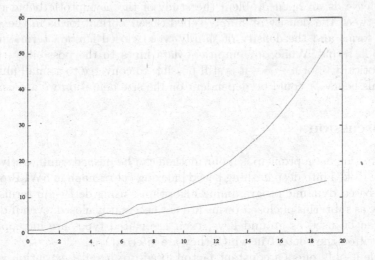

**Fig. 2.** Sparsity of simply-typed terms (lower curve) vs. simply-typed normal forms (upper curve)

Therefore, we see that closed simply-typed normal forms are becoming very sparse much earlier than their plain counterparts. While, e.g., for size 20 there are around 1/16 closed simply-typed terms for each term, at the same size, for each term in normal form there are around 1/60 simply-typed closed terms in normal form. As at sizes above 50 the total number of terms is intractably high, the increased sparsity of the simply-typed terms in normal form becomes the critical element limiting the chances of successful search.

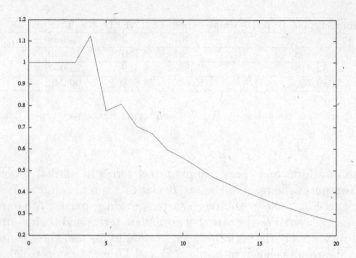

**Fig. 3.** Ratio between the density of simply-typed closed normal forms and that of simply-typed closed lambda terms

We leave as an open problem the study of the asymptotic behavior of the ratio between the density of simply-typed closed normal forms in the set of all normal forms and the density of simply-typed closed lambda terms in the set of lambda terms. While our empirical data hints to the possibility that it is asymptotically 0 for $n \to \infty$, it is still possible to converge to a small finite limit. Also, this behavior could be dependent on the size definition we are using.

## 6    Discussion

An interesting open problem is if our method can be pushed significantly farther. We have looked into deep hashing based indexing (`term_hash` in SWI Prolog) and tabling-based dynamic programming algorithms, using de Bruijn terms. Unfortunately as subterms of closed terms are not necessarily closed, even if de Bruijn terms can be used as ground keys, their associated types are incomplete and dependent on the context in which they are inferred.

While it only offers a constant factor speed-up, parallel execution is a more promising possibility. For exhaustive generation, given the small granularity of the generation and type inference process, the most useful parallel execution mechanism would simply split the task of combined generation and inference process into a number of disjoint sets. For instance, assuming size $n$, and $k \leq n$ `1/1` constructors, one would launch a thread exploring all possible choices, with the remaining $n - k$ size-units to be shared by the applications `a/2` and the weights of indices `s/1`.

For the generation of random terms via Boltzmann sampling, one would simply launch as many threads as the number of processors, with each thread exploring independently the search space.

# 7   Related Work

The problem of counting and generating uniformly random lambda terms is extensively studied in the literature.

In [5] authors considered a canonical representation of closed lambda terms in which variables do not contribute to the overall term size. The same model was investigated in [3], where a sampling method based on a *ranking-unranking* approach was developed. A binary variant of lambda calculus was considered in [9], leading to a generation method employing Boltzmann samplers. The natural size notion was introduced in [10]. The presented results included quantitative investigations of certain semantic properties, such as strong normalization or typability.

Other, non-uniform generation, approaches are also studied in the context of automated software verification. Prominent examples include Quickcheck [13] and GAST [14] – two frameworks offering facilities for random (yet not necessarily uniform) and exhaustive test generation, used in the verification of user-defined function properties and invariants.

In [15] a "type-directed" mechanism for generation of random terms was introduced, resulting in more realistic (from the particular use case point of view) terms, employed successfully in discovering optimization bugs in the Glasgow Haskell Compiler (GHC).

Function synthesis, given a finite set of input-output examples, was considered in [16]. In this approach, the set of candidate functions is restricted to a subset of primitive recursive functions with abstract syntax trees defined by some context-free grammar, yielding an effective method of finding "natural" functions matching the given example set.

A statistical exploration of the structure of the simple types of lambda terms of a given size in [17] gives indications that some types frequent in human-written programs are among the most frequently inferred ones for terms of a given size.

# 8   Conclusion

We have derived from logic programs for exhaustive generation of lambda terms programs that generated uniformly distributed simply-typed lambda terms via Boltzmann samplers.

This has put at test a simple but effective program transformation technique naturally available in logic programming languages: interleaving generators and constraints by integrating them in the same predicate.

For the exhaustive generation, we have also managed to work within the minimalist framework of Horn clauses with sound unification, showing that non-trivial combinatorial problems can be handled without any of Prolog's impure features.

Our empirical study of Boltzmann samplers has revealed an intriguing discrepancy between the case of simply-typed terms and simply-typed normal forms. While these two classes of terms are both known to asymptotically vanish, the significantly faster growth of the sparsity of the later has limited our Boltzmann sampler to sizes below 60.

Our techniques, combining unification of logic variables with Prolog's backtracking mechanism, recommend logic programming as a convenient metalanguage for the manipulation of various families of lambda terms and the study of their combinatorial and computational properties.

The ability to generate uniformly random simply-typed closed lambda terms of sizes above 120 opens the doors for applications to testing compiler components for functional languages and proof assistants, not only for correctness but also for scalability. We hope that simply-typed lambda terms above 120 can be also useful to spot out performance and memory management issues for several algorithms used in these tools, including $\beta$-reduction, lambda lifting and type inference.

# References

1. Hindley, J.R., Seldin, J.P.: Lambda-Calculus and Combinators: An Introduction, vol. 13. Cambridge University Press, Cambridge (2008)
2. Barendregt, H.P.: Lambda calculi with types. In: Handbook of Logic in Computer Science, vol. 2. Oxford University Press (1991)
3. Grygiel, K., Lescanne, P.: Counting and generating lambda terms. J. Funct. Program. **23**(5), 594–628 (2013)
4. Bodini, O., Gardy, D., Gittenberger, B.: Lambda terms of bounded unary height. In: 2011 Proceedings of the Eighth Workshop on Analytic Algorithmics and Combinatorics (ANALCO), pp. 23–32 (2011)
5. David, R., Grygiel, K., Kozik, J., Raffalli, C., Theyssier, G., Zaionc, M.: Asymptotically almost all $\lambda$-terms are strongly normalizing. Logical Meth. Comput. Sci. **9**(1:02), 1–30 (2013)
6. Flajolet, P., Sedgewick, R.: Analytic Combinatorics, 1st edn. Cambridge University Press, New York (2009)
7. Sloane, N.J.A.: The On-Line Encyclopedia of Integer Sequences (2014). https://oeis.org/
8. Tarau, P.: On logic programming representations of lambda terms: de Bruijn indices, compression, type inference, combinatorial generation, normalization. In: Pontelli, E., Son, T.C. (eds.) PADL 2015. LNCS, vol. 9131, pp. 115–131. Springer, Cham (2015). doi:10.1007/978-3-319-19686-2_9
9. Grygiel, K., Lescanne, P.: Counting and generating terms in the binary lambda calculus. J. Funct. Program. **25**, e24 (2015)
10. Bendkowski, M., Grygiel, K., Lescanne, P., Zaionc, M.: A natural counting of lambda terms. In: Freivalds, R.M., Engels, G., Catania, B. (eds.) SOFSEM 2016. LNCS, vol. 9587, pp. 183–194. Springer, Heidelberg (2016). doi:10.1007/978-3-662-49192-8_15
11. de Bruijn, N.G.: Lambda calculus notation with nameless dummies, a tool for automatic formula manipulation, with application to the Church-Rosser theorem. Indagationes Math. **34**, 381–392 (1972)
12. Duchon, P., Flajolet, P., Louchard, G., Schaeffer, G.: Boltzmann samplers for the random generation of combinatorial structures. Comb. Probab. Comput. **13**(4–5), 577–625 (2004)

13. Claessen, K., Hughes, J.: QuickCheck: a lightweight tool for random testing of Haskell programs. In: Proceedings of the Fifth ACM SIGPLAN International Conference on Functional Programming, ICFP 2000, pp. 268–279. ACM, New York (2000)

14. Koopman, P., Alimarine, A., Tretmans, J., Plasmeijer, R.: GAST: generic automated software testing. In: Peña, R., Arts, T. (eds.) IFL 2002. LNCS, vol. 2670, pp. 84–100. Springer, Berlin (2003). doi:10.1007/3-540-44854-3_6

15. Palka, M.H., Claessen, K., Russo, A., Hughes, J.: Testing an optimising compiler by generating random lambda terms. In: Proceedings of the 6th International Workshop on Automation of Software Test, AST 2011, pp. 91–97. ACM, New York (2011)

16. Koopman, P., Plasmeijer, R.: Systematic synthesis of functions, pp. 68–83. The University of Nottingham (2006)

17. Tarau, P.: On Type-directed Generation of Lambda Terms. In: De Vos, M., Eiter, T., Lierler, Y., Toni, F. (eds.) 31st International Conference on Logic Programming (ICLP 2015), Technical Communications, Cork, Ireland, CEUR (2015). http://ceur-ws.org/Vol-1433/

# Selection Equilibria of Higher-Order Games

Jules Hedges[1], Paulo Oliva[2]([⊠]), Evguenia Shprits[3], Viktor Winschel[4], and Philipp Zahn[5]

[1] Department of Computer Science, University of Oxford, Oxford, UK
[2] Department of Electronic Engineering and Computer Science,
Queen Mary University of London, London, UK
p.oliva@qmul.ac.uk
[3] Department of Economics, University of Mannheim, Mannheim, Germany
[4] Department of Management, Technology and Economics,
ETH Zürich, Zürich, Switzerland
[5] Department of Economics, University of St. Gallen, St. Gallen, Switzerland

**Abstract.** In applied game theory the modelling of each player's intentions and motivations is a key aspect. In classical game theory these are encoded in the payoff functions. In previous work [2,4] a novel way of modelling games was introduced where players and their goals are more naturally described by a special class of higher-order functions called *quantifiers*. We refer to these as higher-order games. Such games can be directly and naturally implemented in strongly typed functional programming languages such as Haskell [3]. In this paper we introduce a new solution concept for such higher-order games, which we call *selection equilibrium*. The original notion proposed in [4] is now called *quantifier equilibrium*. We show that for a special class of games these two notions coincide, but that in general, the notion of selection equilibrium seems to be the right notion to consider, as illustrated through variants of coordination games where agents are modelled via fixed-point operators. This paper is accompanied by a Haskell implementation of all the definitions and examples.

## 1 Introduction

In this paper we introduce a representation of simultaneous move games that formally summarises the goals of agents via *quantifiers* and *selection functions*. Both quantifiers and selection functions are examples of higher-order functions (also called functionals or operators) and originate in a game-theoretic approach to proof theory [2,4].

As shown in [2,4], the standard Nash equilibrium concept can be seamlessly generalised to this higher-order representation of games. The original work on these higher-order games used a notion of equilibrium which we will now call *quantifier equilibrium*. In this paper we introduce an alternative notion, which we call *selection equilibrium*. We prove that quantifier and selection equilibria coincide in the case of the classical max and arg max operators, but that, generally, this equivalence does not hold: For other quantifiers and selection functions

© Springer International Publishing AG 2017
Y. Lierler and W. Taha (Eds.): PADL 2017, LNCS 10137, pp. 136–151, 2017.
DOI: 10.1007/978-3-319-51676-9_9

the two different equilibrium concepts yield different sets of equilibria. We give a sufficient condition for the two notions to coincide based on the notion of *closedness* of selection functions. We prove that in general, the selection equilibrium is an equilibrium refinement of the quantifier equilibrium, and present evidence that for games based on non-closed selection functions, the selection equilibrium is the appropriate solution concept.

A Haskell implementation of the theory and examples contained in this paper is available online.[1] We chose not to discuss the actual code here in detail due to lack of space. This code, however, was crucial for the development of the theory here presented. The ability to implement not just the various players, but also the outcome functions and the equilibrium checkers, enabled us to quickly test several different examples of games, with different notions of equilibrium. Careful testing of a variety of situations ultimately led us to the conclusion that the new notion of equilibrium for higher-order games is preferable in general. Although in this paper we could have used any other strongly typed functional language, in the case of sequential games [2–4] the use of Haskell monads is essential. In higher-order *sequential* games one can make use of the fact that the type of selection functions forms a monad, and backwards induction can be simply implemented as the "sequencing" of monads.

## 2    Players, Quantifiers and Selection Functions

A *higher order function* (or *functional*) is a function whose domain is itself a set of functions. Given sets $X$ and $Y$ we denote by $X \to Y$ the set of all functions with domain $X$ and codomain $Y$. There are familiar examples of higher-order functions, such as the max operator, which has type max: $(X \to \mathbb{R}) \to \mathbb{R}$ returning the maximum value of a given real-valued function $p \colon X \to \mathbb{R}$. One will normally write $\max p$ as $\max_{x \in X} p(x)$. A corresponding operator is arg max which returns all the points where the maximum of a function $p \colon X \to \mathbb{R}$ is attained, i.e. arg max: $(X \to \mathbb{R}) \to \mathcal{P}(X)$ using $\mathcal{P}(X)$ for the power-set[2] of $X$. Note that as opposed to max, arg max is naturally a multi-valued function, even when the maximal value is unique.

Of a slightly different nature is the fixed point operator fix: $(X \to X) \to \mathcal{P}(X)$ which calculates all the fixed points of a given self-mapping $p \colon X \to X$, or the anti-fixed-point operator which calculates all points that are not fixed points.

In this section we define two particular classes of higher-order functions: *quantifiers* and *selection functions*. We first establish that these functions provide means to represent agents' goals in an abstract and general way. In particular, these notions usefully generalise utility maximisation and preference relations.

---

[1] http://www.eecs.qmul.ac.uk/~pbo/papers/hog-padl-2017.hs.

[2] As long as our games are finite we can easily replace powersets with lists, which we do in the accompanying implementation.

## 2.1  Game Context

To define players' goals we first need a structure that represents the strategic situation on which these goals are based. To this end we introduce the concept of a *game context* which summarises information of the strategic situation from the perspective of a single player.

**Definition 1 (Game context).** *For a player $\mathcal{A}$ choosing a move from a set $X$, having in sight a final outcome in a set $R$, we call any function $p\colon X \to R$ a possible* game context *for the player $\mathcal{A}$.*

Consider the following *voting contest* which we will use as a running example throughout this paper: three judges are voting simultaneously for one of two contestants $X = \{A, B\}$. The winner is decided by the majority rule maj: $X \times X \times X \to X$. In a setting where judges 1 and 3 have fixed their choices, say $x_1 = A$ and $x_3 = B$, this gives rise to a game context for the second judge, namely

$$x_2 \quad \mapsto \quad \mathrm{maj}(A, x_2, B)$$

which is in fact the identity function since $\mathrm{maj}(A, x_2, B) = x_2$. If, on the other hand, judges 1 and 3 had fixed their choices as $x_1 = x_3 = A$, the game context for player 2 would be the constant function $x_2 \mapsto A$, since his vote does not influence the outcome.

One can think of the game context $p\colon X \to R$ as an *abstraction* of the actual game context that is determined by knowing the rules of the game, and how each opponent played. Notice that in the example above the game context which maps $A$ to $B$, and $B$ to $A$, never arises. It would arise, however, if one replaced the majority rule by the minority rule.

It might seem like we are losing too much information by adopting such an abstraction. We hope that the examples given here will illustrate that this level of abstraction is sufficient for modelling players' individual motivations and goals. And precisely because it is abstract and it captures the strategic context of a player as if it was a single decision problem, it allows for a description of the players' intrinsic motivations, irrespective of how many players are around, or which particular game is being played. This is key for obtaining a modular description of games as well as a modular Haskell implementation.

## 2.2  Quantifiers and Selection Functions

Suppose now that $\mathcal{A}$ makes a decision $x \in X$ in a game context $p\colon X \to R$. First of all, it is important to realise that the only achievable outcomes in the context $p\colon X \to R$ are the elements in the image of $p$, i.e. $\mathrm{Im}(p) \subseteq R$. Out of these achievable outcomes the player should consider some outcomes to be *good* (or *acceptable*). Since the good outcomes must in particular be achievable, it is clear that the set of good outcomes can only be defined in relation to the given context. That dependence, however, can go further than just looking at $\mathrm{Im}(p)$. For instance, an element $r \in R$ might be the maximal attainable value of the mapping $p_1\colon X \to R$, but could be unachievable, sub-optimal or even the worst outcome in a different context $p_2\colon X \to R$.

**Definition 2 (Quantifiers, [2,4]).** *Let $\mathcal{P}(R)$ denote the power-set of the set of outcomes $R$. We call* quantifiers[3] *any higher-order function of type*

$$\varphi\colon (X \to R) \to \mathcal{P}(R)$$

*from contexts $p\colon X \to R$ to non-empty sets of outcomes $\varphi(p) \subseteq R$.*

The approach of [2,4] is to model players $\mathcal{A}$ as quantifiers $\varphi_{\mathcal{A}}\colon (X \to R) \to \mathcal{P}(R)$ We think of $\varphi_{\mathcal{A}}(p) \subseteq R$ as the set of outcomes the player $\mathcal{A}$ considers preferable in a given game context $p\colon X \to R$. It is crucial to recognise that this is a *qualitative* description of a player, in the sense that an outcome is either preferable or it is not, with no numerical measure attached.

It could be, however, that the notion of being a "good outcome" indeed comes from a numeric measure. In fact, the classical example of a quantifier is *utility maximisation*, with the outcome set $R = \mathbb{R}^n$ consisting of $n$-tuples of real-valued payoffs. If we denote by $\pi_i\colon \mathbb{R}^n \to \mathbb{R}$ the $i$-projection, then the utility of the $i^{th}$ player is $\pi_i(r)$. Hence, given a game context $p\colon X \to \mathbb{R}^n$, the good outcomes for the $i^{th}$ player are precisely those for which the $i^{th}$ coordinate, i.e. his utility, is maximal. This quantifier is given by

$$i\text{-max}(p) = \{r \in \text{Im}(p) \mid r_i \geq (\pi_i \circ p)(x') \text{ for all } x' \in X\}$$

where $\text{Im}(p)$ denotes the image of the function $p\colon X \to \mathbb{R}^n$, and $\pi_i \circ p$ denotes the composition of $p$ with the $i$-th projection.

For a very different example of a quantifier, when the set of moves is equal to the set of outcomes $R = X$ there is a quantifier whose good moves are precisely the fixpoints of the context. This quantifier models a player whose aim is to make a choice that is equal to the resulting outcome. If the context has no fixpoint, then the player will be equally satisfied with any outcome. Therefore such a quantifier can be defined as

$$\text{fix}(p) = \begin{cases} \{x \in X \mid p(x) = x\} & \text{if } p(x) = x \text{ for some } x \in X \\ X & \text{otherwise.} \end{cases}$$

Just as a quantifier tells us which outcomes a player considers good in each given context, one can also consider the higher-order function that determines which *moves* a player considers good in any given context.

---

[3] The terminology comes from the observation that the usual existential $\exists$ and universal $\forall$ quantifiers of logic can be seen as operations of type $(X \to \mathbb{B}) \to \mathbb{B}$, where $\mathbb{B}$ is the type of booleans. Mostowski [12] also called arbitrary functionals of type $(X \to \mathbb{B}) \to \mathbb{B}$ *generalised quantifiers*. We are choosing to generalise this further by replacing the booleans $\mathbb{B}$ with an arbitrary type $R$, and allowing for the operation to be multi-valued.

**Definition 3 (Selection functions).** *A selection function is any function of the form*[4]

$$\varepsilon\colon (X \to R) \to \mathcal{P}(X).$$

Similarly to quantifiers, the canonical example of a selection function is maximising one of the coordinates in $\mathbb{R}^n$, defined by

$$i\text{-}\arg\max(p) = \{x \in X \mid (\pi_i \circ p)(x) \geq (\pi_i \circ p)(x') \text{ for all } x' \in X\}.$$

Even in one-dimensional $\mathbb{R}^1$ the arg max selection function is naturally multi-valued: a function may attain its maximum value at several different points.[5]

## 2.3   Relating Quantifiers and Selection Functions

It is clear that quantifiers and selection functions are closely related. One important relation between them is that of *attainment*. Intuitively this means that the outcome of a good move should be a good outcome.

**Definition 4.** *Given a quantifier $\varphi\colon (X \to R) \to \mathcal{P}(R)$ and a selection function $\varepsilon\colon (X \to R) \to \mathcal{P}(X)$, we say that $\varepsilon$ attains $\varphi$ iff for all contexts $p\colon X \to R$ it is the case that*

$$x \in \varepsilon(p) \implies p(x) \in \varphi(p).$$

One can check that the attainability relation holds between the quantifier $i$-max and the selection function $i$-arg max. Any point where the maximum value is attained will evaluate to the maximum value of the function. More interestingly, the fixpoint quantifier is also a selection function, and it attains itself since

$$x \in \mathrm{fix}(p) \implies p(x) \in \mathrm{fix}(p).$$

Let us briefly reflect on the game theoretic meaning of attainability. Suppose we have a quantifier $\varphi$ which describes the outcomes that a player considers to be good. The quantifier might be *unrealistic* in the sense that it has no attainable good outcome. For example, a player may consider it a good outcome if he received a million dollars, but in his current context there may just not be a move available which will lead to this outcome. The attainable quantifiers $\varphi\colon (X \to R) \to \mathcal{P}(R)$ describe realistic players, i.e. for any game context $p\colon X \to R$ there is always a move $x\colon X$ which leads to a good outcome $p(x) \in \varphi(p)$.

Given any selection function $\varepsilon\colon (X \to R) \to \mathcal{P}(X)$, we can form the smallest quantifier which it attains as follows.

---

[4] Where selection functions have been considered previously [2,4] the focus was on single-valued ones. However, as multi-valued selection functions are extremely important in our examples we have adapted the definitions accordingly.

[5] In the following we will assume that quantifiers and selection functions are non-empty. That is, agents will always have a preferred outcome, respectively move, in all situations they have to make a decision. See [9] for a discussion.

**Definition 5.** *Given a selection function* $\varepsilon\colon (X \to R) \to \mathcal{P}(X)$, *define the quantifier* $\overline{\varepsilon}\colon (X \to R) \to \mathcal{P}(R)$ *as*

$$\overline{\varepsilon}(p) = \{p(x) \mid x \in \varepsilon(p)\}.$$

It is easy to check that $\varepsilon$ attains $\overline{\varepsilon}$. Conversely, given any quantifier we can define a corresponding selection function as follows.

**Definition 6.** *Given a quantifier* $\varphi\colon (X \to R) \to \mathcal{P}(R)$, *define the selection function* $\overline{\varphi}\colon (X \to R) \to \mathcal{P}(X)$ *as*

$$\overline{\varphi}(p) = \{x \mid p(x) \in \varphi(p)\}.$$

Again, it is easy to check that the selection function $\overline{\varphi}$ attains the quantifier $\varphi$. We use the same overline notation, as it will be clear from the setting whether we are applying it to a quantifier or a selection function.

# 3  Higher-Order Games

Quantifiers and selection functions as introduced in the previous section can be used to model games. In this section we define higher-order games, illustrate the definition using the voting contest as a running example, and, lastly, discuss two equilibrium concepts.

**Definition 7 (Higher-Order Games).** *An n-players game* $\mathcal{G}$, *with a set* $R$ *of outcomes and sets* $X_i$ *of strategies for the* $i^{th}$ *player, consists of an* $(n+1)$-*tuple* $\mathcal{G} = (\varepsilon_1, \ldots, \varepsilon_n, q)$ *where*

- *for each player* $1 \leq i \leq n$, $\varepsilon_i\colon (X_i \to R) \to \mathcal{P}(X_i)$ *is a selection function describing the i-th player's preferred moves in each game context.*
- $q\colon \prod_{i=1}^{n} X_i \to R$ *is the outcome function, i.e., a mapping from the strategy profile to the final outcome.*

(Note that a strategy profile for a game is simply a tuple $\mathbf{x}\colon \prod_{i=1}^{n} X_i$, consisting of a choice of strategy for each player.)

Intuitively, we think of the outcome function $q$ as representing the 'situation', or the rules of the game, while we think of the selection functions as describing the players. Thus we can imagine the same player in different situations, and different players in the same situation. This allows us to decompose a modelling problem into a global and a local part: modelling the situation (i.e. $q$) and modelling the individual players (i.e. $\varepsilon_1, \ldots, \varepsilon_n$).

*Remark 1 (Classical Game [13]).* The ordinary definition of a normal form game of $n$-players with standard payoff functions is a particular case of Definition 7 when

- for each player $i$ the set of strategies is $X_i$,

**Table 1.** Voting contest with classical players; Nash equilibria in bold.

|  | $J_2$: A | $J_2$: B |  |  | $J_2$: A | $J_2$: B |  |
|---|---|---|---|---|---|---|---|
| $J_1$: A | **1,1,0** | 1,1,0 | $J_3$: $A$ | $J_1$: A | **1,1,0** | 0,0,1 | $J_3$: $B$ |
| $J_1$: B | 1,1,0 | 0,0,1 |  | $J_1$: B | 0,0,1 | **0,0,1** |  |

- the set of outcomes $R$ is $\mathbb{R}^n$, modelling the vector of payoffs obtained by each player,
- the selection function of player $i$ is $i$-$\arg\max$: $(X_i \to \mathbb{R}^n) \to \mathcal{P}(X_i)$, i.e. $\arg\max$ with respect to the $i^{th}$ coordinate, representing the idea that each player is solely interested in maximising their own payoff,
- the $i^{th}$ component of the outcome function $q$: $\prod_{i=1}^n X_i \to \mathbb{R}^n$ can be viewed as the payoff function $q_i$: $\prod_{j=1}^n X_j \to \mathbb{R}$ of the $i^{th}$ player.

*Remark 2.* For an implementation in a simply-typed language (as opposed to dependently typed) such as Haskell, it is convenient either to fix the number of players and store the data in tuples, or to take the sets $X_i$ to be equal and store the data in homogeneous lists. (See also [1].) In the accompanying implementation we opt for the latter, because in our running example the $X_i$ are equal.

## 3.1    Example: Voting Contest

Reconsider the voting contest outlined in Sect. 2.1: There are three players, the judges $J = \{J_1, J_2, J_3\}$, who each vote for one of two contestants $A$ or $B$. The winner is determined by the simple majority rule. We analyse two instances of this game with different motivations of players while keeping the overall structure of the game fixed.

*Classical Players.* Suppose the judges rank the contestants according to a preference ordering. Say judges 1 and 2 prefer $A$ and judge 3 prefers $B$. Table 1 depicts a payoff matrix which encodes this situation, including the rules for choosing a winner (majority) and the goals of each individual player. The two separate tables show the cases when judge 3 has played either $A$ (left table) or $B$ (right table). Within each table, we also have the four possibilities for the voting of judge 2 (columns) and judge 1 (rows). A numeric value such as 1, 1, 0 says that in that particular play judges 1 and 2 got payoff 1, but judge 3 got payoff 0.

How is such a game modelled following Definition 7? The set of strategies in this case is the same as the set of possible outcomes, i.e. $X_i = R = \{A, B\}$. The outcome function $q$: $X_1 \times X_2 \times X_3 \to R$ is the majority function maj: $X \times X \times X \to X$, e.g. $\mathrm{maj}(A, B, B) = B$. It remains for us to find suitable selection functions representing the goals of the three players. Consider two order relations on $X$, call it $B \prec' A$ and $A \prec'' B$. The judges wish to maximise the final outcome

**Table 2.** Voting contest with Keynesian players; Nash equilibria in bold.

|        | $J_2$: A | $J_2$: B |        |        | $J_2$: A | $J_2$: B |        |
|--------|----------|----------|--------|--------|----------|----------|--------|
| $J_1$: A | **1,1,1** | 1,0,1 | $J_3$: A | $J_1$: A | 1,1,0 | **0,1,1** | $J_3$: B |
| $J_1$: B | **1,1,1** | 0,1,0 |        | $J_1$: B | 0,0,1 | **0,1,1** |        |

with respect to their preferred ordering. Hence the three selection functions are

$$\varepsilon_1 = \varepsilon_2 = \prec'\text{-arg max}$$
$$\varepsilon_3 = \prec''\text{-arg max}.$$

Therefore, the game is described by the tuple of higher-order functionals

$$\mathcal{G} = (\prec'\text{-arg max}, \prec'\text{-arg max}, \prec''\text{-arg max}, \text{maj}).$$

*Keynesian Players.* Now, consider the case where the first judge $J_1$ still ranks the candidates according to a preference ordering $B \prec A$. The second and third judges, however, have no preference relations over the candidates per se, but want to vote for the winning candidate. They are *Keynesian*[6] players.

It is possible to model such a game via standard payoff matrices, and Table 2 presents such an encoding. If there is a majority for a candidate and player $J_2$ or $J_3$ votes for the majority candidate they will get a certain payoff, say 1. If they vote for another candidate, their payoff is lower, say 0. Note, however, that in the process of attaching payoffs to strategies, one has to compute the outcome of the votes and then check for the second and the third player whether their vote is in line with the outcome.

Let us now contrast this with the higher-order modelling of games. First note that from the game $\mathcal{G}$ of the previous example, only the "motivation" of players 2 and 3 have changed. Accordingly, we will only need to adjust their selection functions so as to capture their new goal which is to vote for the winner of the contest. Such a goal is exactly captured by equipping $J_2$ and $J_3$ with the *fixpoint selection function* fix: $(X \to X) \to \mathcal{P}(X)$, defined in Sect. 2.2. Note that it is neither necessary to change the structure of the game nor to manually compute anything. The new game with the two Keynesian judges is directly described by the tuple

$$\mathcal{G}_K = (\prec\text{-arg max}, \text{fix}, \text{fix}, \text{maj}).$$

One can say that in the higher-order modelling of games we have equipped the individual players themselves with the problem solving ability that we used to compute the payoff matrices such that they represent the motivations of the Keynesian players.

---

[6] The economist John Maynard Keynes [11] remarked that investors in financial markets can be described as not being interested in the outcome per se but that they want to behave in line with the majority (in order to "buy low and sell high"). This behaviour can be elegantly captured as fixed point goals.

## 3.2  Quantifier Equilibrium

Let us now discuss two different notions of equilibria for higher-order games. Consider a game with $n$ players, and a strategy profile $\mathbf{x} \in \prod_{i=1}^{n} X_i$. Given an outcome function $q\colon \prod_{i=1}^{n} X_i \to R$, the game outcome resulting from this choice of strategy profile is $q(\mathbf{x})$. We can describe the *game context* in which player $i$ unilaterally changes his strategy as

$$\mathcal{U}_i^q(\mathbf{x})(x_i') = q(\mathbf{x}[i \mapsto x_i'])$$

where $\mathbf{x}[i \mapsto x_i']$ is the tuple obtained from $\mathbf{x}$ by replacing the $i^{th}$ entry of the tuple $\mathbf{x}$ with $x_i'$. Note that indeed $\mathcal{U}_i^q(\mathbf{x})$ has type $X_i \to R$, the appropriate type of a game context for player $i$.

We call the $n$ functions $\mathcal{U}_i^q$ ($1 \le i \le n$) the *unilateral maps* of the game. They were introduced in [6] in which it is shown that the proof of Nash's theorem amounts to showing that the unilateral maps have certain topological (continuity and closure) properties. The concept of a context was introduced later in [7], so now we can say that $\mathcal{U}_i^q(\mathbf{x})\colon X_i \to R$ is the game context in which the $i^{th}$ player can unilaterally change his strategy, therefore we call it a unilateral context.

Using this notation we can abstract the classical definition of Nash equilibrium to our framework.

**Definition 8 (Quantifier equilibrium).** *Given a game $\mathcal{G} = (\varepsilon_1, \ldots, \varepsilon_n, q)$, we say that a strategy profile $\mathbf{x} \in \prod_{i=1}^{n} X_i$ is in quantifier equilibrium if*

$$q(\mathbf{x}) \in \overline{\varepsilon_i}(\mathcal{U}_i^q(\mathbf{x}))$$

*for all players $1 \le i \le n$.*

As with the usual notion of Nash equilibrium, we are also saying that a strategy profile is in quantifier equilibrium if no player has a motivation to unilaterally change their strategy. This is expressed formally by saying that preferred outcomes, specified by the selection function when applied to the unilateral context, contain the *outcome* obtained by sticking with the current strategy.

For illustration, we now compute a quantifier equilibrium for the voting contest game with classical players

$$\mathcal{G} = (\prec'\text{-arg}\max, \prec'\text{-arg}\max, \prec''\text{-arg}\max, \mathrm{maj})$$

as described in Sect. 3.1 in the notation of quantifiers and unilateral contexts. We look at two possible strategy profiles: $BBB$ and $BBA$. We claim that $BBB$ is a quantifier equilibrium. Note that $BBB$ has outcome $\mathrm{maj}(BBB) = B$. Let us verify this for player 1. The unilateral context of player 1 is

$$\mathcal{U}_1^{\mathrm{maj}}(BBB)(x) = \mathrm{maj}(xBB) = B,$$

meaning that in the given context the outcome is $B$ no matter what player 1 chooses to play. The maximisation quantifier applied to such a unilateral context gives

$$\overline{\varepsilon_1}(\mathcal{U}_1^{\mathrm{maj}}(BBB)) = \succeq_1\text{-max}(\mathcal{U}_1^{\mathrm{maj}}(BBB)) = \{B\},$$

meaning that, in the given context, player 1's preferred outcome is $B$. Hence, we can conclude by $\mathrm{maj}(BBB) = B \in \{B\} = \overline{\varepsilon_1}(\mathcal{U}_1^{\mathrm{maj}}(BBB))$ that $B$ is a quantifier equilibrium strategy for player 1. This condition holds for each player and allows us to conclude that $BBB$ is a quantifier equilibrium.

On the other hand, we show that $BBA$ is not in quantifier equilibrium. We have that

$$\mathrm{maj}(BBA) = B \notin \{A\} = \overline{\varepsilon_1}(\mathcal{U}_1^{\mathrm{maj}}(BBA)).$$

since $\mathcal{U}_1^{\mathrm{maj}}(BBA)(x) = \mathrm{maj}(xBA) = x$. In other words, the strategy profile $BBA$ gives rise to a game context $\mathcal{U}_1^{\mathrm{maj}}(BBA)$ where player 1 has an incentive to change his strategy to $A$, so that the new outcome $\mathrm{maj}(ABA) = A$ is better than the previous outcome $B$.

This game has three quantifier equilibria: $\{AAA, AAB, BBB\}$. They are exactly the same as the Nash equilibria in the normal form representation (cf. Table 1). We will discuss this coincidence in more detail in Sect. 4.2.

## 3.3   Selection Equilibrium

The definition of quantifier equilibrium is based on quantifiers. However, we can also use selection functions directly to define an equilibrium condition.

**Definition 9 (Selection equilibrium).** *Given a game $\mathcal{G} = (\varepsilon_1, \ldots, \varepsilon_n, q)$, we say that a strategy profile $\mathbf{x} \in \prod_{i=1}^{n} X_i$ is in selection equilibrium if*

$$x_i \in \varepsilon_i(\mathcal{U}_i^q(\mathbf{x}))$$

*for all players $1 \leq i \leq n$, where $x_i$ is the $i^{th}$ component of the tuple $\mathbf{x}$.*

As in the previous subsection, let us illustrate the concept above using the voting contest with classical players from Sect. 3.1. The set of selection equilibria is $\{AAA, AAB, BBB\}$, the same as the set of quantifier equilibria.

Consider $BBB$ and the rationale for player 1. As seen above, his unilateral context is

$$\mathcal{U}_1^{\mathrm{maj}}(BBB)(x) = \mathrm{maj}(xBB) = B.$$

Hence, given this game context his selection function calculates

$$\varepsilon_1(\mathcal{U}_1^{\mathrm{maj}}(BBB)) = \{B\}$$

As before, given that he is not pivotal, an improvement by switching votes is not possible. The same condition holds analogously for the other players.

Let us now investigate the strategy profile $BBA$. The unilateral context is

$$\mathcal{U}_1^{\mathrm{maj}}(BBA)(x) = \mathrm{maj}(xBA) = x.$$

Given this context, the selection function tells us that player 1 would switch to $A$:

$$\varepsilon_1(\mathcal{U}_1^{\mathrm{maj}}(BBA)) = \{A\}.$$

Hence, $BBA$ is not a selection equilibrium.

# 4    Relationship Between Equilibrium Concepts

In this section we show that selection equilibrium is a strict refinement of quantifier equilibrium. Moreover, we show that for a special class of selection functions, which we call *closed selection functions*, the two notions coincide. The obvious question then arises: which concept is more reasonable when games involve non-closed selection functions? We will argue by example that in such cases selection equilibrium is the adequate concept.

## 4.1    Closed Selection Functions

Selection functions such as *i-arg max(p)*, which one obtains from utility functions as discussed in Sect. 2.2, are examples of what we call *closed selection functions*.

**Definition 10 (Closedness).** *A selection function* $\varepsilon\colon (X \to R) \to \mathcal{P}(X)$ *is said to be* closed *if whenever* $x \in \varepsilon(p)$ *and* $p(x) = p(x')$ *then* $x' \in \varepsilon(p)$.

Intuitively, a closed selection function is one which chooses optimal moves only based on the outcomes they generate. Two moves that lead to the same outcome are therefore indistinguishable, they are either both good or bad. It is easy to see that the selection function arg max is closed. Agents modelled via closed selection functions do not put any preferences on moves that lead to identical outcomes.

An example of a non-closed selection function is the fixpoint operator

$$\text{fix}\colon (X \to X) \to \mathcal{P}(X).$$

defined in Sect. 2.2. To see that fix is non-closed, we might have two points $x \neq x'$ which both map to $x$ (i.e. $p(x) = p(x') = x$) so that $x$ is a fixed point but $x'$ is not.

One can consider translating quantifiers into selection functions and back into quantifiers, or conversely.

**Proposition 1.** *For all* $p\colon X \to R$ *we have*

*(i)* $\overline{\overline{\varphi}}(p) = \varphi(p)$ *if* $\varphi$ *is an attainable quantifier of type* $(X \to R) \to \mathcal{P}(R)$
*(ii)* $\varepsilon(p) \subseteq \overline{\overline{\varepsilon}}(p)$ *for any selection functions of type* $(X \to R) \to \mathcal{P}(X)$.

*Proof.* These are easy to derive. Let us briefly outline $\varepsilon(p) \subseteq \overline{\overline{\varepsilon}}(p)$. Suppose $x \in \varepsilon(p)$ is a good move in the game context $p\colon X \to R$. By Definition 5 we have that $p(x) \in \overline{\varepsilon}(p)$. Finally, by Definition 6 we have that $x \in \overline{\overline{\varepsilon}}(p)$.    □

The proposition above shows that on attainable quantifiers the double-overline operation calculates the same quantifier we started with. On general selection functions, however, the mapping $\varepsilon \mapsto \overline{\overline{\varepsilon}}$ can be viewed as a *closure* operator.[7] Intuitively, the new selection function $\overline{\overline{\varepsilon}}$ will have the same good *outcomes* as the original one, but it might consider many more *moves* to be good as well, as it does not distinguish moves which both lead to equally good outcomes.

---

[7] Note that we might have a strict inclusion $\varepsilon(p) \subset \overline{\overline{\varepsilon}}(p)$ in case we have $x_1 \neq x_2$, with $x_1 \in \varepsilon(p)$ and $x_2 \notin \varepsilon(p)$ but $p(x_1) = p(x_2)$.

**Proposition 2.** *A selection function $\varepsilon$ is* closed *if and only if $\varepsilon = \bar{\bar{\varepsilon}}$.*

*Proof.* Assume first that $\varepsilon$ is closed, i.e.

(i) $x \in \varepsilon(p)$ and $p(x) = p(x')$ then $x' \in \varepsilon(p)$.

By Proposition 1 is it enough to show that if $x' \in \bar{\bar{\varepsilon}}(p)$ then $x' \in \varepsilon(p)$. Assuming $x' \in \bar{\bar{\varepsilon}}(p)$, and by Definition 6 we have

(ii) $p(x') \in \bar{\varepsilon}(p)$.

By Definition 5, (ii) says that $p(x') = p(x)$ for some $x \in \varepsilon(p)$. By (i) it follows that $x \in \varepsilon(p)$.
Conversely, assume that $\varepsilon = \bar{\bar{\varepsilon}}$ and that $x \in \varepsilon(p)$ and $p(x) = p(x')$. We wish to show that $x' \in \varepsilon(p)$. Since $x \in \varepsilon(p)$ then $p(x) \in \bar{\varepsilon}(p)$. But since $p(x) = p(x')$ we have that $p(x') \in \bar{\varepsilon}(p)$. Hence, $x' \in \bar{\bar{\varepsilon}}(p)$. But since $\varepsilon = \bar{\bar{\varepsilon}}$ it follows that $x' \in \varepsilon(p)$.     $\square$

## 4.2   Selection Refines Quantifier Equilibrium

The following theorem shows that selection equilibrium is a refinement of quantifier equilibrium.

**Theorem 1.** *Every selection equilibrium is a quantifier equilibrium.*

*Proof.* Recall that by definition, for every context $p$ we have $x \in \varepsilon_i(p) \implies p(x) \in \bar{\varepsilon_i}(p)$, since $\bar{\varepsilon_i}(p) = \{p(x) \mid x \in \varepsilon_i(p)\}$. Assuming that $\mathbf{x}$ is a selection equilibrium we have $x_i \in \varepsilon_i(\mathcal{U}_i^q(\mathbf{x}))$ Therefore $\mathcal{U}_i^q(\mathbf{x})(x_i) \in \bar{\varepsilon_i}(\mathcal{U}_i^q(\mathbf{x}))$. It remains to note that $\mathcal{U}_i^q(\mathbf{x})(x_i) = q(\mathbf{x})$, because $\mathbf{x}[i \mapsto x_i] = \mathbf{x}$.     $\square$

However, for closed selection functions the two notions coincide:

**Theorem 2.** *If $\varepsilon_i = \bar{\bar{\varepsilon_i}}$, for $1 \leq i \leq n$, then the two equilibrium concepts coincide.*

*Proof.* Given the previous theorem, it remains to show that under the assumption $\varepsilon_i = \bar{\bar{\varepsilon_i}}$ any strategy profile $\mathbf{x}$ in quantifier equilibrium is also in selection equilibrium. Fix $i$ and suppose $\mathbf{x}$ is such that $q(\mathbf{x}) \in \bar{\varepsilon_i}(\mathcal{U}_i^q(\mathbf{x}))$. Since $\mathcal{U}_i^q(\mathbf{x})(x_i) = q(\mathbf{x})$, we have $\mathcal{U}_i^q(\mathbf{x})(x_i) \in \bar{\varepsilon_i}(\mathcal{U}_i^q(\mathbf{x}))$. By the definition of $\bar{\bar{\varepsilon_i}}$ it follows that $x_i \in \bar{\bar{\varepsilon_i}}(\mathcal{U}_i^q(\mathbf{x}))$. Therefore, since $\varepsilon_i = \bar{\bar{\varepsilon_i}}$, we obtain $x_i \in \varepsilon_i(\mathcal{U}_i^q(\mathbf{x}))$.$\square$

The theorem above explains why in the voting contest with classical preferences the strategy profiles that were quantifier equilibrium were the same as those in selection equilibrium. This example can be modelled with closed selection functions. Moreover, since $\arg\max$ can be easily shown to be closed, in the classical modelling of games via maximising players, our two notions of equilibrium also coincide. The following theorem shows that they both indeed also coincide with the standard notion of Nash equilibrium.

**Theorem 3.** *In a classical game (see Remark 1) the standard definition of Nash equilibrium and the equilibrium notions of Definitions 8 and 9 are equivalent.*

*Proof.* Suppose the set of outcomes $R$ is $\mathbb{R}^n$ and that the selection functions $\varepsilon_i$ are $i$-arg max, i.e. maximising with respect to $i^{th}$ coordinate. Unfolding Definition 9 and that of a unilateral context $\mathcal{U}_i^q(\mathbf{x})$, we see that a tuple $\mathbf{x}$ is an equilibrium strategy profile if for all $1 \leq i \leq n$

$$x_i \in i\text{-arg}\max_{x \in X_i} q(\mathbf{x}[i \mapsto x]).$$

But $x_i$ is a point on which the function $p(x) = q(\mathbf{x}[i \mapsto x])$ attains its maximum precisely when $p(x_i) \in \max_{x \in X_i} p(x)$. Hence

$$q(\mathbf{x}) = q(\mathbf{x}[i \mapsto x_i]) = p(x_i) = \max_{x \in X_i} p(x) = \max_{x \in X_i} q(\mathbf{x}[i \mapsto x])$$

which is the standard definition of a Nash equilibrium: for each player $i$, the outcome obtained by not changing the strategy, i.e. $q(\mathbf{x})$, is the best possible amongst the outcomes when any other available strategy is considered, i.e. $\max_{x \in X_i} q(\mathbf{x}[i \mapsto x])$. □

Theorem 3 above shows that in the case of classical games the usual concept of a Nash equilibrium coincides with both the quantifier equilibrium and the selection equilibrium. On the other hand, for general games, Theorem 1 proves that every selection equilibrium is a quantifier equilibrium.

$$\text{selection equilibria} \subsetneq \text{quantifier equilibria}$$

In the following section we give examples showing that the inclusion above is strict, i.e. that there are games where selection equilibrium is a strict refinement of quantifier equilibrium. By Theorem 2 these examples necessarily make use of players modelled by non-closed selection functions.

### 4.3    Illustrating the Two Solution Concepts

In Sect. 3.1 we have discussed the representation of the *voting contest with Keynesian players* game both in normal form as well as in higher-order functions. Here, we will turn to analysing the equilibria of its higher-order representation

$$\mathcal{G}_K = (\prec\text{-arg}\max, \text{fix}, \text{fix}, \text{maj}).$$

We begin with quantifier equilibria (see Table 3). These include the strategy profiles where judges (players) $J_2$ and $J_3$ are both coordinated but also profiles where either $J_2$ or $J_3$ is in the minority. Readers are encouraged to download the Haskell implementation, and interactively verify entries of this table.

We illustrate the rationale for the strategy profile $AAB$ of the Keynesian player 3. The outcome of $AAB$ is $\text{maj}(AAB) = A$. The unilateral context of player 3 is

$$\mathcal{U}_3^{\text{maj}}(AAB)(x) = \text{maj}(AAx) = A$$

**Table 3.** Players: max, fix, fix

| Strategy | Outcome | Quantifier eq. | Defects | Selection eq. | Defects |
|----------|---------|----------------|---------|---------------|---------|
| $AAA$ | $A$ | ✓ | | ✓ | |
| $AAB$ | $A$ | ✓ | | - | $J_3$ |
| $ABA$ | $A$ | ✓ | | - | $J_2$ |
| $ABB$ | $B$ | ✓ | | ✓ | |
| $BAA$ | $A$ | ✓ | | ✓ | |
| $BAB$ | $B$ | - | $J_1$ | - | $J_1, J_2$ |
| $BBA$ | $B$ | - | $J_1$ | - | $J_1, J_3$ |
| $BBB$ | $B$ | ✓ | | ✓ | |

meaning that the outcome is (still) $A$ if player 3 unilaterally changes from $B$ to $A$. The fixed point quantifier applied to this context gives

$$\overline{\varepsilon_3}(\mathcal{U}_3^{\text{maj}}(AAB)) = \text{fix}(\mathcal{U}_3^{\text{maj}}(AAB)) = \{A\}$$

meaning that $A$ is the outcome resulting from an optimal choice. Hence, we can conclude by

$$\text{maj}(AAB) = A \in \{A\} = \overline{\varepsilon_3}(\mathcal{U}_3^{\text{maj}}(AAB))$$

that player 3 is happy with his choice of move $B$ according to the quantifier equilibrium notion. This already demonstrates the problem with the *quantifier equilibrium* notion, since the Keynesian player 3 has voted for $B$ but $A$ is the winner, so he should not be happy at all!

Now, let us turn to the selection equilibria. Table 3 also contains the selection equilibria and it shows that they are a strict subset of the quantifier equilibria. Consider again the strategy profile $AAB$, focusing on the third player. In the case of the selection equilibrium we have

$$B \notin \{A\} = \text{fix}(\mathcal{U}_3^{\text{maj}}(AAB)) = \varepsilon_3(\mathcal{U}_3^{\text{maj}}(AAB))$$

meaning that player 3 is not happy with his current choice of strategy $B$ with respect to the strategy profile $AAB$.

*Remark 3.* Given Theorem 2 it follows immediately that fix: $(X \to X) \to \mathcal{P}(X)$ is not a closed selection function. Indeed, it is easy to calculate that

$$\overline{\overline{\text{fix}}}(p) = \{x \mid p(x) = p(y), \text{ for some } y \text{ such that } y = p(y)\},$$

i.e. $\overline{\overline{\text{fix}}}(p)$ is the inverse image of $\text{fix}(p)$, so it contains not only all fixed points of $p$ but also points that map through $p$ to a fixed point.

The selection equilibria are precisely those in which $J_2$ and $J_3$ are coordinated, and $J_1$ is not pivotal in any of these. For illustration, consider the strategy

$AAA$, which is a selection equilibrium of this game. Suppose the moves of $J_1$ and $J_2$ are fixed, but $J_3$ may unilaterally change strategy. The unilateral context is

$$\mathcal{U}_3^{\mathrm{maj}}(AAA)(x) = \mathrm{maj}(AAx) = A$$

Thus the unilateral context is a constant function, and its set of fixpoints is

$$\mathrm{fix}(\mathcal{U}_3^{\mathrm{maj}}(AAA)) = \{A\}.$$

This tells us that $J_3$ has no incentive to unilaterally change to the strategy $B$, because he will no longer be voting for the winner.

On the other hand, for the strategy $ABB$ the two Keynesian players are indifferent, because if either of them unilaterally changes to $A$ then $A$ will become the majority and they will still be voting for the winner. This is still a selection equilibrium (as we would expect) because the unilateral context is the identity function, and in particular $B$ is a fixpoint.

As a last point, let us compare the selection and quantifier equilibria of Table 3 with the Nash equilibria in the normal form game. The payoff matrix in Table 2 also depicts Nash equilibria payoffs as marked in bold. Note that the latter are the same as the selection equilibria. Thus, in general selection equilibrium appears to be the adequate solution concept.

*Coordination.* As a last point, consider a game where all players want to vote for the winner of the contest. Table 4 represents the payoffs of this game; Nash equilibria are in bold. Clearly the only two equilibria are when all judges vote unanimously for a given contestant. Judges $J_1, J_2$ and $J_3$ want to vote for the winner, so the selection functions are all given by the fixpoint operator.

**Table 4.** Nash equilibria of coordination game

| | $J_2$: A | $J_2$: B | | | $J_2$: A | $J_2$: B | |
|---|---|---|---|---|---|---|---|
| $J_1$: A | **1,1,1** | 1,0,1 | $J_3$: A | $J_1$: A | 1,1,0 | 0,1,1 | $J_3$: B |
| $J_1$: B | 0,1,1 | 1,1,0 | | $J_1$: B | 1,0,1 | **1,1,1** | |

The selection equilibria of the higher-order representation of this game are exactly the coordinated strategies. This game is a good example of why quantifier equilibria are not suitable for modelling games with non-closed selection functions: every strategy is a quantifier equilibrium of this game, but the selection equilibrium captures the intuition perfectly that the equilibria should be the strategy profiles that are maximally coordinated, namely $AAA$ and $BBB$.

## 5  Conclusion

In this paper, we introduced a representation of strategic games based on *quantifiers* and *selection functions* as well as a new equilibrium concept, and showed by example that the selection equilibrium is the appropriate concept as it works well even when players are described by non-closed selection functions. We focused on simultaneous move games. Yet, the theory as well as the implementation naturally extend to sequential games. Moreover, multi-valued selection functions as formulated here have sparked new research avenues, for instance on so called "open games" [5,8,10], a compositional approach to game theory.

# References

1. Botta, N., Ionescu, C., Brady, E.: Sequential decision problems, dependently typed solutions. In: Proceedings of PLMMS 2013 (2013)
2. Escardó, M., Oliva, P.: Selection functions, bar recursion and backward induction. Math. Struct. Comput. Sci. **20**(2), 127–168 (2010)
3. Escardó, M., Oliva, P.: What sequential games, the Tychonoff theorem and the double-negation shift have in common. In: Proceedings of the Third ACM SIG-PLAN Workshop on Mathematically Structured Functional Programming (MSFP 2010), pp. 21–32 (2010)
4. Escardó, M., Oliva, P.: Sequential games and optimal strategies. Proc. R. Soc. Lond. A Math. Phys. Eng. Sci. **467**(2130), 1519–1545 (2011)
5. Ghani, N., Hedges, J.: A compositional approach to economic game theory. arXiv:1603.04641 (2016)
6. Hedges, J.: A generalization of Nash's theorem with higher-order functionals. Proc. R. Soc. Lond. A Math. Phys. Eng. Sci. **469**(2154) (2013). http://rspa.royalsocietypublishing.org/content/469/2154/20130041
7. Hedges, J.: Monad transformers for backtracking search. In: Proceedings of the 5th Workshop on Mathematically Structured Functional Programming, pp. 31–50. Open Publishing Association (2014)
8. Hedges, J.: Towards compositional game theory. Ph.D. thesis, Queen Mary University of London (2016)
9. Hedges, J., Oliva, P., Sprits, E., Winschel, V., Zahn, P.: Higher-order decision theory. arXiv preprint cs.GT, arXiv:1506.01003 (2015)
10. Hedges, J., Sprits, E., Winschel, V., Zahn, P.: Compositionality and string diagrams for game theory. arXiv:1604.06061 (2015)
11. Keynes, J.M.: General Theory of Employment, Interest and Money. Macmillan, London (1936)
12. Mostowski, A.: On a generalization of quantifiers. Fundamenta Mathematicae **44**, 12–36 (1957)
13. Osborne, M., Rubinstein, A.: Course in Game Theory. MIT Press, Cambridge (1994)

# DALI for Cognitive Robotics: Principles and Prototype Implementation

Stefania Costantini[✉], Giovanni De Gasperis, and Giulio Nazzicone

DISIM, Università di L'Aquila, L'Aquila, Italy
stefania.costantini@univaq.it

**Abstract.** DALI is a logic Prolog-based Multi Agent System Language and Framework (publicly available on GitHub) developed at University of L'Aquila since 1999, and includes features aimed at user monitoring and training in Ambient Intelligent applications. In this paper, we show how such features can be integrated and extended in view of cognitive robotic applications; we then illustrate the extensions to the DALI implementation that allow DALI agents to interact with robotic platforms even through the cloud.

## 1 Introduction

Quoting from http://www.ieee-ras.org/cognitive-robotics, "There is growing need for robots that can interact safely with people in everyday situations. These robots have to be able to anticipate the effects of their own actions as well as the actions and needs of the people around them. To achieve this, two streams of research need to merge, one concerned with physical systems specifically designed to interact with unconstrained environments and another focusing on control architectures that explicitly take into account the need to acquire and use experience."

Several papers on cognitive robotics can be found in the proceedings of main Conferences on Artificial Intelligence (e.g., ECAI, IJCAI) and on Agents (e.g., AAMAS). The importance of developing "intelligent" adaptive robots can be particularly appreciated in view of the societal issue of helping the elderly and the disabled; in fact life expectancy is increased, and consequently the number of persons needing personalized assistance is increasing as well. ICT (Information and Communication Technologies) can potentially (and partly already are) of great help. According to the guidelines provided by the European Union (http://ec.europa.eu/health/ehealth/policy/index_en.htm), the eHealth scenario "refers to tools and services using information and communication technologies (ICTs)" that can improve prevention, diagnosis, treatment, monitoring and management but, also, "Bringing ICT and healthcare together is not simply a matter of digitizing and communicating matters of health, but rather opening a new world of doing things in ways that were not possible or even conceivable before...". Cognitive robotic systems can potentially also help in any situation where there is an impaired or disabled person, or more generally any person in need of special

Y. Lierler and W. Taha (Eds.): PADL 2017, LNCS 10137, pp. 152–162, 2017.
DOI: 10.1007/978-3-319-51676-9_10

**Envisaged Smart Healthcare Architecture**

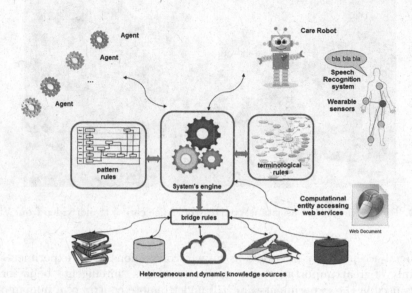

**Fig. 1.** Envisaged Smart Healtcare Architecture

assistance. This may include children, not as a substitute but as a support to parents, family and caregivers.

In [1] we have outlined a comprehensive system (depicted in Fig. 1 and called Friendly&Kind, for short F&K) based upon logical agents for monitoring patients, where a patient's personal agent can be embodied in a robot. Some of the monitoring can be performed locally, where however agents are able, upon need, to interact with human specialists, knowledge bases, and with the health system. This while performing routine care chores and, possibly, entertaining the patient. This should alleviate the healthcare and social security systems from the burden of having to provide full-time highly specialized human assistants while allowing elderly people to leave at home rather than be moved to an institution. The level of synergic knowledge retrieval and integration that such a system can provide goes beyond the capabilities of a human nurse or personal assistant.

It has been demonstrated that, understandably, humans prefer friendly interfaces and robots that show some kind of intelligent and also affective and "emotional" behavior. There is interesting ongoing work, e.g., by the group of Prof. Johan Hoorn at Vrije Universiteit Amsterdam about social robotics, which considers the impact of robots on the user from the point of view of ethics [2], interaction with the disabled [3] and even acceptable robot appearance. Some of this work is reported in a famous documentary "Alice cares" (https://vimeo.com/116760085, a scene from this documentary is reported in Fig. 2), which shows the positive interaction among three old women and a friendly humanoid care robot. From a cognitive point of view and for exploring

**Fig. 2.** Text reading robot assistant, courtesy of "Alice cares" trailer video from Vimeo

the social acceptability of robots as human companions these experiments are certainly of great importance. However, as concerns "intelligent" behavior the robots used in the experiments are still under remote control of a human operator.

In the perspective of making such robots really intelligent and autonomous, research results from many fields of Artificial Intelligence, Automated Reasoning and Intelligent Software Agents can be usefully exploited. We strongly believe that in this and in other fields it can be advantageous to define a robot's cognitive part as an agent or Multi-Agent System (MAS) defined via declarative agent-oriented languages. In fact, the behavior of a robot which is aimed at assisting a human user should be based on user observation, monitoring and training. I.e., the robot should be equipped with a basic user profile defining the user's needs, habits, and preferences; such profile should be then refined via the robot's own observation of the user's behavior over time; the robot should then be able to supervise and check the user's activities, and to teach (or remind) a user of how to perform tasks. In all this, the robot should be able to recognize relevant complex events from sets of simple ones, and to check and to adapt its own behavior upon changing circumstances.

There are many logic agent-oriented languages and architectures in computational logic apt to these aims, among which MetateM, 3APL, GOAL, AgentSpeak, Impact, KGP and DALI (the reader may refer to the surveys [4–6] and to the references therein), that might be usefully exploited in robotics, as in fact many of them already have, or at least many of the examples provided in the literature concern potential robotic applications.

The DALI language [11,12] has been empowered and experimented over the years concerning capabilities for the definition and management of an agent's memory and experience and for user monitoring and training also by learning new behavioral patterns (via deep learning or via knowledge exchange); DALI agents are able to perform complex event processing, and to dynamically check and modify their own behavior also in terms of a special interval temporal logic (cf. [7–10] and the references therein). However all these features, though experimented in software agents, have never been applied since recently to robotic applications because DALI lacked a suitable plug-in, that we have now developed.

Such extension to the basic DALI implementation allows action commands to be exchanged between DALI agents and any robotic platform by using the YARP middleware. In addition, we have implemented ServerDALI which allows to locate DALI agents and MAS on a server. This is relevant, as for instance in the architecture of Fig. 1 the caregiver agents will presumably be copies of the same one, to which robots' cognitive functioning can refer; so, a cloud solution eliminates the need of equipping the (possibly diverse) robot hardware with sophisticated software; moreover, computationally heavy automated reasoning tasks can be more efficiently executed on the server.

The novel contribution of this paper is twofold: on the one hand, we have re-elaborated and extended past work on DALI in the perspective of robotic applications for the care of persons in need; on the other hand, we have realized and experimented a practical efficient implementation constructed out of open-source components. At the present stage, we have been experimenting the use of a declarative language for defining the cognitive part of robots, and for our experiments we have adopted simulators rather than real robot hardware. So, in this context we are not concerned with physical aspects concerning sensors, actuators, vision, etc., that are however widely studied by specialists.

In Sect. 2 we recall the basic DALI language, while in Sect. 3 we discuss, also by means of small though significant examples the potential applicability of DALI in robotic user monitoring and training. In Sect. 4 we illustrate the extension to robotics of the DALI implementation. Finally, in Sect. 5 we conclude.

## 2   The Basic DALI Language and Architecture

DALI [11,12] (cf. [13] for a comprehensive list of references) is an Agent-Oriented Logic Programming language. The DALI Prolog-based Multi Agent System Language and Framework has been developed at University of L'Aquila since 1999.

DALI agents are able to deal with several kinds of events: external events, internal, present and past events.

**External events** are syntactically indicated by the postfix $E$. Reaction to each such event is defined by a reactive rule, of the form $EvE :> Reaction$ where $:>$ is a special token. The agent remembers to have reacted by converting an external event into a *past event* (postfix $P$). An event perceived but not yet reacted to is called "present event" and is indicated by postfix $N$.

In DALI, **actions** (indicated with postfix $A$) may have or not preconditions: in the former case, the actions are defined by actions rules, in the latter case they are just action atoms. An action rule is characterized by the new token $:<$. Similarly to events, actions are recorded as past actions.

**Internal events** is the feature that makes DALI agent agents proactive. An internal event is syntactically indicated by the postfix $I$, and its description is composed of two rules. The first one contains the conditions (knowledge, past events, procedures, etc.) that must be true so that the reaction (in the second rule) may happen. Thus, a DALI agent is able to react to its own conclusions. Internal events are automatically attempted with a default frequency customizable by means of directives in the initialization file.

The DALI communication architecture implements the DALI/FIPA protocol, which consists of the main FIPA primitives, plus few new primitives which are particular to DALI and provides the possibility of defining meta-rules for filtering incoming and out-coming messages, and for accessing and querying external ontologies in the semantics web.

DALI provides a plugin to an answer set solver, so complex reasoning tasks such as, e.g., planning and preference handling can be performed in Answer Set Programming (ASP), which is a state-of-the art technology for dealing with hard computational problems (cf., among many, [14] and the references therein); several efficient ASP solvers are in fact freely available and are periodically checked and compared over well-established benchmarks, and over challenging sample applications proposed at the yearly ASP competition (cf. the ASPCOMP web sites).

## 3    DALI Advanced Features and Possible Applications to Robotics

The robotic applications that we particularly envisage concern (since [15]) user monitoring and training in any context, but especially for the care of elderly and disabled persons. In our setting, agents interact with users (i) with the objective of training a user in some particular task, and (ii) with the aim of monitoring the user for ensuring some degree of consistence and coherence in user behavior.

Agents are able to be aware, by prior knowledge or via some form of learning, of the behavioral patterns that the user is adopting, and to learn rules and plans also from other agents (by imitation or by being told). Assume as a simple example that an agent has been somehow able to learn that the user normally takes a drink when coming back home. This can be represented by a rule such as:

$$drink :\text{-} arrive\_home.$$

This learned rule can possibly be associated with a certainty factor. When the rule becomes later confronted with subsequent experience, its certainty factor will be updated accordingly. Whenever this factor exceeds a threshold, this may lead to assert new meta-rules, such as:

$$USUALLY\ drink\ WHEN\ arrive\_home.$$

User monitoring can be performed via temporal-logic-like rules like the following one:

$$NEVER\ drink\_alchool\ AND\ take\_medicine.$$

Such a rule acts as a constraint which has priority over former ones; so, the agent will actively discourage the user to drink while taking medicines. In [16] the semantics of such expressions is defined, also in relation to the possibility of defining the *interval* where some events/actions must or must not occur.

The following example concerns a robot aiding to supervise a baby, thus relieving caregivers from some of their tasks. If the baby is hungry, the robot should feed the baby with available baby food (feeding is an action, indicated with postfix $A$) paying attention to choose the healthier among those that the baby likes. Conjunction *food*$(F)$, *available*$(F)$ provides a number of values for $F$, among which one is chosen. In particular, the choice will correspond to a maximum in the partial order imposed by the binary predicates *best_preferred* and *healthier* in the given order. This construct for complex preference, the p-set, was originally introduced in [17].

*baby_is_hungryE* :>
   {*feed_babyA*$(F)$ : *food*$(F)$, *available_babyf*$(F)$ :  *best_preferred, healthier*}.

In the example below, the robot again assists parents taking care of a child. The child has to go to school (mandatory goal, indicated by postfix $G$) and is about to skip breakfast because she prefers cereals that unfortunately are finished. The agent, based upon the monitoring condition (never skip breakfast) will be able to suggest alternative food, in particular the best preferred among available options.

*go to schoolG* : *NEVER skip_breakfast*$(D)$ :: *cereals_finished* :::
   *suggestA*(*alternative_food*) *IN* {*cookies, cake_slice* : *best_preferred*}.

The monitoring component can however also include meta-axioms such as for instance the following one, which states that a user action which is necessary to reach a mandatory objective should necessarily be undertaken. The agent can fulfill this statement either by convincing the user to do so, or to resort to human caregivers' help:

*ALWAYS do*(*user, A*) *WHEN mandatory_goal*($G$), *required*($G, A$)

Such a meta-rule could be applied to practical cases such as the following:

*mandatory_goal*(*healthy*).
*required*(*healthy, take_medicineA*).

ASP modules can be exploited in order to plan actions which might be performed in given situations, and to extract *necessary* actions, which are those actions included in all possible plans. Given ASP module $M$ (defined in a separate text file), in the example below reaction to event *evE* can be either any action which can be inferred (from $M$) as a possible reaction, or a *necessary* action, again according to $M$. Events are indicated with postfix $E$, reaction is indicated with :>. Connective > expresses preference: the former option is preferred over the latter if the condition after the :- holds; *necessary* and *action* are distinguished predicates applicable over ASP modules' results. So, in this sample rule necessary actions are preferred in a critical situation. Otherwise, any of the two options may be taken.

$$evE :> necessary(M,N)|action(M,A) \ : \ M > A :- critical\_situation.$$

The above examples are witnesses of a re-elaboration of past work on DALI in the perspective of cognitive robotics applications. Though small, the examples should have practically demonstrated that DALI has indeed the potential for acting as an agent language in this realm. However, a suitable interface between DALI agents and robotic hardware or simulators was lacking. Such an interface has been recently implemented, and is presented in the next section.

## 4   The Extended DALI Implementation

The DALI programming environment at the current stage of development [18] offers a multi-platform folder environment including Sicstus Prolog programs (as DALI is implemented in Sicstus), shells scripts, and Python scripts.

For the development of DALI agents and MAS, a programmer can simply use any text editor to write DALI agents' programs and the necessary start/configuration scripts; more proficiently, she could use a web-based system-independent integrated development environment where agents editing is managed through an HTML5/AJAX-based online editor, with start/stop command buttons and agents logs output for runtime verification, handling signals and events from the DALI engine running in the background. The system is designed so as to be able to interact with other services by means of JSON data events. Such an external service can be a virtual robotics simulator. Thus, an entire complex anthropomorphic cognitive robot like the iCub [19] could be controlled by a DALI MAS.

The software components diagram in Fig. 3 shows how DALI has been encapsulated and integrated with other modules through a Python "glue code" layer, called PyDALI. Each DALI agent is an instance of the Prolog program "DALI Interpreter". The multi-platform open source library *pexpect* (http://github.com/pexpect/pexpect) has been adopted for building a Python middle layer to automate the interaction with the Sicstus Prolog environment, seen as an instance of the class PySicstus. In this way, by abstracting via the PyDALI class, a DALI agent instance process can be configured, loaded, started, executed and terminated. A MAS can then be handled via the most abstract class "MAS".

The Python code can then been imported in any Python program by using the open source Twisted (http://github.com/twisted/twisted) programming library. This allows the interaction of DALI agents with other software modules/server/clients by means of asynchronous JSON events. In particular, what we call the *Multi-standard DALI Bus* is in practice a middle layer communication protocol that converts any JSON event coming from the outside

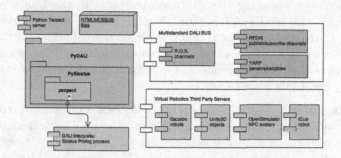

Fig. 3. Software components diagram of the extended DALI architecture

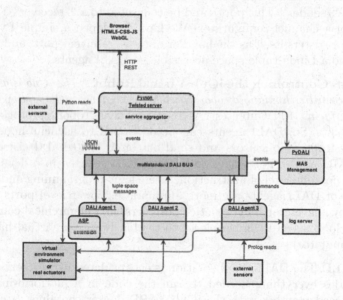

Fig. 4. Runtime deployment diagram of the extended DALI architecture

world to an internal FIPA event in a Linda tuple space[1], that the DALI MAS thus receives as an external event. Specific actions performed within the DALI MAS can generate FIPA events that are converted to JSON event so as to send commands to external actuators, that can be either real robotic actuators or virtual robotic components in a virtual robotics simulator. A typical runtime deployment diagram can be seen in Fig. 4.

---

[1] *Linda* is a model of coordination and communication among parallel processes providing a logically global *associative memory*, called a "tuplespace", in which processes store and retrieve tuples. It is available for Sicstus Prolog and it is therefore used as a communication middleware in the DALI implementation.

The central Multi-standard DALI bus collects asynchronous data events from different sources, translating them into counterparts in the Linda tuple space whenever an agent is the destination. It also collects action messages from agents and translates them into JSON structures compatible with the destination, through the Python service aggregator/container. There may also be external sensors that directly generate Linda tuple messages, or external sensors mediated by the Python container.

**YARP Integration.** YARP, "Yet An other Robotic Platform" (http://github. com/robotology/yarp) *"supports building a robot control system as a collection of programs communicating in a peer-to-peer way, with an extensible family of connection types (tcp, udp, multicast, local, MPI, mjpg-over-http, XML/RPC, tcpros,...) that can be swapped in and out to match your needs."*. A C++ program, typically embedded in a robot, generates raw data and sends them to the YARP port "/sender". This port could be connected to a "/receiver" YARP port by means of a channel configurator. We have developed a simple Python program which registers itself as the handler of the "/receiver" port, and translates the data into a Linda tuple space accessible by DALI agents.

**DALI MAS Controlling the iCub Virtual Robot**. *"The iCub is a 53 degree-of-freedom cognitive humanoid robot which has been developed as an open-systems research platform"* [19]. iCub uses YARP extensively as robotic protocol for internal data events. So, DALI agents can be developed to asynchronously receive data events from iCub sensors and send outcomes of logical decisions/actions through YARP ports. Ports have to be accurately selected in order to work at the highest possible level of abstraction, where logic programming and reasoning capabilities of DALI agents are more appropriate. Lower level ports should be controlled by conventional cybernetic controllers, in a hierarchical control structure where loop speed is higher closer to the hardware (or virtual hardware in case of a simulator).

**ServerDALI.** The DALI cloud solution is encapsulated in "docker" container, that[2] includes everything needed to run the code in a platform-independent way. Composed together with the iCub YARP docker container, a cloud computing based MAS could control the cognitive aspect of an embodied robot. The ServerDALI application allows a DALI MAS to be made available to users also via web or mobile applications. ServerDALI and a sample web interface have been programmed using PHP, CSS3, Javascript and HTML5. The entire MAS is made available analogously to a single object, so its external users are not required to possess any notion about Agents or Artificial Intelligence. This is accomplished via a special agent (called Ermes) which is added to any MAS and acts as an interface between the MAS and the external web based environment; in particular, via the ServerProlog library PHP and JSON objects can be translated into messages that Ermes can then dispatch, and vice versa. This solution can be generalized to other agent-oriented frameworks and to different external languages.

---

[2] *Docker* is an open-source multi-platform tool to automate the deployment of Linux lightweight containers, see http://www.docker.com/technologies/overview.

# 5 Conclusions

In this paper we have showed the potential usefulness of the DALI logical agent-oriented programming language in the cognitive robotic domain; we particularly envisage applications for user monitoring and training concerning elderly or disabled persons, or children (in cooperation with parents or caregivers). We have then illustrated in some detail the extensions to the previously-existing DALI implementation which allow DALI agents to be actually exploited in the robotic realm. Therefore, DALI agents can now be developed to act as high level cognitive robotic controllers, and can be automatically integrated with conventional embedded controllers. The cloud package ServerDALI allows a DALI MAS to be integrated in any practical environment. Realistic experiments are planned in the near future in the context of the F&K project.

# References

1. Aielli, F., Ancona, D., Caianiello, P., Costantini, S., De Gasperis, G., Di Marco, A., Ferrando, A., Mascardi, V.: Friendly&Kind with your health: human-friendly knowledge-intensive dynamic systems for the e-health domain. In: Bajo, J., et al. (eds.) PAAMS 2016. CCIS, vol. 616, pp. 15–26. Springer, Heidelberg (2016)
2. van Kemenade, M., Konijn, E.A., Hoorn, J.F.: Robots humanize care - moral concerns versus witnessed benefits for the elderly. In: Verdier, C., Bienkiewicz, M., Fred, A.L.N., Gamboa, H., Elias, D. (eds.) Proceedings of HEALTHINF 2015, pp. 648–653. SciTePress (2015)
3. Paauwe, R.A., Keyson, D.V., Hoorn, J.F., Konijn, E.A.: Minimal requirements of realism in social robots: designing for patients with acquired brain injury. In: Proceedings of the 33rd Annual ACM Conference on Human Factors in Computing Systems, pp. 2139–2144. ACM (2015)
4. Fisher, M., Bordini, R.H., Hirsch, B., Torroni, P.: Computational logics and agents: a road map of current technologies and future trends. Comput. Int. J. **23**(1), 61–91 (2007)
5. Bordini, R.H., Braubach, L., Dastani, M., ElSeghrouchni, A.F., Gomez-Sanz, J., Leite, J., O'Hare, G., Pokahr, A., Ricci, A.: A survey of programming languages and platforms for multi-agent systems. Informatica (Slovenia) **30**(1), 33–44 (2006)
6. d'Inverno, M., Fisher, M., Lomuscio, A., Luck, M., de Rijke, M., Ryan, M., Wooldridge, M.: Formalisms for multi-agent systems. Knowl. Eng. Rev. **12**(3), 315–321 (1997)
7. Costantini, S., De Gasperis, G.: Memory, experience and adaptation in logical agents. In: Casillas, J., Martínez-López, F.J., Vicari, R., De la Prieta, F. (eds.) Management Intelligent Systems. AISC, vol. 220, pp. 17–24. Springer, Heidelberg (2013)
8. Costantini, S., Dell'Acqua, P., Pereira, L.M.: Conditional learning of rules and plans by knowledge exchange in logical agents. In: Bassiliades, N., Governatori, G., Paschke, A. (eds.) RuleML 2011. LNCS, vol. 6826, pp. 250–265. Springer, Heidelberg (2011). doi:10.1007/978-3-642-22546-8_20
9. Costantini, S.: ACE: a flexible environment for complex event processing in logical agents. In: Baldoni, M., Baresi, L., Dastani, M. (eds.) EMAS 2015. LNCS, vol. 9318, pp. 70–91. Springer, Heidelberg (2015). doi:10.1007/978-3-319-26184-3_5

10. Costantini, S., De Gasperis, G.: Runtime self-checking via temporal (meta-)axioms for assurance of logical agent systems. In: Proceedings of LAMAS 2014, 7th Workshop on Logical Aspects of Multi-agent Systems, held at AAMAS 2014, pp. 241–255 (2014)

11. Costantini, S., Tocchio, A.: A logic programming language for multi-agent systems. In: Flesca, S., Greco, S., Ianni, G., Leone, N. (eds.) JELIA 2002. LNCS, vol. 2424, pp. 1–13. Springer, Heidelberg (2002). doi:10.1007/3-540-45757-7_1

12. Costantini, S., Tocchio, A.: The DALI logic programming agent-oriented language. In: Alferes, J.J., Leite, J. (eds.) JELIA 2004. LNCS, vol. 3229, pp. 685–688. Springer, Heidelberg (2004). doi:10.1007/978-3-540-30227-8_57

13. Costantini, S.: The DALI agent-oriented logic programming language: summary and references 2016 (2016). http://www.di.univaq.it/stefcost/info.htm

14. Baral, C.: Knowledge Representation, Reasoning and Declarative Problem Solving. Cambridge University Press, New York (2003)

15. Costantini, S., Dell'Acqua, P., Pereira, L.M., Toni, F.: Towards a model of evolving agents for ambient intelligence. In: Proceedings of the Symposium on Artificial Societies for Ambient Intelligence (ASAmI 2007) (2007)

16. Costantini, S.: Self-checking logical agents. In: 8th Latin American Works, LA-NMR 2012. CEUR Workshop Proceedings, vol. 911. CEUR-WS.org (2012). 3–30 Invited Paper, Extended Abstract in Proceedings of AAMAS 2013

17. Costantini, S., Formisano, A.: Modeling preferences and conditional preferences on resource consumption and production in ASP. J. Alg. Cogn. Inf. Logic 64(1), 3–15 (2009)

18. De Gasperis, G., Costantini, S., Nazzicone, G.: DALI multi agent systems framework, July 2016. http://github.com/AAAI-DISIM-UnivAQ/DALI

19. Metta, G., Natale, L., Nori, F., Sandini, G., Vernon, D., Fadiga, L., Von Hofsten, C., Rosander, K., Lopes, M., Santos-Victor, J., et al.: The iCub humanoid robot: an open-systems platform for research in cognitive development. Neural Netw. 23(8), 1125–1134 (2010)

# Funky Grooves: Declarative Programming of Full-Fledged Musical Applications

Henrik Nilsson[1(✉)] and Guerric Chupin[2]

[1] School of Computer Science, University of Nottingham, Nottingham, UK
nhn@cs.nott.ac.uk
[2] ENSTA ParisTech, Palaiseau, France
guerric.chupin@ensta-paristech.fr

**Abstract.** There are many systems and languages for music that essentially are declarative, often following the synchronous dataflow paradigm. As these tools, however, are mainly aimed at artists, their application focus tends to be narrow and their usefulness as general purpose tools for developing musical applications limited, at least if one desires to stay declarative. This paper demonstrates that Functional Reactive Programming (FRP) in combination with Reactive Values and Relations (RVR) is one way of addressing this gap. The former, in the synchronous dataflow tradition, aligns with the temporal and declarative nature of music, while the latter allows declarative interfacing with external components as needed for full-fledged musical applications. The paper is a case study around the development of an interactive cellular automaton for composing groove-based music.

**Keywords:** Functional reactive programming · Reactive values and relations · Synchronous dataflow · Hybrid systems · Music

## 1 Introduction

Time, simultaneity, and synchronisation are all inherent aspects of music. Further, there is much that is declarative about music, such as musical notation and many underpinning aspects of music theory. This suggests that a time-aware, declarative paradigm like synchronous dataflow [5] might be a good fit for musical applications. Indeed, there are numerous successful examples of languages and systems targeting music that broadly fall into that category, such as CSound[1], Max/MSP[2], and Pure Data[3] just to mention three.

However, systems like these primarily target artists and are not in themselves general purpose languages. It may be possible to extend them to support novel applications, but this usually involves non-declarative programming and working

---

[1] http://www.csounds.com/.
[2] https://cycling74.com/products/max/.
[3] https://puredata.info/.

© Springer International Publishing AG 2017
Y. Lierler and W. Taha (Eds.): PADL 2017, LNCS 10137, pp. 163–172, 2017.
DOI: 10.1007/978-3-319-51676-9_11

around limitations such as lack of support for complex data structures [7, p. 170] or difficulties to express dynamically changing behaviour [7, p. 156][1].

With this application paper, we aim to demonstrate that Functional Reactive Programming (FRP) [8,13] in combination with Reactive Values and Relations (RVR) [15] is a viable and compelling approach to developing full-fledged musical applications in a declarative style, and, by extension, other kinds of interactive applications where time and simultaneity are central. To cite Berry [2]:

> From the points of view of modeling and programming, there is actually not much difference between programming an airplane or an electronic orchestra.

A more detailed account of this work is available as a technical report [12].

FRP combines the full power of polymorphic functional programming with synchronous dataflow, thus catering for the aforementioned temporal aspects while not being restricted by being tied to any specific application domain. Its suitability for musical applications has been demonstrated a number of times. For example, it constitutes an integral part of the computer music system Euterpea[4], which supports a broad range of musical applications [10], and it has been used for implementing modular synthesizers [9].

Generally, though, the core logic is only one aspect of a modern, compelling software application. In particular, musical applications usually require sophisticated, tailored GUIs and musical I/O, such as audio or MIDI. In practice, such requirements necessitate interfacing with large, complex, and often platform-specific imperative frameworks. In contrast to earlier work [9], we do consider external interfacing here: RVR was developed specifically to meet that need in a declarative manner.

The paper constitutes a case study of the development of a medium-sized musical application inspired by the reacTogon [4], an interactive (hardware) cellular automaton for groove-based music. The FRP system used is Yampa [13]. To challenge our frameworks, we have adapted and extended the basic idea of the reacTogon considerably to create a useful and flexible application that fits into a contemporary studio setting. Through an overview of the developed application and highlights of techniques and code fragments, we hope to convince the reader that our approach works in practice for real applications and has many merits. The source code for the application is publicly available on GitLab[5].

## 2    Background

### 2.1    Time in Music

Change over time is an inherent aspect of music. Further, at least when considered at some level of abstraction, such as a musical score or from the perspective of music theory, music exhibits both discrete-time, and continuous-time aspects

---

[4] http://www.euterpea.com/.

[5] https://gitlab.com/chupin/arpeggigon.

[6, p. 127]. In music theory, this is referred to as *striated* and *smooth* time, a distinction usually attributed to the composer Pierre Boulez [3]. For example, the notes in a musical score begin at discrete points in time. On the other hand, *crescendo* is the gradual increase of the loudness, *ritardando* is the gradual decrease of the tempo, and *portamento* is the gradual change of the pitch from one note to another. Contemporary electronic musical genres provide many other examples of gradual change as an integral part of the music, such as smooth filter sweeps or rhythmic changes of the volume.

Of course, there are many more aspects of time in music than discrete vs. continuous [6, pp. 123–130]. However, for musical applications, support for developing mixed discrete- and continuous-time systems, often referred to as *hybrid systems*, is a good baseline.

## 2.2 Functional Reactive Programming and Yampa

Functional Reactive Programming (FRP) [8] is a declarative approach to implementing reactive applications centred around programming with time-varying values in the synchronous dataflow tradition [5]. In this paper, we are using the arrows-based [11] FRP system Yampa [13]. It is realised as an embedding in Haskell and it supports hybrid systems whose structure may change over time. Thus, as discussed in Sect. 2.1, it is a good fit for musical applications. Further, the arrows-based programming model is close to the visual "boxes and arrows" approach. This also goes well with musical applications, as evidenced by systems like Max/MSP and similar. We outline some of the basic aspects of Yampa in the following for the benefit of readers not familiar with it. A more in-depth account can be found in e.g. the accompanying technical report [12].

Yampa is based on two central concepts: *signals* and *signal functions*. A signal is a function from time to values of some type:

$$Signal\ \alpha \approx Time \rightarrow \alpha$$

*Time* is (notionally) continuous, represented as a non-negative real number. (We will return to discrete time shortly.) The type parameter $\alpha$ specifies the type of values *carried* by the signal. A *signal function* is a function from *Signal* to *Signal*:

$$SF\ \alpha\ \beta \approx Signal\ \alpha \rightarrow Signal\ \beta$$

When a value of type $SF\ \alpha\ \beta$ is applied to an input signal of type $Signal\ \alpha$, it produces an output signal of type $Signal\ \beta$. Signal functions are *first class entities* in Yampa. Signals, however, are not: they only exist indirectly through the notion of signal function.

Programming in Yampa consists of defining signal functions compositionally using Yampa's library of primitive signal functions and a set of combinators. Some central arrow combinators are *arr* that lifts an ordinary function to a stateless signal function, serial composition ⋙, parallel composition &&&, and the fixed point combinator *loop*. Figure 1 illustrates these combinators pictorially. In practice, Paterson's arrow notation [14] is often used to facilitate writing

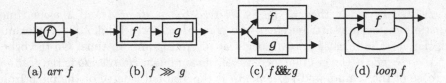

**Fig. 1.** Basic signal function combinators.

arrow code. It is a variation of Haskell's **do**-notation and essentially allows diagrams to be described textually by naming the arrows.

The *Event* type models discrete-time signals:

**data** *Event a = NoEvent | Event a*

A signal function whose output signal is of type *Event T* for some type *T* is called an *event source*. The value carried by an event occurrence may be used to convey information about the occurrence.

A family of *switching* primitives enable the system structure to change in response to events. The simplest such primitive is *switch*:

*switch* :: *SF a* (*b, Event c*) → (*c → SF a b*) → *SF a b*

Once the switching event occurs, *switch* applies its second argument to the value carried by the event and switches into the resulting signal function. Yampa also includes *parallel* switching constructs that maintain *dynamic collections* of signal functions connected in parallel [13].

### 2.3 Reactive Values and Relations

A Reactive Value (RV) [15] is a typed mutable value with access rights and change notification. RVs provide a light-weight and *uniform* interface to GUI widgets and other external components such as files and network devices. Each entity is represented as a collection of RVs, each of which encloses an individual property. RVs can be transformed and combined using a range of combinators, including lifting of pure functions and lenses.

Reactive Relations (RR) specify how RVs are related *separately* from their definitions. An RR may be uni- or bi-directional. Once RVs have been related, changes will be propagated automatically among them to ensure that the stated relation is respected.

## 3 The Arpeggigon

Our application is called *Arpeggigon*, from *arpeggio* and *hexagon*. It was inspired by Mark Burton's hardware reacTogon: a "chain reactive performance

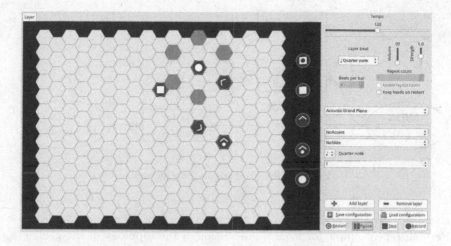

**Fig. 2.** The Arpeggigon (Color figure online)

arpeggiator" [4]. However, we have expanded considerably upon the basic idea to create a software application we believe is both genuinely useful in a contemporary studio setting and a credible test case for our approach.

### 3.1 The reacTogon

Central to the design of the reacTogon is the Harmonic Table[6]: a way to arrange musical notes on a hexagonal grid. The various directions correspond to different musically meaningful intervals. For example, each step along the vertical axis corresponds to a perfect fifth. The reacTogon uses this layout to implement a cellular automaton. See Fig. 2 for our adaptation of the idea. *Tokens* of a few different kinds are placed on the grid, at most one token per cell. These tokens govern how *play heads* move around the grid, as well as the initial position and direction of the play heads. When a play head hits a token, the kind of token determines what happens next. First, for most tokens, a note corresponding to the position of the token is played. Second, either the direction of the play head is changed, it is split into new play heads, or it is absorbed. Thus, arpeggiated chords or other sequences of notes are described. These can further be transposed in response to playing a keyboard, allowing the reacTogon to be performed.

### 3.2 Features and Architecture

Our Arpeggigon is a software realization of the reacTogon concept. The main features our Arpeggigon provides over the reacTogon are:

- Multiple layers: one or more cellular automata run in parallel. Layers can be added, removed, and edited dynamically through a tabbed GUI.

---

[6] https://en.wikipedia.org/wiki/Harmonic_table_note_layout.

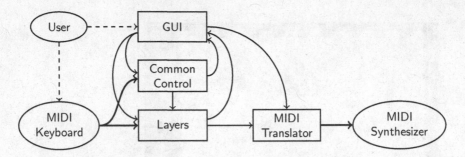

**Fig. 3.** The Arpeggigon architecture

- Extended attributes for tokens, such as note length, accent, and slide.
- Per-cell repeat count for local modification of the topology of the grid.
- MIDI integration.
- Saving and loading of configurations.

Figure 2 shows a screenshot. Dynamic addition and removal of layers means that both the core logic of the application and the GUI must support structural changes while the application is running. Note the different kinds of tokens to the right of the grid. They can be dragged and dropped onto the grid to configure a layer, even while the Arpeggigon is running. The play heads are coloured green.

Figure 3 illustrates the architecture of the Arpeggigon. The rectangles represent the main system components. The thin arrows represent internal communication, the thick ones MIDI I/O, and the dashed ones user interaction.

GUI is the graphical user interface. It includes a model of the state of global parameters, such as the overall system tempo, and the current configuration of each layer. Common Control is responsible for system-wide aspects, such as generating a global clock (reflecting the system tempo) that keeps the layers synchronised. Layers is the instances of the actual automata, each generating notes. MIDI Translator translates high-level internal note events and control signals into low-level MIDI messages, merging and serialising the output from all layers.

GUI communicates the current system configuration to Common Control and Layers. Note that this data is time-varying as the user can change the configuration any time. Layers needs to communicate the positions of the play heads back to GUI for animation purposes. This is thus also a time-varying signal.

## 4 Implementation

### 4.1 Layers

At its core, each layer of the Arpeggigon is a cellular automaton that advances one step per layer beat. Its semantics is embodied by a transition function:

$$advanceHeads :: Board \rightarrow BeatNo \rightarrow RelPitch \rightarrow Strength \rightarrow [PlayHead]$$
$$\rightarrow ([PlayHead], [Note])$$

In essence, given the current configuration of tokens on the hexagonal grid, henceforth the *board*, it maps the state of the play heads (position, direction, and a repeat counter) to an updated play head state and a list of notes to be played at this beat. The number of play heads may change as a play head may be split or absorbed. The remaining parameters give the current transposition of the layer, the strength with which notes should be played, and the beat number within a bar allowing specific notes in a bar to be accented (played stronger).

Using the *scanl*-like Yampa function *accumBy*, *advanceHeads* is readily lifted into an event-processing signal function:

$$automaton :: [PlayHead] \rightarrow SF\ (Board, DynamicLayerCtrl, Event\ BeatNo)$$
$$(Event\ [Note], [PlayHead])$$

The static parameter is the initial state of the play heads. The first of the three input signals carries the current configuration of the board, originating from GUI (Fig. 3). The second carries a record of dynamic control parameters for the layer, including transposition, play strength, and the length of a layer beat, originating from GUI and MIDI Keyboard. These two are continuous-time signals, reflecting the fact that the configuration of the board can change and a key be struck on the MIDI keyboard at any time, not just at a beat. The third is the discrete-time layer beat clock, from Common Control, carrying the beat number within a bar. The output signals are the notes to be played, to be sent to MIDI Translator, and the state of the play heads for animation purposes, to be sent back to GUI. Note the close correspondence to the architecture in Fig. 3.

## 4.2   Synchronisation

As an example of turning Yampa's continuous-time capabilities to musical applications, consider automating gradual tempo changes. Imagine two sliders to set a fast and a slow tempo, a button to select between them, and a further slider to set the rate at which the tempo should change. The following signal function derives a smoothly changing tempo from these controls, regulated to within 0.1 bpm of the desired tempo. Note the feedback (enabled by **rec**):

$$smoothTempo :: Tempo \rightarrow SF\ (Bool, Tempo, Tempo, Rate)\ Tempo$$

```
smoothTempo tempo0 = proc (select1, tempo1, tempo2, rate) → do
  rec
    let desiredTempo = if select1 then tempo1 else tempo2
        diff         = desiredTempo − currentTempo
        rate'        = if      diff > 0.1   then rate
                       else if diff < −0.1 then − rate
                       else                       0
      currentTempo ← arr (+tempo0) ≪ integral ≺ rate'
    returnA ≺ currentTempo
```

### 4.3  GUI and Interaction

The GUI of the Arpeggigon is written using the cross-platform widget toolkit
GTK+. The Arpeggigon does not generate any audio by itself; it needs to be
connected to an external, MIDI-capable hardware or software synthesizer. MIDI
I/O is handled by the JACK Audio Connection Kit.

All code for interfacing with the external world is structured using reactive
values and relations (RVR). Much of this code is of course monadic (in the IO
monad). However, as it is mostly concerned with creating and interconnecting
interface entities, the code has a fairly declarative reading as a sequence of entity
definitions and specifications of how they are related.

As a case in point, consider the following code for the system tempo slider:

```
globalSettings :: IO (VBox, ReactiveFieldReadWrite IO Int)
globalSettings = do
    globalSettingsBox ← vBoxNew False 10
    tempoAdj          ← adjustmentNew 120 40 200 1 1 1
    tempoLabel        ← labelNew (Just "Tempo")
    boxPackStart globalSettingsBox tempoLabel PackNatural 0
    tempoScale        ← hScaleNew tempoAdj
    boxPackStart globalSettingsBox tempoScale PackNatural 0
    scaleSetDigits tempoScale 0
    let tempoRV =
        bijection (floor, fromIntegral) 'liftRW' scaleValueReactive tempoScale
    return (globalSettingsBox, tempoRV)
```

In essence, this code defines a box, a label, and a slider, and visually relates
them by placing the last two inside the box. This is all standard GTK+.
A read/write, integer-valued reactive value (RV) is finally defined and related
to the real-valued value of the slider: *scaleValueReactive* associates a slider with
an RV, while *liftRW* derives a new RV from an existing one by specifying two
conversion functions, one for reading and one for writing.

Finally, the RVR part and the Yampa part of the Arpeggigon are connected
by the following function:

```
yampaReactiveDual ::
    a → SF a b → IO (ReactiveFieldWrite IO a, ReactiveFieldRead IO b)
```

This creates two reactive values: one for the input and one for the output of the
signal function. After writing a value to the input, the corresponding output at
that point in time can be read.

# 5    Conclusions

This paper demonstrated how Functional Reactive Programming in combination with Reactive Values and Relations can be used to develop a realistic, non-trivial musical application. On the whole, we found that these two frameworks together were very well suited for this task. The performance was good, including critical aspects like jitter, without much effort so far having been spent on optimisation. Heap usage and overall memory footprint was modest. See the accompanying technical report for details [12]. Further, as most of the techniques we demonstrated are not limited to a musical context, we suggest that this is a good approach for programming time-aware, interactive applications in general.

**Acknowledgments.** The authors would like to thank Ivan Perez and Henning Thielemann for support and advice with the reactive libraries and the Haskell JACK bindings respectively, Michel Mauny for co-supervising the second author's summer internship with the Functional Programming Laboratory in Nottingham, and François Pessaux and anonymous reviewers for helpful feedback.

# References

1. Baudart, G., Mandel, L., Pouzet, M.: Programming mixed music in ReactiveML. In: 1st Workshop on Functional Art, Music, Modeling and Design (FARM), Boston, USA, pp. 11–22. ACM, September 2013
2. Berry, G.: Formally unifying modeling and design for embedded systems - a personal view. In: Margaria, T., Steffen, B. (eds.) ISoLA 2016. LNCS, vol. 9953, pp. 134–149. Springer, Heidelberg (2016). doi:10.1007/978-3-319-47169-3_11
3. Boulez, P.: Penser la musique aujourd'hui. Gallimard, Paris (1964)
4. Burton, M.: The reacTogon: a chain reactive performance arpeggiator (2007). https://www.youtube.com/watch?v=AklKy2NDpqs
5. Caspi, P., Pilaud, D., Halbwachs, N., Plaice, J.A.: LUSTRE: a declarative language for programming synchronous systems. In: 14th Symposium on Principles of Programming Languages (POPL). ACM, New York (1987)
6. Cont, A.: Antescofo: anticipatory synchronization and control of interactive parameters in computer music. In: International Computer Music Conference (ICMC), Belfast, Ireland, pp. 33–40, August 2008
7. Cont, A., Anticipation, M.M.: From the time of music to music of time. Ph.D. thesis. University of California San Diego (UCSD) and University of Pierre et Marie Curie (Paris VI) (2008)
8. Elliott, C., Hudak, P.: Functional reactive animation. In: 2nd International Conference on Functional Programming (ICFP), pp. 163–173, June 1997
9. Giorgidze, G., Nilsson, H.: Switched-On Yampa. In: Hudak, P., Warren, D.S. (eds.) PADL 2008. LNCS, vol. 4902, pp. 282–298. Springer, Heidelberg (2007). doi:10.1007/978-3-540-77442-6_19
10. Hudak, P., Quick, D., Santolucito, M., Winograd-Cort, D.: Real-time interactive music in Haskell. In: 3rd International Workshop on Functional Art, Music, Modelling and Design (FARM), Vancouver, BC, Canada, pp. 15–16. ACM, September 2015

11. Hughes, J.: Generalising monads to arrows. Sci. Comput. Program. **37**, 67–111 (2000)
12. Nilsson, H., Chupin, G.: The Arpeggigon: Declarative programming of a full-fledged musical application. Technical report, November 2016. http://eprints.nottingham.ac.uk/38657
13. Nilsson, H., Courtney, A., Peterson, J.: Functional reactive programming, continued. In: Haskell Workshop, Pittsburgh, PA, USA, pp. 51–64. ACM, October 2002
14. Paterson, R.: A new notation for arrows. In: International Conference on Functional Programming (ICFP), Firenze, Italy, pp. 229–240, September 2001
15. Perez, I., Nilsson, H.: Bridging the GUI gap with reactive values and relations. In: 8th ACM SIGPLAN Symposium on Haskell, Vancouver, Canada, pp. 47–58. ACM (2015)

# A Domain-Specific Language
# for Software-Defined Radio

Geoffrey Mainland[✉]

Department of Computer Science, Drexel University, Philadelphia, PA, USA
mainland@drexel.edu

**Abstract.** Software-defined radio (SDR) is a demanding domain; real-world wireless protocols require high data rates and low latency. Existing SDR platforms, typically based on FPGAs, provide the necessary substrate for meeting these requirements, but the high-level tools available to program them are not capable of fully exploiting the underlying hardware to meet rigorous performance requirements. Ziria [11] demonstrated that a high-level language can compete in this demanding space, but its design was ad-hoc and overly influenced by the needs of the compiler writer since its surface language does double duty as the compiler's intermediate language.

We present a re-formulation of Ziria's surface language that includes a new type system that allows this language, which is effectful, to elaborate into a pure, monadic language where effects such as input/output and reference manipulation can be distinguished purely by type. This re-formulation and its elaboration into a core language is embodied in a new compiler for Ziria, kzc. By choosing an appropriate type system, awkward syntactic distinctions currently made by Ziria can be eliminated, although our new implementation maintains source compatibility with the original compiler due to a large body of existing Ziria code (a full 802.11 physical layer implementation). Our contribution is a description of the surface language, its type system, and its elaboration into a core language. We also show that far from being limited to the SDR domain, the constructs built-in to Ziria are applicable to other resource-constrained domains that require high-speed data processing.

## 1 Introduction

Software-defined radio promises to bring the productivity benefits of software—fast development cycles and modular reuse of code—to the world of radio protocols. Radio platforms for SDR, such as USRP [3] and BladeRF [2], provide the necessary hardware for high-performance radio protocol implementations, but existing tools for programming these devices fall short on one or more dimensions. The fundamental issue is the tension between ease of programming and performance.

Although most SDR hardware incorporates an FPGA, which could be programmed directly, doing so requires not only the use of proprietary tools, but also fairly low-level knowledge of the underlying FPGA. Instead, platforms like GNU

© Springer International Publishing AG 2017
Y. Lierler and W. Taha (Eds.): PADL 2017, LNCS 10137, pp. 173–188, 2017.
DOI: 10.1007/978-3-319-51676-9_12

Radio [4] offer a high-level toolkit of signal processing blocks written in Python and C++. These blocks are composed using a graph-based model where vertices, i.e., blocks, represent computation, and edges represent communication. While simple to program, this model does not result in high-speed, low-latency protocol implementations. As a programming model, the graph-based paradigm also has a number of shortcomings. First, it does not specify when a vertex's state is initialized. Although edges represent "communication," how control messages and data flow are differentiated is not well-defined, and it is unclear how one vertex could send a control message to another vertex, perhaps one to which it is not directly connected. There is also no well-defined method for control messages to reconfigure data flow in the graph. Finally, since each vertex is a black box, there is no opportunity to jointly optimize multiple vertices' operations.

SORA [14] was the first SDR programming platform to provide a purely software-based 802.11 a/b/g implementation that operated at speeds comparable to commodity 802.11 hardware. This was achieved with a carefully hand-tuned C++ implementation. The SORA implementation is so carefully tuned, that modifying it while maintaining performance is very difficult. For example, SORA relies crucially and frequently on lookup tables (LUTs) for performance, but these LUTs appear simply as array constants in the C source. Questions such as how these LUTs were generated (by hand?), how one should choose when to write a function as a LUT, and how one might go about changing an existing LUT are left unanswered.

Implementing radio protocols directly in FPGA hardware is typically accomplished using MATLAB/Simulink; both WARP [9] and SOFDM [5] take this approach. The resulting programs are graph-based system models that are synthesized to FPGA bitstreams. However, though they can fully exploit the underlying FPGA, these models are large, difficult to construct and reason about, and they are intimately tied to particular platform traits such as the FPGA clock rate and the bit width of the A/D converter in the radio front end. Furthermore, the MATLAB/Simulink environment does not offer constructs tailored to the SDR domain.

Ziria [11] is a high-level language for wireless physical layer (PHY) protocols, i.e., the portion of the radio stack that converts radio signals into bits, which are then passed on to another protocol handler, such as a MAC protocol. Ziria provides *both* programmability and SORA-level performance. This is achieved by a number of compiler optimizations—in effect, instead of an expert C programmer doing the work of translating a high-level specification of a wireless PHY protocol into efficient low-level C code, the Ziria compiler does the work. The optimizer's job is made easier by the nature of the restricted application domain: whole-program analysis is possible, arrays sizes are statically known, and communication between components is performed via built-in language constructs.

In this work, we show how to reformulate the Ziria surface language so that terms' types differentiate between the three effects that are meaningful in our setting: memory assignment/dereference, reading from a queue, and writing to a queue. The existing surface language uses syntactic constructs to distinguish between code that performs memory assignment/dereferencing and code that performs IO via queues; our reformulation shows how this syntactic distinction can be eliminated in favor of a type-based distinction. This reformulation also enables elaboration of the effectful surface language into a pure, monadic core language. In other work [8], we show that novel source-to-source transformations on this core language can jointly optimize across multiple Ziria components, fusing them into a single loop; we include benchmarks demonstrating the performance effects of these optimizations in Sect. 6. Concretely, the contributions of this work are as follows:

- A type system, with a limited form of quantification, that expresses what are currently syntactic distinctions in Ziria as type distinctions.
- A method for elaborating the effectful Ziria surface language into a pure, monadic core language.
- A new continuation-based compilation model for Ziria.

Our contributions are embodied in kzc[1], a wholly new open source compiler for the Ziria language that is source-compatible with the existing compiler, wplc[2].

## 2   Background

We first give a brief overview of the Ziria surface language to provide necessary context. The surface language we describe is identical to the language described by Stewart et al. [11], and this section does not represent novel work. Ziria provides an imperative core wrapped with combinators for producer-consumer computations that operate over streams of data. We illustrate both components of the language in Listing 2.1, which is the Ziria implementation of the 802.11 scrambler [1, Sect. 16.2.4]. The purpose of the scrambler is to transform the transmitted bit stream so that it does not contain long runs of ones or zeros, either of which would make detection at the receiver more difficult.

Line 2 allocates mutable storage for the scrambler's state; this state is initialized with the (immutable) value of the parameter init_scrmbl_st. Both init_scrmbl_st and scrmbl_st are arrays of seven bits. After initializing the scrambler state, the scambler enters a **repeat** loop in line 4 that continually reads a bit from its input data stream using **take**, updates the scrambler state, transforms the consumed bit using the scrambler state, and finally outputs the transformed bit in line 14 using **emit**. Although not shown in this snippet, Ziria also allows immutable values to be bound with **let** (instead of **var**). The surface language does not include an explicit dereference construct, instead making dereferencing implicit, as shown on line 9.

The syntactic distinction between ref manipulation and input/output is made using **do** and **seq** blocks; a **seq** block sequences IO, whereas a **do** block sequences ref manipulation. The **repeat** language construct takes an IO action

---

[1] The Kyllini Ziria compiler. Ziria is another name for Mount Kyllini in Greece.
[2] The wireless programming language compiler.

```
1   fun comp scrambler(init_scrmbl_st: arr[7] bit) {
2     var scrmbl_st : arr[7] bit := init_scrmbl_st;
3
4     repeat seq {
5       x ← take;
6
7       var tmp : bit;
8       do {
9         tmp := (scrmbl_st[3] ^ scrmbl_st[0]);
10        scrmbl_st[0:5] := scrmbl_st[1:6];
11        scrmbl_st[6] := tmp;
12      };
13
14      emit (x^tmp)
15    }
16  }
```

Listing 2.1. Ziria implementation of 802.11 scrambler.

```
scrambler('1011101)
≫
seq {
  var buf : arr[8] bit;
  for i in [0, 8] { x ← take; do { buf[i] := x;} };
  emits buf;
}
```

Listing 2.2. Composition along the data path.

and repeats it forever. The resulting computation is termed a *stream transformer* because it continually reads input, transforms it, and writes the transformed value to its output. Both **do** and **seq** blocks compose computations along the *control* path, and the syntax for this sort of composition is deliberately reminiscent of Haskell's do syntax, as seen in line 5.

## 2.1  Composition Along the Data Path

Given the scrambler, which ensures the bits we are transmitting will be sufficiently varied between 1 and 0, we need a way to compose it with other data producer/consumer components. Instead of composition along the control path, we want to compose the scrambler *along the data path*, which is accomplished using the *par* operator, ≫.

Listing 2.2 shows an example of composition along both the control and data paths using the previously defined scrambler function. The first component in the data path is the scrambler computation. Note that producer-consumer computations are higher-order; the argument to scrambler here is a bit array constant of length 7, which serves to initialize the scrambler's state. The second element in the data path reads 8 elements from its input, collecting them in a buffer, and then outputs them all at once using **emits**. The only difference between **emit** and **emits** is that the latter acts as though each element of its array argument were emitted one-by-one. Because the second element in the data path terminates, it is a *stream computer*. The distinction between a *stream transformer* and a *stream computer* is apparent from their types, the topic to which we now turn.

## 3   Typing Ziria Programs

The first contribution of this paper is a new type system for the Ziria surface language that makes a distinction between three effects: ref manipulation (assignment and dereferencing), reading (using **take**), and writing (using **emit**). The kzc compiler performs type inference using this type system, elaborating source language terms to a core language we describe in Sect. 4. We first informally sketch our types system.

Like Stewart et al. [11], we make use of an indexed type reminiscent of both monads and arrows [6], but we use a limited form of quantification to distinguish between effects. For example, we assign the scrambler in Listing 2.1 the moral type arr[7] bit → ST T bit bit. The type to the left of the arrow is the argument to scrambler. The type ST is indexed by three types: T, which indicates that this term is a *stream transformer*, and the two types, both bit, specifying the input and output types, respectively, of the computation. The second half of the *par* in listing 2.2 is instead assigned the type ST (C ()) bit (arr[8] bit). Because this computation terminates with the unit value, i.e., it is a *stream computer*, the first index to ST is now C (). The computation reads values of type bit and writes values of type arr[8] bit, so those types make up the final two indices.

The question remains: how do we differentiate between effects using types? For pure expressions, the answer is simple: pure expressions have a non-ST type. Expressions that manipulate references but *do not* perform IO could be assigned a type that quantifies over the input and output types of the data stream. For example, the expression x := 1; could be typed as $\forall \alpha \beta.$ ST (C ()) $\alpha \beta$. Similarly, computations that only read or write could be typed by quantifying over the appropriate index to ST.

Unfortunately, the simple quantification strategy does not allow us to properly differentiate between terms that perform IO using take and emit and those that do not. Consider the following example:

```
seq { x ← take; return 1; }
```

What type should we assign this term? Its type must certainly have the form ST (C int) $\alpha \beta$ for some $\alpha$ and $\beta$. It is also clear that we need to quantify over $\beta$ because the expression does not write to the data stream. However, although it does read from its input stream, the term is *agnostic to the type* of the data it reads, so it seems reasonable to quantify over *both* $\alpha$ and $\beta$. We conclude that this expression should have type $\forall\, \alpha\, \beta.\ \mathsf{ST}\ (\mathsf{C}\ \mathsf{int})\ \alpha\ \beta$. Similar reasoning leads us to assign the same type to this term, which *does not* perform any input or output:

```
seq { return 1; }
```

The root of the problem is that our quantification scheme does not allow us to differentiate between terms that are polymorphic in the value read from the data stream and terms that do not read from the data stream at all.

Our solution will be to add a fourth index to the ST type—but what should this index be? Since we want to know whether or not a term reads a value from its input stream, we could make the index a type-level Boolean. We could also add an additional type-level construct analogous to the $\mathsf{C}\ \alpha/\mathsf{T}$ construct we use to differentiate between transformers and computers, but this makes the type system more complicated. Instead of adding something new, we will reuse existing type system mechanisms—in particular, unification. Our new type index will be left free until a read occurs, at which point it will be unified with the type index that specifies the type of the input stream. Therefore, when these two indices are equal, we know a read has occurred, and if they are not equal, we know that a read *has not* occurred.

## 3.1   A Type System for Differentiating Effects

Figure 1 shows the language of types for Ziria terms. We do not include array types here as they clutter the presentation, and adding them is not difficult. Base types, $\tau$, are as one would expect. Types in ST allow quantification over base types in the indices of ST. The first index, $\omega$, specifies whether this computation is a stream transformer ($\mathsf{T}$) or a stream computer ($\mathsf{C}\ \tau$). We will shortly see the details of how the other three indices are used to indicate read/write behavior. For completeness, we include the details of reference handling. Note that types are stratified so that although references can always be passed to a function, they can never be returned from a function, i.e., only "downward reference funargs" are allowed. This ensures that a reference can never escape its defining scope, eliminating the need for garbage collection. This reduction in expressivity is perfectly acceptable in our domain.

$$
\begin{aligned}
\nu, \tau &::= \alpha, \beta, \gamma \\
&\ \ \mid\ () \\
&\ \ \mid\ \mathsf{bool} \\
&\ \ \mid\ \mathsf{int} \\
\omega &::= \mathsf{C}\ \tau \\
&\ \ \mid\ \mathsf{T} \\
\mu &::= \forall \bar{\alpha}.\mathsf{ST}\ \omega\ \tau\ \tau\ \tau \\
\rho &::= \tau \\
&\ \ \mid\ \mathsf{ref}\ \tau \\
\sigma &::= \tau \\
&\ \ \mid\ \mu \\
\phi &::= \rho \\
&\ \ \mid\ \rho_1 \ldots \rho_n \to \sigma \\
\Gamma &::= \cdot \\
&\ \ \mid\ x : \theta, \Gamma \\
\theta &::= \tau \\
&\ \ \mid\ \mathsf{ref}\ \tau \\
&\ \ \mid\ \mu \\
&\ \ \mid\ \rho_1 \ldots \rho_n \to \sigma
\end{aligned}
$$

**Fig. 1.** Ziria type language.

The declarative formulation of the Ziria typing relation is shown in Fig. 2. We include the T-DEREF rule even though, as stated earlier, dereferences are *implicit* in the surface language. We return to this point in Sect. 4. Rule T-TAKE forces the second and third index of the ST type to both be $\alpha$, although it still quantifies over $\alpha$. This type reflects the fact

$$\boxed{\Gamma \vdash e : \theta}$$

$$\frac{\Gamma \vdash e_1 : \tau_1 \quad x : \text{ref } \tau_1, \Gamma \vdash e_2 : \text{ST } \omega \, \alpha \, \beta \, \gamma}{\Gamma \vdash \text{letref } x = e_1 \text{ in } e_2 : \text{ST } \omega \, \alpha \, \beta \, \gamma} \quad \text{(T-LetRef)}$$

$$\frac{x : \text{ref } \tau \in \Gamma}{\Gamma \vdash !x : \forall \alpha \, \beta \, \gamma. \, \text{ST } (\text{C } \tau) \, \alpha \, \beta \, \gamma} \quad \text{(T-Deref)}$$

$$\frac{x : \text{ref } \tau \in \Gamma \quad \Gamma \vdash e : \tau}{\Gamma \vdash x := e : \forall \alpha \, \beta \, \gamma. \, \text{ST } (\text{C } ()) \, \alpha \, \beta \, \gamma} \quad \text{(T-Assign)}$$

$$\frac{\Gamma \vdash c : \tau}{\Gamma \vdash \text{return } c : \forall \alpha \, \beta \, \gamma. \, \text{ST } (\text{C } \tau) \, \alpha \, \beta \, \gamma} \quad \text{(T-Return)}$$

$$\frac{\Gamma \vdash c_1 : \text{ST } (\text{C } \nu) \, \alpha \, \beta \, \gamma \quad x : \nu, \Gamma \vdash c_2 : \text{ST } \omega \, \alpha \, \beta \, \gamma}{\Gamma \vdash x \leftarrow c_1; \, c_2 : \text{ST } \omega \, \alpha \, \beta \, \gamma} \quad \text{(T-Bind)}$$

$$\frac{\Gamma \vdash c_1 : \text{ST } (\text{C } \nu) \, \alpha \, \beta \, \gamma \quad \Gamma \vdash c_2 : \text{ST } \omega \, \alpha \, \beta \, \gamma}{\Gamma \vdash c_1; \, c_2 : \text{ST } \omega \, \alpha \, \beta \, \gamma} \quad \text{(T-Seq)}$$

$$\frac{}{\Gamma \vdash \text{take} : \forall \alpha \, \beta. \, \text{ST } (\text{C } \alpha) \, \alpha \, \alpha \, \beta} \quad \text{(T-Take)}$$

$$\frac{\Gamma \vdash e : \tau}{\Gamma \vdash \text{emit } e : \forall \alpha \, \beta. \, \text{ST } (\text{C } ()) \, \alpha \, \beta \, \tau} \quad \text{(T-Emit)}$$

$$\frac{\Gamma \vdash c : \text{ST } (\text{C } ()) \, \alpha \, \beta \, \gamma}{\Gamma \vdash \text{repeat } c : \text{ST } \text{T } \alpha \, \beta \, \gamma} \quad \text{(T-Repeat)}$$

$$\frac{\Gamma_1 \oplus \Gamma_2 = \Gamma \quad \Gamma_1 \vdash c_1 : \text{ST } \omega_1 \, \alpha \, \alpha \, \beta \quad \Gamma_2 \vdash c_2 : \text{ST } \omega_2 \, \beta \, \beta \, \gamma}{\Gamma \vdash c_1 \ggg c_2 : \text{ST } (\omega_1 \sqcup \omega_2) \, \alpha \, \alpha \, \gamma} \quad \text{(T-Par)}$$

$$\text{C } \alpha \sqcup \text{T} = \text{C } \alpha$$
$$\text{T} \sqcup \text{C } \alpha = \text{C } \alpha$$
$$\text{T} \sqcup \text{T} = \text{T}$$

$$\frac{\Gamma \vdash c : \forall \overline{\alpha}. \, \text{ST } \omega \, \tau_1 \, \tau_2 \, \tau_3}{\Gamma \vdash c : [\overline{\alpha \mapsto \tau}] \, \text{ST } \omega \, \tau_1 \, \tau_2 \, \tau_3} \quad \text{(T-Inst)}$$

$$\frac{\overline{\alpha} \notin fvs(\Gamma) \quad \Gamma \vdash c : \text{ST } \omega \, \tau_1 \, \tau_2 \, \tau_3}{\Gamma \vdash c : \forall \overline{\alpha}. \, \text{ST } \omega \, \tau_1 \, \tau_2 \, \tau_3} \quad \text{(T-Gen)}$$

**Fig. 2.** Declarative typing relation for Ziria.

that we are reading from the data stream, although we are polymorphic in the value being read. During type inference, use of take is what causes unification of the two type indices as mentioned above. Rule T-Emit says that **emit** is polymorphic in the input type of the data stream, but it constrains the fourth index of the ST type (the *data stream output type* index) to be $\tau$, the type of the value being emitted. Table 1 maps types to their conceptual meanings, showing how types differentiate between effects. The essential idea is that a term with an ST type in which the second and third indices (the *data stream input type* indices) are identical reads from its input data stream, even if it is polymorphic in the type that is read. If the second and third indices *differ*, then the term does not read from its input stream. As a final example, the following identify transformer has the type $\forall \alpha. \, \text{ST } \alpha \, \alpha \, \alpha$:

Table 1. Conceptual meaning of quantification in ST types.

| Type | Conceptual meaning |
|---|---|
| $\forall \alpha\ \beta\ \gamma.\ \mathsf{ST}\ \omega\ \alpha\ \beta\ \gamma$ | A computation that may assign or dereference memory but does not perform IO |
| $\forall \alpha\ \gamma.\ \mathsf{ST}\ \omega\ \alpha\ \alpha\ \gamma$ | A computation that reads one or more values from the data stream but does nothing with the read value(s) |
| $\forall \gamma.\ \mathsf{ST}\ \omega\ \tau\ \tau\ \gamma$ | A computation that reads one or more values of type $\tau$ from the data stream |
| $\mathsf{ST}\ \omega\ \tau_1\ \tau_1\ \tau_2$ | A computation that reads one or more values of type $\tau_1$ from the input data stream and writes one or more values of type $\tau_2$ to the output data stream |

```
repeat seq { x ← take; emit x; }
```

In implementing the kzc compiler, we certainly wanted to differentiate between pure and impure code for purposes of optimization; that is easily done via the ST type. However, we also want to differentiate between impure code that uses memory references and code that may perform IO. The new type system in Fig. 2 allows for this. In the original incarnation of Ziria, this distinction was made syntactically via seq and do, and programmers had to manually "lift" code that used references into the ST monad. With the new type system, it is now possible to eliminate the do/seq distinction from the surface language; we plan to add a new alternative syntax that does this, but for compatibility reasons we have not yet done so.

### 3.2   Typing Composition Along the Control Path

The rules T-BIND and T-SEQ support composition along the control path. The only notable aspect of these rules is the way the first index of the ST type assigned to the overall term relates to the first index of the ST type of each subterm. The first subterm being sequenced must be a computer, i.e., it must compute a value and terminate, so the its $\omega$ index must be C $\nu$. The second subterm *may or may not* terminate. That is, it may be a transformer, so its $\omega$ index is unconstrained. The overall term then has an $\omega$ index matching that of the second subterm being sequenced. Note that we could remove the T-SEQ rule and treat sequencing as syntactic sugar for bind.

### 3.3   Typing Composition Along the Data Path

Typing composition along the data path is done by the rule T-PAR. Unlike the rules for composition along the control path, the subterms $c_1$ and $c_2$ of T-PAR have types whose $\tau$ indices (the third through fourth indices in the ST type) that may differ between the two subterms' types. Since $\gg$ represents composition along the data path, the terms' types are instead constrained so that the data stream output index of the type of $c_1$ matches the data stream input type indices of the type of $c_2$.

The T-PAR rule uses of the join operator, $\cdot \sqcup \cdot$, to determine the $\omega$ type index of the result of the par. This operator guarantees that two stream transformers may be composed on the data path, as may a stream computer and a stream transformer, but it prevents two stream computers from being composed along the data path. We could imagine adding a fourth case to the join operator, $\mathsf{C}\ \alpha \sqcup \mathsf{C}\ \alpha = \mathsf{C}\ \alpha$, but this complicates the semantics as it requires additional synchronization on the final computed result. This change would also complicate the implementation; with the current semantics, we are guaranteed that at most one side of the par will ever terminate and call the par's continuation.

The final subtlety in T-PAR is the context splitting operation, $\oplus$. The context splitting operation $\oplus$ splits the portion of the context that contains variables that have type ref $\tau$, leaving the rest of the context as-is. This ensures that the type environments for the two subterms, $\Gamma_1$ and $\Gamma_2$, contain completely distinct sets of references, thus preventing race conditions. An additional check on function calls ensures aliasing does not occur, $\oplus$ can perform a purely syntactic check on $\Gamma$; see Mainland [8] for details.

### 3.4   Type Inference in Practice

The described typing relation is declarative. When, then, do we apply rules T-GEN and T-INST? Similar to standard syntax-directed systems based on Hindley-Milner, we instantiate types immediately and generalize at "let"; for example, when inferring the type of a function body, we immediately instantiate any occurrence of **take** or **emit**, and we then generalize once we have inferred the type of the entire function body. Inference makes use of the standard unification algorithm. We plan to formalize the inference algorithm, but on its own it is standard—the novel aspect of inference is the use of the indexed type ST to differentiate between various effects and the process of elaborating to the core language, which we describe in the next section.

### 3.5   Types for Streaming Combinators

The type system we have presented supports a general form of stream combinator and is not specific to the SDR domain or the Ziria language. The technique we use to reflect read operations in the ST type by forcing unification of two type indices is even more general. In effect, we are differentiating between two kinds of polymorphism: polymorphism that arises because read values are used polymorphically, as in the identity function, and polymorphism that arises because values aren't read at all. Because we are simply forcing type equality—in our case, via the typing rule for take—we minimize the number of extra features that need to be added to the type system. We expect these techniques to be transferable to any domain where typed streaming combinators are useful.

# 4   Elaborating to Core

The kzc compiler performs type inference on the Ziria surface language and elaborates it to the core language given in Fig. 3. Unlike the surface language, the core language contains only a single syntactic category: expressions. There is no need for a syntactic distinction between pure terms, terms that use memory references, and terms that perform IO, because the type system described in Sect. 3 provides the needed distinctions. Also unlike the surface language, the core language makes memory dereferencing explicit. Explicit memory reference operations in the core language make some analyses in the compiler easier to perform; for example, it allows the compiler to determine that an expression is pure merely based on its type. However, forcing the programmer to use explicit dereferencing in the surface language seems overly burdensome; despite our use of monadic bind, we want the surface language to be as close to typical "curly brace and semicolon" imperative code as possible while still being fundamentally functional.

Elaboration makes use of a new form of judgment:

$$\mathscr{F}; \Gamma \vdash^{val} e : \tau \rightsquigarrow \mathscr{F}'; e'$$

Like the typing judgment, the elaboration judgment assigns a type $\tau$ to a term $e$. However, it also elaborates a surface language term $e$ to a core term $e'$. Recall from Sect. 3.1 that references are not first-class in Ziria—they can never be returned from a function or otherwise escape the scope of their originating binder. This judgment form is a *value elaboration*; it elaborates a Ziria term, which may contain implicit dereferences, into a core term in which all dereferences are made explicit. The extra component $\mathscr{F}$ that is threaded through the elaboration judgment is the elaborated term's *value context*; it is a function from core terms to core terms that transforms an elaborated term so that all implicit dereferences are bound.

$$
\begin{aligned}
e, c ::= \; & k & \text{(constant)} \\
| \; & x & \text{(variable)} \\
| \; & unop\ e \\
| \; & e_1\ binop\ e_2 \\
| \; & \text{if } e_1 \text{ then } e_2 \text{ else } e_3 \\
| \; & \text{let } x : \tau = e_1 \text{ in } e_2 \\
| \; & \text{letfun } f(\overline{x_i : \rho_i}) : \sigma = e_1 \text{ in } e_2 \\
| \; & \text{letref } x : \text{ref } \tau = e_1 \text{ in } e_2 \\
| \; & f\ e_1 \dots e_n \\
| \; & !x \\
| \; & x := e \\
| \; & \text{return } e \\
| \; & (x : \tau) \leftarrow c \ ; \ c & \text{(bind)} \\
| \; & c \ ; \ c & \text{(sequence)} \\
| \; & \text{take} \\
| \; & \text{emit } e \\
| \; & \text{repeat } c \\
| \; & c_1 \ggg c_2 & \text{(par)}
\end{aligned}
$$

**Fig. 3.** The expression core language.

The intuition behind the function $\mathscr{F}$ is that it will insert the necessary bindings around an elaborated term to ensure that dereferenced values are properly bound. For example, if we have a surface language term $x + y$ where $x$ and $y$ are references of type ref int, it will be elaborated to a term $x' + y'$, where $x'$ and $y'$ are fresh variables, along with a value context:

$$\lambda e.(x' : \text{int}) \leftarrow !x \ ; (y' : \text{int}) \leftarrow !y \ ; e$$

The value context will continue to accumulate bindings until it is applied. Figure 4 shows a fragment of the elaboration rules; we do not include the full set of rules due to space constraints. Note that in rule V-If, the subterms are all elaborated with empty value contexts, i.e., the identity function, and the resulting value contexts are applied immediately to the subterms. This ensures, for example, that dereferences required for the then branch are performed only within the then branch. The $\mathbf{binop}_{\tau_1, \tau_2}$ meta-function maps a surface language binary operator $binop$ whose arguments have types $\tau_1$ and $\tau_2$ to the type of the operator's result; this allows us to, for example, overload $+$ at multiple numeric types.

$$\boxed{\mathscr{F}; \Gamma \vdash^{val} e : \tau \rightsquigarrow \mathscr{F}'; e'}$$

$$\frac{\Gamma \vdash v : \mathsf{ref}\ \tau \qquad v'\ \mathrm{fresh}}{\mathscr{F}; \Gamma \vdash^{val} v : \tau \rightsquigarrow \mathscr{F} \circ \lambda e. \boxed{(v' : \tau) \leftarrow !v\ ;\ e}\ ; v'} \quad \text{(V-VAR)}$$

$$\frac{\mathscr{F}; \Gamma \vdash^{val} e_1 : \tau_1 \rightsquigarrow \mathscr{F}'; e_1' \qquad \mathscr{F}'; \Gamma \vdash^{val} e_2 : \tau_2 \rightsquigarrow \mathscr{F}''; e_2' \qquad \mathbf{binop}_{\tau_1, \tau_2}(binop)\ \mathrm{defined}}{\mathscr{F}; \Gamma \vdash^{val} e_1\ binop\ e_2 : \mathbf{binop}_{\tau_1, \tau_2}(binop) \rightsquigarrow \mathscr{F}''; e_1'\ [\![binop]\!]\ e_2'} \quad \text{(V-BINOP)}$$

$$\frac{\mathsf{id}; \Gamma \vdash^{val} e_1 : \mathsf{bool} \rightsquigarrow \mathscr{F}_1; e_1' \qquad \mathsf{id}; \Gamma \vdash^{val} e_2 : \tau \rightsquigarrow \mathscr{F}_2; e_2' \qquad \mathsf{id}; \Gamma \vdash^{val} e_3 : \tau \rightsquigarrow \mathscr{F}_3; e_3'}{\mathscr{F}; \Gamma \vdash^{val} \mathsf{if}\ e_1\ \mathsf{then}\ e_2\ \mathsf{else}\ e_3 : \tau \rightsquigarrow \mathscr{F}; \mathscr{F}_1\ (\mathsf{if}\ e_1'\ \mathsf{then}\ (\mathscr{F}_2 e_2')\ \mathsf{else}\ (\mathscr{F}_3 e_3'))} \quad \text{(V-IF)}$$

**Fig. 4.** Value elaboration relation for Ziria.

The process of maintaining a value context and elaborating to a pure, monadic language allows us to provide an impure surface language to the user, who does not have to worry about manually sequencing dereferencing, while reaping the benefits of a pure, monadic core language within the compiler.

## 5  Compilation Model

Stewart et al. [11] describe a `tick-proc` compilation model for compiling Ziria terms to C. In this model, each Ziria computation compiles to two blocks of code: a `tick` block that determines whether the computation needs to consume from the data stream to proceed, in which case it jumps to the upstream computation, or if it has data to emit, in which case it jumps to the downstream component. If the computation can proceed without IO, the `proc` block of code is executed. This compilation model results in overhead for every sequenced computation, since each sequenced computation requires both a `tick` and a `proc` block even if the computation itself does not perform IO.

Our compilation model is based on the observation that the only time one computation needs to "jump" to another computation is inside a *par* construct, $c_1 \gg c_2$, when $c_2$ is executing and needs to read from upstream, or when $c_1$ is executing and needs to write downstream. Conceptually, we track the current continuation of both $c_1$ and $c_2$. When we are executing $c_2$ and encounter a **take**, we save the current continuation and jump to $c_1$'s saved continuation. When we then encounter an **emit** in $c_1$, we save its current continuation, save a pointer to the emitted value, and jump to $c_2$'s current continuation with the pointer as an argument. This gives rise to a coroutine-style execution model.

Since our compiler is a whole-program compiler, we can map this execution model to C code by using either GCC-style first-class labels, which are available in clang, gcc, and Intel's icc, or we can use a single switch statement to trampoline between continuations. Like the original Ziria compiler, for single-threaded Ziria code we completely avoid queues by storing a pointer to emitted values instead of queueing the values. Unlike the original Ziria compiler, we can also avoid copying emitted values in most cases using a data flow analysis that makes use of the fact that dereferences are explicit in our core language [8]. Our new compilation model imposes zero overhead for sequencing computation that do not perform IO.

# 6   Evaluation

The type system described in Sect. 3, elaboration to the core language described in Sect. 4, and compilation model described in Sect. 5 are all implemented in the kzc compiler. The existing Ziria WiFi implementation can be compiled with kzc, which also passes the extensive Ziria test suite. In this section we provide a performance evaluation to demonstrate that kzc works and that the new implementation strategies it uses do not impose additional overhead—in fact, kzc produces better code than the existing Ziria compiler, wplc. The performance results we provide are fully described by Mainland [8]; we do not claim the demonstrated performance improvements as contributions in this paper. All data was collected on an i7–4770 CPU running at 3.40 GHz under Ubuntu 16.04, generated C code was compiled with GCC 5.4[3], all runs were repeated 100 times, and we assume a normal distribution. All Ziria programs evaluated in this section are taken from the publicly available Ziria release [12].

The transmitter and receiver performance of kzc and wplc are shown in Figs. 5a and b. The ratios of the data rates of the two implementations are given in Fig. 6a. Code compiled by kzc is always as fast as code compiled by wplc, and in most cases it is at least 10% faster. The relative performance of individual pipeline blocks is broken out in Fig. 6b. We use the same runtime primitives as wplc, so the performance differences between the two implementations can be attributed directly to the differences in their compilation models. Our original expectation was that there was limited room for improvement in the transmitter and receiver pipelines because they use primitive blocks like FFT, IFFT, and

---

[3] -march=native -mtune=native -Ofast.

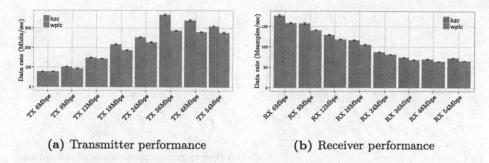

(a) Transmitter performance          (b) Receiver performance

**Fig. 5. Transmitter and receiver data rates.** The receiver consumes a quadrature signal consisting of pairs of 16-bit numbers representing IQ samples. The transmitter consumes bits. Error bars show one standard deviation above and below the mean.

Viterbi, which tend to be the bottlenecks. However, we are pleased that we were nonetheless able to gain a 10% performance increase over an already highly-optimizing compiler.

# 7   Related Work

## 7.1   SDR

Our work is directly based on the original Ziria compiler [11]. Although we do not reuse any code from the Ziria compiler, we evaluate our implementation using Ziria's WiFi implementation, including its standard library routines, written in C, such as FFT, IFFT, and Viterbi.

Most SDR platforms are based on FPGAs [9,10]. Platforms supporting development of SDR applications on commodity CPUs have become more common [3,14], in particular due to the availability of the GNU Radio [4] environment. There are numerous approaches to programming SDR applications; however, these platforms do not provide the combination of performance and powerful abstractions needed for SDR, instead relying on graph-based models of signal processing.

Mainland [8] describes a number of source-to-source transformations on the core language from Sect. 4 and additional optimizations that are responsible for much of the performance increase over wplc shown in Sect. 6.

## 7.2   Capturing Effects in Types

If we were to re-cast Ziria as an embedded DSL, especially if we were to embed it in Haskell, extensible effects [7] would be an obvious path to differentiating between pure terms, terms that manipulate memory references, and terms that perform IO. However, utilizing extensible effects in our setting would require a substantially more general—and more complicated—type system. The type system we present in Sect. 3 has just enough features to support our

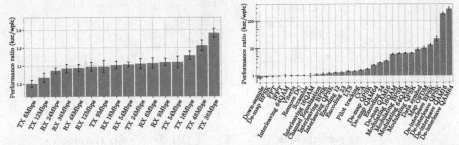

**(a)** Performance improvement of transmitter/receiver pipelines at different 802.11 data rates

**(b)** Performance improvement of individual blocks

**Fig. 6. Performance improvement ratios.** These figures show the relative improvement of kzc over wplc both for entire transmitter/receiver pipelines and for individual blocks. The vertical axis gives the ratio of the throughput of the kzc-compiled version to the throughput of the wplc-compiled version. Error bars show the bound of the ratio when the two metrics being compared range from one standard deviation below the mean to one standard deviation above the mean. Note that Fig. 6a uses a linear scale, whereas Fig. 6b uses a log scale.

requirements, and we have not previously seen the technique of constraining two type indices to be equal in order to distinguish between a term that consumes a value, but is polymorphic in its input, and a term that is polymorphic in its input because it doesn't consume anything at all.

It is not clear how to type Ziria's *par* combinator ($\gg$) in an EDSL setting. We see this as an argument for a non-embedded DSL. Choosing a stand-alone DSL also allows us to provide syntax that is more familiar to Ziria's likely customers, imperative programmers, and provide an impure surface language.

### 7.3   Elaboration to a Pure Language

Our technique for elaborating the impure surface language into a pure, monadic core language is reminiscent of the technique described by Swamy et al. [13] for adding monadic programming to ML. Our elaboration is constrained to a single monad (ST) and, again, provides just enough type system support for the feature we desire. Implementing a more general, extensible system of elaboration would require a significantly more complicated type system and compiler.

## 8   Conclusions and Future Work

We have presented a type system and elaboration procedure for mapping the high-level, impure language Ziria to a pure, monadic core language where terms' effects are distinguished by their type rather than syntactically. We have also described an improved compilation model for Ziria that avoids unnecessary control flow and imposes zero additional overhead for sequencing computations that do not perform IO. All work we describe is implemented in the kzc compiler, and benchmarks show our implementation improves upon the existing Ziria system.

Although a more complicated type system could perhaps capture our elaboration procedure and technique for tracking effects in types, we believe we have hit a domain-specific sweet-spot—a more general type system would require a more complex implementation. Far from being limited to the software-defined radio domain, our techniques apply to general producer-consumer computations where combinators like take and emit are provided as language built-ins. Providing these built-in communication primitives allows kzc to use our efficient compilation method—the compiler is able to know when communication between components is occurring and can optimize this communication across components.

## 8.1  Future Work

Our immediate goal is to eliminate the **seq**/**do** distinction in the surface language via a new Ziria dialect, thereby providing a more natural surface language for SDR programmers. In order to provide backwards-compatibility, this will likely require adding a simple module system to allow for code written in both Ziria dialects to coexist in the same program. We will not abandon whole-program compilation, as this is vital for cross-component optimizations such as fusion [8].

Longer term, we plan to target the FPGA hardware in common SDR platforms directly by generating HDL, such as VHDL or Verilog, directly from Ziria and gradually moving portions of the 802.11 pipeline into hardware. We are also actively working on implementing blocks like FFT, IFFT, and Viterbi directly in Ziria, with promising results. Eventually, we hope to re-implement SOFDM [5] in Ziria and use that experience to make Ziria a viable language for hardware development. We also plan to broaden the applicability Ziria, including applications such as wireless MAC protocols and video codecs. Finally, we plan to fully formalize our algorithmic inference algorithm.

## References

1. IEEE Std 802.11[TM]–2012, pp. 1–2793, March 2012
2. bladeRF Software Defined Radio, September 2016. https://www.nuand.com/
3. USRP Software Defined Radio (SDR) online catalog, September 2016. https://www.ettus.com/product
4. Blossom, E.: GNU radio: tools for exploring the radio frequency spectrum. Linux J. **2004**(122), 4 (2004)
5. Chacko, J., Sahin, C., Nguyen, D., Pfeil, D., Kandasamy, N., Dandekar, K.: FPGA-based latency-insensitive OFDM pipeline for wireless research. In: Proceedings of the 2014 IEEE Conference on High Performance Extreme Computing Conference (HPEC 2014), Waltham, MA, pp. 1–6, September 2014

6. Hughes, J.: Generalising monads to arrows. Sci. Comput. Program. **37**(1–3), 67–111 (2000)
7. Kiselyov, O., Sabry, A., Swords, C.: Extensible effects: an alternative to monad transformers. In: Proceedings of the 2013 ACM SIGPLAN Symposium on Haskell (Haskell 2013), Boston, MA, pp. 59–70, September 2013
8. Mainland, G.: Better living through operational semantics: an optimizing compiler for radio protocols (2016, in submission)
9. Murphy, P., Sabharwal, A., Aazhang, B.: Design of WARP: a flexible wireless open-access research platform. In: Proceedings of the 14th European Signal Processing Conference (EUSIPCO 2006), Florence, Italy, pp. 1–5, September 2006
10. Ng, M.C., Fleming, K.E., Vutukuru, M., Gross, S., Arvind, Balakrishnan, H.: Airblue: a system for cross-layer wireless protocol development. In: Proceedings of the 6th ACM/IEEE Symposium on Architectures for Networking and Communications Systems (ANCS 2010), La Jolla, CA, pp. 4:1–4:11 (2010)
11. Stewart, G., Gowda, M., Mainland, G., Radunovic, B., Vytiniotis, D., Agulló, C.L.: Ziria: an optimizing compiler for wireless PHY programming. In: Proceedings of the 20th International Conference on Architectural Support for Programming Languages and Operating Systems (ASPLOS 2015), Istanbul, Turkey, March 2015
12. Stewart, G., Vytiniotis, D., Mainland, G., Radunovic, B., de Vries, E.: Ziria, version 85cc34db, April 2016. https://github.com/dimitriv/Ziria
13. Swamy, N., Guts, N., Leijen, D., Hicks, M.: Lightweight monadic programming in ML. In: Proceeding of the 16th ACM SIGPLAN International Conference on Functional Programming (ICFP 2011), Tokyo, Japan, pp. 15–27, September 2011
14. Tan, K., Zhang, J., Fang, J., Liu, H., Ye, Y., Wang, S., Zhang, Y., Wu, H., Wang, W., Voelker, G.M.: Sora: high performance software radio using general purpose multi-core processors. In: Proceedings of the 6th USENIX Symposium on Networked Systems Design and Implementation (NSDI 2009), Boston, MA, pp. 75–90, April 2009

# A Declarative DSL for Customizing ASCII Art

Felix S. Klock II[(✉)]

Mozilla Research, San Francisco, USA
pnkfelix@mozilla.com

**Abstract.** When writing source comments or blog posts, developers often choose to express diagrams as ASCII art, accepting the drawback that it is ugly. mon-artist is a software library, inspired by a2s, that converts blocks of text-based art into SVG elements far more pleasing to the eye than the original text. mon-artist allows custom SVG generation by revising the rules used for detecting and rendering graphical "paths" within the text, and uses a declarative DSL to encode its rendering rules.

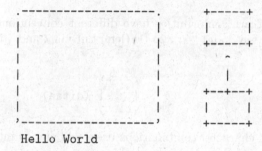

Hello World

## 1 Introduction

When authoring technical diagrams in source comments or blog posts, developers must choose between using some external tool or staying within their text editor. External tools, such as a vector graphics application, a picture description language, or scanning in a drawing, are inconvenient and remove one from the task at hand. However, text-based art usually implies an ugly rendering for the end audience.

mon-artist is a software library that will convert blocks of text-based art into scalable vector graphics (SVG) elements that are often far more pleasing to the eye than the original lines of text. Our handling of ASCII art is inspired by a2s [1], but our support for customized connective rules is novel.

### 1.1 Goals

We want to translate ASCII art into embeddable SVG.

Y. Lierler and W. Taha (Eds.): PADL 2017, LNCS 10137, pp. 189–197, 2017.
DOI: 10.1007/978-3-319-51676-9_13

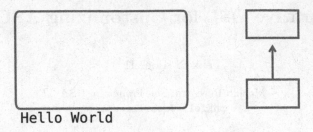

```
Hello World
```

**Fig. 1.** Example ASCII art and rendered SVG

**Correspondence.** The output should not wildly deviate from the input. Consider the input from page 1, which yields Fig. 1: two equivalently sized rectangles on the right-hand side, with their top and bottom edges coincident with the top and bottom edges of the rectangle on the left. Also: the left rectangle has rounded corners, "Hello World" lies beneath it, and an arrow points up between the right rectangles.

**Customizable Rules.** Different art communities have different conventions. E.g. rounded corners are encoded via . and ' in a2s [1] (left) but via / and \ in ditaa [2] (right):

```
.----.                          /----\
|    | (a2s)                     |    | (ditaa)
'----'                          \----/
```

Also, one cannot predict what character combinations users will embed into their diagrams, especially when supporting Unicode combinations.

Rather than hard code all rendering logic into the tool, we allow the end user to add or override rules. In addition, the rendering rules dictate how to *find* objects in the diagram. If characters are not found to be part of some path via the rules, they are instead rendered as text.

**Compositional Rules.** It should be easy to anticipate how the rendering process is affected by adding rules. Most rules are *compositional*: each dictates how a single cell in the grid is rendered (more precisely, how the portion of a path flowing through that cell is rendered).

**Expose Underlying SVG.** Some SVG attributes can be inferred from the art itself (e.g. whether a stroke should be solid or dashed), but many attributes have no natural ASCII art representation. Therefore, the syntax provides a way to inject attributes directly via markup in the text.

**Not Arbitrary Artwork.** We cannot ensure ideal rendering of arbitrary ASCII art. We assume authors are willing to tailor their diagrams, and in some cases, the rendering rules.

## 2    Review of SVG

This paper uses a small subset of the functionality provided by SVG. An SVG document is XML made up of a sequence of either <path> or <text> elements.

A <path> can carry stroke, fill, and d attributes; stroke says how to draw the path, and fill indicates how to fill the space it encloses.

The d attribute describes the path's shape, encoded in a compact command language describing a pen moving across a plane. The M command starts a new subpath and *moves* the pen's position to the argument coordinate, without drawing. Commands like L, A, Q, and C draw lines, arcs, quadratic bezier and cubic bezier curves from the current position to some new position. The Z command closes the current subpath, drawing a line directly to the first coordinate in the subpath.

Uppercase letters indicate that the coordinates are to be interpreted as an *absolute* (relative to some global origin), while lowercase letters indicate that the argument coordinates are interpreted as *relative* to the current pen position.

## 3    Rules Encoded via Oriented Tuples

Each rule dictates how to render a character it matches, in the context of the immediately neighboring characters on the current path.

Each ASCII art diagram is a grid formed by lines of characters. Each element of the grid has eight immediate neighbors, referenced via compass based notation by combining N(orth), S(outh), E(ast) and W(est).

A path is a sequence of cells, where each cell is an immediate neighbor of its predecessor according to the compass coordinates.

Paths are discovered by attempting to match the rendering rules against neighboring cells in the ASCII art grid. The rules are kept in a list, where earlier rules take precedence.

A rule matches a fragment by matching the current character as well as matching the immediate neighbors on the path. Each rule takes the form ⟨*match*⟩ draw ⟨*rendering*⟩, first saying what pair or triple of characters the rule matches, and then how to render the central matched character.

The core model provides four kinds of ⟨*match*⟩ forms:

| | | | | |
|------|------|------|------|------|
| loop | ⟨*prevchar*⟩ | ⟨*dir*⟩ | ⟨*currchar*⟩ | ⟨*dir*⟩ | ⟨*nextchar*⟩ |
| step | ⟨*prevchar*⟩ | ⟨*dir*⟩ | ⟨*currchar*⟩ | ⟨*dir*⟩ | ⟨*nextchar*⟩ |
| start | | | ⟨*currchar*⟩ | ⟨*dir*⟩ | ⟨*nextchar*⟩ |
| end | ⟨*prevchar*⟩ | ⟨*dir*⟩ | ⟨*currchar*⟩ | | |

You can read the match pattern specified in each rule as a triple (or pair) of sets of characters, joined by the directions that link them.

Each of ⟨*prevchar*⟩, ⟨*currchar*⟩, ⟨*nextchar*⟩, is a character or set of characters, or `ANY` as the set of all non-whitespace unicode characters. A ⟨*dir*⟩ is a non-empty set of compass directions; `ANY` is the full set of eight directions.

All SVG paths have to start somewhere. We distinguish between *closed* paths, which always end at the same position as they start, and *open* paths, which can have distinct start and end points.

All closed paths are initially matched via `loop`. For example, the matcher `loop '/' NE '+' E '-'` states that a closed path can start at a `+` if there is a `-` east of the `+` and the last character in the path is a `/` southwest of the `+`.

The bulk of any path is made up of characters that neither start nor end the path, which are matched by `step`. For example, `step '-' E '-' E '-'` specifies a path can proceed eastward through three dashes `---` in a row.

All open paths are initially matched by `start`. This has only two characters because the first character in an open path has no predecessor; so ⟨*prevchar*⟩⟨*dir*⟩ is absent. Likewise, the `end` rule, which specifies how to terminate an open path, is missing the ⟨*dir*⟩⟨*nextchar*⟩.

# 4    The Path Search Process

Given a list of rule instances, a backtracking depth-first search finds paths in the character grid, starting from each unused cell.

After finding a path through a sequence of cells, we mark those cells as "used", to avoid wasting time initiating searches from used points. However, used cells *can* be made part of other paths that start from an unused cell. Thus, characters can be reused in distinct paths.

At a high-level, the ASCII art processing, inspired by the source code for `a2s` [1], works as follows: First attempt to match as many closed paths as possible, marking cells from successfully matched paths as "used" during the search. Second, match open paths from the characters that remain on the grid.

A search for an open path may in fact yield a suffix of a longer path. Therefore, after successfully matching an open path via a forward search, we additionally attempt to extend the path backwards; our simple declarative rules are reversible.

After accumulating as many closed and open paths as possible, and removing their characters from the grid, we finally scan the grid row by row and accumulate any remaining characters into `<text>` elements.

# 5    Rendering Templates

After accumulating paths, the next step is to render them into SVG `<path>` elements. This has two parts: how to build the `d` attribute of `<path>`, and how to add other attributes. The ⟨*rendering*⟩ in a rule provides answers for both.

Since one rule can match distinct locations on the grid, we use a template system to substitute coordinates into the rules. A ⟨*rendering*⟩ is a template string, followed by an optional collection of XML key/value attribute pairs.

## 5.1   Template Strings

The template string specifies what text should be injected into the d attribute for the <path> to render the ⟨*currchar*⟩ of the rule, in the context of the neighboring cells specified by the rule.

Curly braces are used to delimit expressions within a template string that are to be evaluated during rendering and replaced with numbers or coordinates.

There are nine "primitive points" one can reference within a template string. One of them {C}, lies at the center of a cell. The other eight lie along edges of the cell, shown on the left side of Fig. 2.

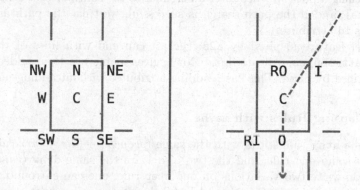

**Fig. 2.** Primitive points

For example, the rule start '-' W="+" draw "M {E} L {W}" says that if you start a path with a dash and then continue westward to join with a dash or plus, then the resulting d attribute for the <path> should start by moving (M) to the middle of the east edge ({E}) of the cell with the first dash, and then draw a line (L) to the middle of the west edge ({W}).

Rules compose with other rules. Therefore rules should end with a pen position consistent with the rules that could follow it.

In addition to the template syntax already listed, one can alternatively specify one of the primitive points along the edge in terms of the previous or next cell, by writing {I}, {O}, {RI}, or {RO}. {I} is the edge from which we came; likewise {O} is the outgoing neighbor. {RI} and {RO} are the *reflections* of those points through the center. For example, if the incoming neighbor is to the northeast of the current cell, then {I} is the same as {NE} and {RI} is the same as {SW} (illustrated in the dashed path on right side of Fig. 2).

## 5.2   Attribute Injection

A template string is intended to handle local rendering of the current character. However, sometimes you want a single character to have a global effect on a path.

A simple example, inspired by a2s, is making a vertical line dashed by putting a: anywhere on the line.

To express this, each ⟨*rendering*⟩ ends with a list of zero or more (key, value)-attributes. When the rendering system encounters a use of such a rule, it adds all such attributes to the path currently being rendered.

## 5.3    Path Identification

The id attribute is used to uniquely identify the path so other content can reference it. We use an a2s-inspired markdown style syntax for encoding id: if while matching a path we encounter a neighbor to the south or east that has the form [name], and if the path search is successful, we treat the path as having name as its id attribute.

Another feature inspired by a2s: the art can end with lines of the form: [name]: attributes. All attributes for a given name are then added to the path identified by name. This eases adding attributes without adding new rules.

## 5.4    Collapsing Rules with maybe

Sometimes a step rule starts with the same ⟨*prevchar*⟩ ⟨*dir*⟩ ⟨*currchar*⟩ components as some end rule, and the two also share the same draw ⟨*rendering*⟩. Rather than write two variations on one step rule, one can surround its ⟨*dir*⟩ ⟨*nextchar*⟩ with the text (maybe and ). All this means is one step using maybe can expand into two rules: a core step and an end.

# 6    Example Rule Set and Rendering

Below is a relatively small self-contained example rule set. It demonstrates some of the functionality, such as the use of template expressions like {O}, {E}, or {RO}. It also shows the use of the ⟨*prevchar*⟩ and ⟨*nextchar*⟩ to constrain the application of rules to certain contexts.

```
# '+' is corner of loop; it joins with lines. Move to center
loop "|-/\\" ANY  '+'  (N,S)        "|"      draw "M {C}"
loop "|-/\\" ANY  '+'  (E,W)        "-"      draw "M {C}"
# '-', '|', and '+' can start if next works. Draw line across.
start         '-'  (E,W)        "-+"     draw "M {RO} L {O}"
start         '|'  (N,S)        "|+"     draw "M {RO} L {O}"
start         '+'  ANY          ANY      draw "M {C}"
# '.'and '`' make rounded corners. Draw curve through center.
step ANY (E,NE,N,NW,W) '.'  (E,SE,S,SW,W) "-|\\/" draw "Q {C} {O}"
step ANY (E,SE,S,SW,W) '\''  (E,NE,N,NW,W) "-|\\/" draw "Q {C} {O}"
# ... for a loop, draw curve from incoming edge to outgoing one.
loop ANY (E,NE,N,NW,W) '.'  (E,SE,S,SW,W) "-|\\/" draw "M {I} Q {C} {O}"
```

```
loop ANY (E,SE,S,SW,W) '\'' (E,NE,N,NW,W) "-|\\/" draw "M {I} Q {C} {O}"
# '-'and '|' connect w/ most things. Draw line to outgoing edge.
step "+-.'" (E, W)       '-' (maybe (E, W)   "-+.'>") draw "L {O}"
step "+|.'" (N, S)       '|' (maybe (N, S)   "|+.'" ) draw "L {O}"
# '+' is a corner; ensure compatible. Just draw line to center
# (the rest of corner is handled by next character, if present).
step "|-/\\>" ANY         '+' (maybe (N,S) "|")     draw "L {C}"
step "|-/\\>" ANY         '+' (maybe (E,W) "-")     draw "L {C}"
step "|-/\\>" ANY         '+'      (NE,SW) "/")     draw "L {C}"
step "|-/\\>" ANY         '+'      (NW,SE) "\\")    draw "L {C}"
# '/', '\' are diagonals. Draw line to outgoing corner.
step ANY (NE, SW) '/' (maybe (NE, SW) "/+.'")    draw "L {O}"
step ANY (NW, SE) '\\' (maybe (NW, SE) "\\+.'")  draw "L {O}"
# Special case arrowhead code (1st does not touch; 2nd + 3rd do)
end  '-' E '>'       draw "L {C} l 3,0 m -3,-3 l 3,3 l -3,3 m 0,-3"
step '-' E '>' E '+' draw "L {E} m -2,0 l 4,0 m -4,-3 \
                    l 4,3 l -4,3 m 0,-3 m 4,0"
step '+' W '>' W '-' draw "M {E} m -2,0 l 4,0 m -4,-3 \
                    l 4,3 l -4,3 m 0,-3 m 4,0 M {E} L {C}"
```

Figures 1 and 2 were both rendered using the tool. Figure 3 shows how the limited rules given above can yield interesting output, based on the following input.

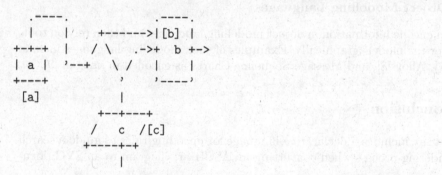

```
[a]: stroke-dasharray="5,3"
[b]: stroke-dasharray="15,2"
[c]: fill="yellow"
```

# 7   Related Work

## 7.1   ASCII Art Rendering

There exist pre-existing software ASCII art renderers. Examples include ditaa [2] and a2s [1]; the design of the latter heavily influenced this work. However,

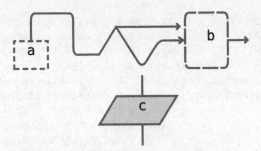

**Fig. 3.** Rendered demo

we are not aware of any such tool that allows the user to customize the rendering process for arbitrary character combinations.

## 7.2   Picture Description Languages

There are many domain specific languages for describing pictures in an abstract manner, such as Metapost [3], Tikz/PGF [4], Graphviz [5], and `mermaid` [6].

None of these attempt to reflect the desired image in the rendering of the source text itself, however.

## 7.3   Object Modelling Languages

One can encode information in object modelling languages and then rely on tools to render the models graphically. Examples of such modelling languages include UML [7], Alloy [8], and Message Sequence Charts as encoded in `mscgen` [9].

## 8   Conclusion

`mon-artist` includes a declarative language for encoding rules to guide a search and rendering process when converting an ASCII art diagram to an SVG document.

The language was originally designed to be user extensible; it remains to be seen whether such extension is actually *usable* in practice.

Nonetheless, I have made heavy use of the tool in my own diagram authoring, and found the ability to modify the rules to accommodate idiosyncracies in a particular diagram (e.g. the use of -> in type signatures, which needed to remain text, not a path) was useful.

# References

1. O'Dell, D.H.: ASCIIToSVG: an ASCII art diagram to SVG converter. https://9vx. org/dho/a2s/index.html
2. Sideris, S.: DITAA, DIagrams Through ASCII Art. http://ditaa.sourceforge.net/
3. Hobby, J.D.: A user's manual for MetaPost. AT&T Bell Laboratories, Murray Hill (1992)
4. Tantau, T.: The TikZ and PGF packages: manual for version 3.0.0. (2015)
5. Gansner, E.R., North, S.C.: An open graph visualization system and its applications to software engineering. Softw. Pract. Exp. **30**, 1203–1233 (2000)
6. Sveidqvist, K.: Mermaid - generation of diagrams and flowcharts from text in a similar manner as markdown. https://knsv.github.io/mermaid/
7. Booch, G., Rumbaugh, J., Jacobson, I.: Unified Modeling Language User Guide. Addison-Wesley Object Technology Series, 2nd edn. Addison-Wesley Professional, Reading (2005)
8. Jackson, D.: Alloy: a lightweight object modelling notation. ACM Trans. Softw. Eng. Methodol. **11**, 256–290 (2002)
9. McTernan, M.: Mscgen. http://www.mcternan.me.uk/mscgen/

# Using Iterative Deepening for Probabilistic Logic Inference

Theofrastos Mantadelis[(⊠)] and Ricardo Rocha

CRACS & INESC TEC, Faculty of Sciences, University of Porto,
Rua do Campo Alegre, 1021, 4169-007 Porto, Portugal
{theo.mantadelis,ricroc}@dcc.fc.up.pt

**Abstract.** We present a novel approach that uses an iterative deepening algorithm in order to perform probabilistic logic inference for ProbLog, a probabilistic extension of Prolog. The most used inference method for ProbLog is exact inference combined with tabling. Tabled exact inference first collects a set of SLG derivations which contain the probabilistic structure of the ProbLog program including the cycles. At a second step, inference requires handling these cycles in order to create a noncyclic Boolean representation of the probabilistic information. Finally, the Boolean representation is compiled to a data structure where inference can be performed in linear time. Previous work has illustrated that there are two limiting factors for ProbLog's exact inference. The first factor is the target compilation language and the second factor is the handling of the cycles. In this paper, we address the second factor by presenting an iterative deepening algorithm which handles cycles and produces solutions to problems that previously ProbLog was not able to solve. Our experimental results show that our iterative deepening approach gets approximate bounded values in almost all cases and in most cases we are able to get the exact result for the same or one lower scaling factor.

**Keywords:** Probabilistic logic programming · Inference engine · Cycle handling · Iterative deepening · ProbLog

## 1 Introduction

ProbLog [8] is a probabilistic framework that extends Prolog with probabilistic facts. ProbLog's most fundamental task is the efficient computation of a query's success probability and, for that, ProbLog employs several inference methods and uses several different state-of-the-art technologies. The most used inference method for ProbLog is *exact inference*. ProbLog is also able to compute conditional probabilities, solve multiple queries and compute the probabilities of answers. State-of-the-art Probabilistic Logic Programming (PLP) systems, such as ProbLog, often use a three step inference mechanism: (i) SLD/SLG logic resolution; (ii) Boolean formula preprocessing; and (iii) knowledge compilation.

© Springer International Publishing AG 2017
Y. Lierler and W. Taha (Eds.): PADL 2017, LNCS 10137, pp. 198–213, 2017.
DOI: 10.1007/978-3-319-51676-9_14

Inference in PLP systems impose several challenges which still have not been fully addressed. Currently, an important limitation is the efficiency of knowledge compilation of highly connected graphs. At the Boolean formula preprocessing step, big cyclic graph based problems are also almost intractable. Motivated by the need of providing a solution for these problems, several approximation methods have been proposed. One of the most prominent and used for ProbLog is *program sampling* [8]. Program sampling is able to compute a result for many queries that would be intractable for exact inference, but program sampling is usually much more time consuming than exact inference when the problem is tractable, making it often an unusable inference method. Initial work in ProbLog [8], proposed an approach based in the $k$-best derivations. This approach works for the calculation of lower bound probabilities with a small $k$. The early stopped derivations which are used to compute the upper bound probability become intractable even for a small $k$. The scaling of $k$-best derivations approach was proven in most cases worst than tabled exact inference, thus making it unusable.

SkILL [4], a Stochastic Inductive Logic Learner which produces First Order Logic theories from probabilistic annotated data, uses MetaProbLog[1] as its inference engine to analyse the probabilistic data. In particular, SkILL uses MetaProbLog's exact inference to compute the success probability of induced theories. When exact inference for a theory is intractable, SkILL then computes the probability of that theory by using MetaProbLog's program sampling inference. Whenever SkILL resolves to program sampling, the time overhead is significant. Motivated by the above observations and SkILL's usage of MetaProbLog, we have identified the need to be able to compute an approximation for intractable queries in speeds comparable to exact inference.

To address the mentioned problems, we propose a new inference method based on *iterative deepening search*. The underlying idea is to perform the Boolean formula preprocessing step in a bounded fashion producing two Boolean formulae: *one more specific* and *one more general* than the exact Boolean formula. Afterwards, we compute the probability of the two bounded formulae as lower and upper bounded probabilities. Finally, after completing an iteration, we can increase the bound and compute the next iteration until we either reach an exact probability, a desirable bound interval, a maximum bound, or time out. Our approach thus incrementally computes the Boolean formula preprocessing step and as a result generates and compiles subformulae that incrementally grow/shrink towards the exact formula creating a lower/upper probability bound, respectively. In this way, we are able to compute good approximations in a very fast way even for the hardest problems.

The main contributions of this paper are:

1. The application of iterative deepening to handle cycles in probabilistic logic programs in order to compute lower and upper bounds.

---

[1] MetaProbLog is an implementation of the ProbLog semantics and can be found at: www.dcc.fc.up.pt/metaproblog. Other implementations are ProbLog1 and ProbLog2 and can be found at: http://dtai.cs.kuleuven.be/problog.

2. The full integration and compatibility of the new algorithm with all existing optimizations and system features in MetaProbLog, such as: variable compaction [12], general (stratified) negation, multiple queries and evidence.
3. An experimental evaluation of iterative deepening using three key datasets against exact inference and program sampling inference. The iterative deepening algorithm clearly over performed the other inference methods in two datasets and equally performed with exact inference at the third dataset.

The rest of the paper is structured as follows. First, we briefly introduce ProbLog and the distribution semantics in Sect. 2.1. We then present AND-OR graphs, which are a fundamental step for our method, in Sect. 2.2. The detailed description of our algorithm is given in Sect. 3. Section 4 contains the experimental evaluation. Finally, future work and conclusions are presented in Sect. 6.

## 2   ProbLog

We start by giving a brief introduction to ProbLog which follows the *distribution semantics* [16], and by defining the success probability of logic programs. Then, we describe the exact inference method and how the collective proofs are represented as AND-OR graphs.

### 2.1   ProbLog and the Distribution Semantics

ProbLog programs use the syntax of Prolog and extend it with probabilistic facts [8]. A ProbLog program $T$ consists of a set of facts annotated with probabilities $p_i :: pf_i$ (called *probabilistic facts*) together with a set of standard definite clauses or definite clauses that also contain positive and/or negative probabilistic facts in their body $h : -b_1, \ldots, b_n$ (called *background knowledge* (BK)). A probabilistic fact $pf_i$ is true with probability $p_i$. These facts correspond to random variables, which are assumed to be mutually independent. We define $L_T = \{p_1 :: pf_1, \ldots, p_n :: pf_n\}$ as the set of all probabilistic facts in a ProbLog program. Formally, a ProbLog program is of the form $T = L_T \cup BK$. Finally, as syntactic sugar, ProbLog implementations allow probabilistic heads to definite clauses.

We define as possible world $L_T = L_{true} \cup L_{false}$ and $L_{true} \cup L_{false} = \emptyset$, where $L_{true}$ and $L_{false}$ are the sets containing all probabilistic facts of the ProbLog program $T$ that are set to true and false, respectively. It is clear that a ProbLog program $T$ has a number of possible worlds exponential to the number of probabilistic facts ($2^N$ where $N$ is the number of probabilistic facts).

The probability of a possible world ($P_{world}$) equals to the product of the probability of all probabilistic facts in $L_{true}$ and 1 - probability of all probabilistic facts in $L_{false}$, i.e.,

$$P_{world} = \prod_{p_i :: pf_i \in L_{true}} p_i \cdot \prod_{p_j :: pf_j \in L_{false}} (1 - p_j),$$

where $L_{true} \cup L_{false} = L_T$ and $L_{true} \cap L_{false} = \emptyset$. The sum of the probabilities of all possible worlds equals to:

$$\sum_{w_i \in Worlds} P_{w_i} = 1.0.$$

The most fundamental task of ProbLog is to calculate the success probability of a query. In ProbLog, inquiring the success probability of a query means asking for the probability that a randomly selected possible world satisfies that query. Such worlds contain the probabilistic facts needed to satisfy the query, but can also contain more probabilistic facts. The success probability $P_s(q|T)$ of a query $q$ is the summation of the probabilities of all possible worlds for which there exists a substitution $\theta$ such that $q\theta$ is entailed by $T$, i.e., $P_s(q|T) = \sum_{w_i \in Worlds} P(q|w_i) \cdot P_{w_i}$, where $P(q|w_i) = 1.0$ if there exists a substitution $\theta$ such that $w_i \cup BK \models q\theta$ and $P(q|w_i) = 0.0$ otherwise. The equation states that we are able to calculate the success probability of a query by summing the probabilities of all worlds that satisfy the query.

The naive approach of enumerating all possible worlds and then summing the ones that satisfy the query quickly becomes computationally intractable. For that reason ProbLog uses different strategies to calculate the success probability of a query. The most used inference method of ProbLog is the exact inference method with general (stratified) negation and tabling support. ProbLog complies to the closed world assumption and for that reason the ProbLog's general negation mechanism is limited to stratified programs [10]. Exact inference is a three step inference approach:

1. **SLG resolution** is used to prove the query and collect the proofs that compactly represent the possible worlds where the query succeeds. For the purpose of this paper, we will use SLG resolution for ProbLog programs as presented in [10].
2. **Boolean formula preprocessing** takes the compact representation of the possible worlds in order to perform cycle handling [10] and optimize it as a Boolean formula [11].
3. **Knowledge compilation** is used to compile the collected Boolean formula to Reduced Ordered Binary Decision Diagrams (ROBDDs) [1], or to smooth decomposable Deterministic Negated Normal Form (sd-DNNF) [7], or to Sentient Decision Diagrams (SDDs) [6].

## 2.2   AND-OR Graphs

We represent the collected proofs as an AND-OR graph. An AND-OR graph is a directed graph composed by AND and OR nodes. An AND node indicates that all child nodes must be true, while an OR node indicates that at least one of the child nodes must be true. The SLG derivations of a query $q$ with respect to a logic program can be represented as an AND-OR graph. To solve a query $q$, the different clauses $(c_{i \in 1..m} : -l_{i,1}, ..., l_{i,n}.)$ of the predicate $q$ are processed as follows. For each different clause $c_i$ all literals $l_{i,j}$ in the body are grouped as children of an AND node. The different AND nodes are then grouped as children of an OR node labeled with $q$.

An AND-OR graph of a query has the following characteristics: (i) cycles that appear in the logic program also appear in the AND-OR graph; (ii) for each subgoal $g$ there is only one OR node; (iii) an OR-node has multiple parents if the subgoal is repeated and goals proven as facts are represented by special OR nodes without children, called terminal nodes; and (iv) the edge from a child node to a parent node states that the parent depends on the child node.

Formally, an AND-OR graph for a query $q$ is a directed graph $G = (V_{and}, V_{or}, V_{term}, E)$ with $V_{and}$ a set of AND nodes, $V_{or}$ a set of labeled OR nodes, $V_{term} \subset V_{or}$ a set of terminal nodes, $V_{nonterm} = V_{or} \backslash V_{term}$ and $E \subseteq R$ a set of directed edges, where $R = (V_{and} \times V_{or}) \cup (V_{nonterm} \times V_{and}) \cup (V_{nonterm} \times V_{or})$ and the OR node with label $q$ as root.

In order to compile the collected proofs, ProbLog must first process the AND-OR graph and produce a Boolean formula that does not contain cyclic references but, often, converting a cyclic AND-OR graph to a non cyclic one is a hard task [10]. Furthermore, compiling an AND-OR graph to any of the knowledge compilation approaches has complexity exponential to the tree width of the AND-OR graph [7]. In this paper, we propose a new method to iteratively compute the Boolean formula to two Boolean formulae, one *more specific* and one *more general*. In that way, we are able to compute lower and upper bounds with lower complexity than computing the exact probability.

Figure 1 presents the probabilistic graph for the following ProbLog program, which will be used as our running example.

```
0.5::e(a,b).     0.4::e(a,c).     0.6::e(a,f).
0.2::e(b,a).     0.8::e(b,c).     0.7::e(b,f).
0.9::e(c,a).     0.1::e(c,b).     0.3::e(c,f).


p(X, Y) :- e(X, Y).
p(X, Y) :- e(X, Z), Z \= Y, p(Z, Y).
```

In order to prove the query $p(a, f)$, SLG resolution collects the AND-OR graph presented in Fig. 2. The query defines the entry point of the AND-OR graph which we annotate by shading the node gray. With rhombus we annotate the AND nodes; with ellipses we annotate the OR nodes (notice that all OR nodes are labeled with a logical goal); and with rectangles we annotate the leaf nodes which are the probabilistic facts. The AND-OR graph represents not only the relevant information used to proven the query by SLG resolution but also any cycle found in the proving. For example, observe that the OR nodes $\{p(a, f); p(b, f); p(c, f)\}$ all have paths (by following the directed edges) through AND nodes that would return to the initial OR node, thus creating the cycles.

When computing the exact probability of query $q$, one requires to handle the cycles that are introduced in the AND-OR graph. ProbLog uses the algorithm presented at [10], which treats positive cycles [3] as failures. The algorithm is implicitly transforming the AND-OR graph to a larger one (in the worst case

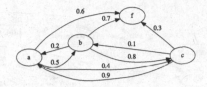

**Fig. 1.** An example probabilistic graph.

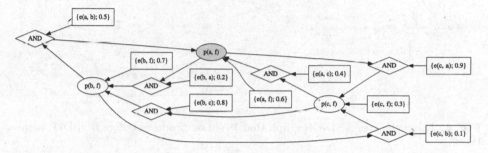

**Fig. 2.** The AND-OR graph collected by SLG resolution for query $p(a, f)$ for the probabilistic graph of Fig. 1.

exponentially larger) Figure 3 presents the transformed graph where the cycles have been fully handled; we annotate the detected cycles with double octagons. The reader can notice that some nodes, such as $\{p(b, f); p(c, f)\}$, appear in different paths and that others, such as $\{p(a, f) = cycle, p(b, f) = cycle\}$, are characterized as cycles when they appear twice in the same path. The cycle handling algorithm, uses a set of logical rules and memoization that permits the re-usage of computations. This re-usage allows a significant reduction of the work and size of the expansion. Still, the cycle handling remains an exponentially hard task and often generates a very large AND-OR graph where the knowledge compilation step often fails.

## 3   Iterative Deepening Cycle Handling

The proposed approach does not modify at all the first step (SLG resolution); it introduces a new cycle handling algorithm at the second step (Boolean formula preprocessing) which is fully compatible with all existing optimizations; and it modifies the third step by calling it multiple times in order to compute the probabilities of different bounds.

The underlying idea of our approach is similar to the iterative deepening depth first search (DFS) algorithm but, instead of searching for a specific node, we are interested in traversing the whole graph structure (or as much of it as possible) and transform it to a cyclic free graph.

Algorithm 1 presents the generalized AND-OR graph to ROBDD definitions approach with iterative deepening modifications, which includes the relevant parts of the original cycle handling algorithm together with the extensions

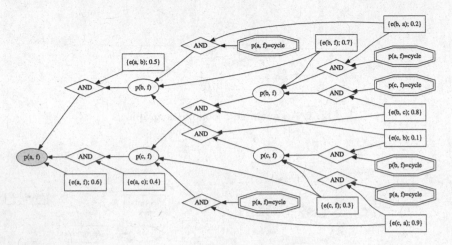

**Fig. 3.** The cyclic free AND-OR graph that ProbLog produces before ROBDD compilation.

required to implement an iterative deepening strategy. Optimizations and the handling for general negation has been omitted for simplification. The extensions are noted as underlined text. Our inference method calls Algorithm 1 for a user-defined number of iterations and, at each iteration, the bound is increased by a user-defined step.

Algorithm 1 recursively traverses the AND-OR graph structure calling at each recursion level the auxiliary procedure PREPROCESSING_METHOD() (line 2 in Algorithm 1), which is responsible of handling an AND-OR graph that contains a single OR node. ProbLog supports several different preprocessing methods. In this work, we used the Recursive Node Merging preprocessing method [11]. The preprocessing procedure is responsible for writing the AND-OR graph as a depth breadth trie. MetaProbLog uses depth breadth tries in order to perform optimizations on the writing of Boolean formulae. For the purposes of this paper, the reader can assume that a depth breadth trie is a simple representation of the Boolean formula. For more details on the preprocessing methods we direct the reader to [11]. We note that these optimizations are independent from this work but our implementation is fully compatible and fully supports them.

Whenever an AND-OR subgraph $T_{nested}$ is found, the algorithm needs to choose the appropriate of four different conditions. First, the algorithm verifies if $T_{nested}$ introduces a positive cycle [3] and handles it as a failure [10] (lines 5–6 in Algorithm 1). The second condition occurs when the $T_{nested}$ has been processed earlier and the results can be reused (lines 7–10 in Algorithm 1). If neither the first nor second condition apply, the algorithm checks whether $T_{nested}$ was encountered within the introduced bound of the iteration. If $T_{nested}$ is within the bound (lines 11–15 in Algorithm 1), then the algorithm will recursively try to compute the newly found reference. Otherwise, if it is out of the bound

---

**Algorithm 1.** The generalized AND-OR graph to ROBDD definitions approach with iterative deepening

---

**input** The AND-OR graph $T$, the depth breadth trie $DBT$ where the generated ROBDD definitions are stored, the ancestor AND-OR graphs $A_T$ of the AND-OR graph $T$, the reference $L_{begin}$ to the next free ROBDD definition, the current depth ($Depth$) in the AND-OR graph, the available bound ($Bound$) of this iteration and a Boolean starting value for $Assumed$.

**output** Updates $DBT$ to contain the ROBDD definitions generated for $T$ and returns the representative reference $L_{end}$ and the Boolean variable $\underline{Assumed}$ that indicates whether an assumption was taken.

**call as** $(L_{end}, \underline{Assumed}) := \text{PROCESS}_{AND-OR}(T, DBT, \emptyset, L_{begin}, 1, \underline{Bound}, \underline{false})$.

---

1: **function** $\text{PROCESS}_{AND-OR}(T, DBT, A_T, L_{begin}, \underline{Depth}, \underline{Bound}, \underline{Assumed})$
2:    $(L_{end}, T_{nested}) := \text{PREPROCESSING\_METHOD}(T, \underline{DBT}, L_{begin})$
3:    **if** $T_{nested} \neq$ **null then** {$T$ contains a sub AND-OR graph $T_{nested}$}
4:       $A_{T_{nested}} := A_T \cup \{T\}$
5:       **if** $T_{nested} \in A_{T_{nested}}$ **then** {$T_{nested}$ introduces a cycle}
6:          Replace the occurrence of $T_{nested}$ in AND-OR graph $T$ with **false**.
7:       **else if** $\text{IS\_MEMOIZED}(T_{nested}, A_{T_{nested}}, \underline{Bound - Depth})$ **then**
8:          $(L_{T_{nested}}, \underline{Assumed_{T_{nested}}}) := \text{GET\_MEMOIZED\_RESULT}(T_{nested}, A_{T_{nested}}, \underline{Bound - Depth})$
9:          Replace the occurrence of $T_{nested}$ in AND-OR graph $T$ with $L_{T_{nested}}$.
10:          $\underline{Assumed := Assumed \cup Assumed_{T_{nested}}}$
11:       **else if** $\underline{Depth < Bound}$ **then** {$T_{nested}$ is not a cycle, neither is memoized and current depth is still in bound}
12:          $(L_{T_{nested}}, \underline{Assumed_{T_{nested}}}) := \text{PROCESS}_{AND-OR}(T_{nested}, DBT, A_{T_{nested}}, L_{end}+1, \underline{Depth+1}, \underline{Bound}, \underline{Assumed})$
13:          Replace the occurrence of $T_{nested}$ in AND-OR graph $T$ with $L_{T_{nested}}$.
14:          $L_{end} := L_{T_{nested}}$
15:          $\underline{Assumed := Assumed \cup Assumed_{T_{nested}}}$
16:       **else** {Current depth is out of bound}
17:          Assume $L_{T_{nested}}$ is false for lower inference and true of upper inference
18:          Replace the occurrence of $T_{nested}$ in AND-OR graph $T$ with $L_{T_{nested}}$.
19:          $\underline{L_{end} := L_{T_{nested}}}$
20:          $\underline{Assumed := true}$
21:       **return** $\text{PROCESS}_{AND-OR}(T, DBT, A_T, L_{end}+1, \underline{Depth+1}, \underline{Bound}, \underline{Assumed})$
22:    **else** {$T$ is fully processed}
23:       $\text{MEMOIZE}(T, A_T, \underline{Bound - Depth}, L_{end}, \underline{Assumed})$
24:       **return** $(L_{end}, \underline{Assumed})$

---

(lines 16–20 in Algorithm 1), then the algorithm will assume either false or true depending on whether it is a lower or upper iteration. After replacing the AND-OR subgraph, the algorithm continues recursively by increasing by one the used depth (line 21 in Algorithm 1). Finally, when an AND-OR graph is fully processed (contains a single node), the result is memoized for reuse and the result is returned (lines 22–24 in Algorithm 1).

For cyclic handling, we use a memoization technique that compares the subsets of the ancestors of AND-OR graphs [10]. This technique allows us to discover cycles and to widen our re-usage compared with the normal DFS strategy. When the algorithm memorizes a computed AND-OR graph, it keeps track of the ancestors in list $A_T$ (called the *ancestor list*) of the AND-OR graph in order to identify the possibly introduced cycles. With iterative deepening, the algorithm also requires to memoize the number of recursions remaining $(Bound - Depth)$ and whether an assumption was taken $(Assumed)$ for computing the AND-OR graph (line 23 in Algorithm 1). When the algorithm checks whether a memoized result can be reused, in addition of checking the ancestor list, it also needs to check whether the number of used recursions of the stored AND-OR graph is equal or greater than the currently remaining recursions. In case the memorized recursions are less than the currently remaining recursions, it means that the memorized AND-OR graph reference contains less probabilistic information than what the current iteration is able to compute and thus the memorized result is not reused. This way we can allow iterations with different bounds to use previously computed results.

For example, assume that the AND-OR graph $t(1)$ with the ancestor list $A_{t(1)}$ at the lower iteration with $Bound = 5$ in the recursion with $Depth = 3$ has been computed as the ROBBD definition $L_{t(1)}$ with no assumptions. The algorithm then memoizes the term: $and-or\_graph(t(1), A_{t(1)}, 2, L_{t(1)}, false)$ and can reuse this computations of $t(1)$ in any lower iteration with ancestor list $A_{t(1)}^{new}$ as long $Bound - Depth \leq 2$ and $A_{t(1)} \subseteq A_{t(1)}^{new}$.

When the current depth equals the bound of the current iteration, any occurrence of a sub graph is assumed to be *false* for lower bounded iterations and *true* for upper bounded iterations. In this way, we lose probabilistic information but we ensure that the probability will be a lower/upper bound of the exact probability. This simple strategy gives us lower and upper bounds for AND-OR graphs that do not contain general negation. By memorizing and returning for each AND-OR subgraph whether an assumption was taken to compute the result, we know if the stored result of the AND-OR graph is the equivalent of the exact result for that AND-OR graph. This allows us to detect when we computed an iteration that provides an equivalent to exact Boolean formulae regardless the actual probability results.

Returning to our example, we illustrate how the AND-OR graph of Fig. 1 would appear for the first two iterations of our iterative deepening algorithm. The first iteration would produce the AND-OR graph presented in Fig. 4 and the second iteration would produce the AND-OR graph presented in Fig. 5. For this specific example, on the third iteration, the computed AND-OR graph would be identical with the AND-OR graph computed by the exact method, which is presented in Fig. 3. With octagons we annotated the nodes that the iterative deepening approach assumed true or false.

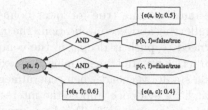

**Fig. 4.** AND-OR graph after one iteration of the iterative deepening algorithm.

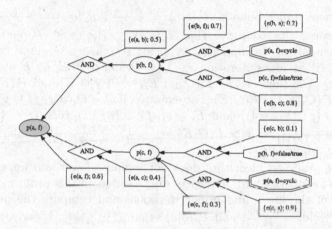

**Fig. 5.** AND-OR graph after two iterations of the iterative deepening algorithm.

After each iteration of the iterative deepening algorithm, ProbLog compiles the computed Boolean formulae using a knowledge compilation approach in order to efficiently compute the probability. For our implementation and description, we used ROBDDs.

Finally, this algorithm is executed iteratively with the user being able to choose: (i) the starting bound; (ii) the step; and (iii) several ending conditions, such as, specific bound, lower to upper probability difference being less than a value, or reach a time limit. The algorithm also automatically terminates if it detects the computation of the exact probability.

Implementation-wise, we have introduced three different inference methods that the user can use, namely: *lower iterative*; *upper iterative*; and *bounded iterative* (the combination of the two). These new methods are compatible with all features and optimization techniques that exact inference uses.

## 3.1 General Negation and Conditional Probability

ProbLog programs with general negation impose a complication to the iterative algorithm assumption taking. Whenever the algorithm takes an assumption, the number of enclosing negations of the assumed subgraph define whether the assumption should be false or true. If the enclosed graph is an odd number of times enclosed then we must assume true for lower bound and false for upper bound. In order to handle the above complication, the moment we encounter a general negation, we need to push it deeper in the computation by using De Morgan's laws, i.e., in practice we are transforming the next AND-OR subgraph. This mechanism causes a small overhead when general negation is encountered.

ProbLog queries that have evidence impose the interesting theoretical question whether the results are bounded. In ProbLog, we define the probability of a query $q$ with evidence $e$ as $P(q|e) = \frac{P(q \cap e)}{P(e)}$. Our iterative method computes lower and upper bounds, $P_l(q|e) = \frac{P_l(q \cap e)}{P_l(e)}$, $P_u(q|e) = \frac{P_u(q \cap e)}{P_u(e)}$, respectively. We would like to prove that $P_l(q|e) \leq P(q|e) \leq P_u(q|e)$. Unfortunately, we can prove the opposite by using set theory. Assume two sets $Q$, $E$ such that (i) at lower iteration $i$, $Q_i = Q$ and $\emptyset \neq E_i \subset E$ and that (ii) $Q_i \cap E_i = Q \cap E$ then clearly $P_l(Q_i \cap E_i) = P(Q \cap E)$ and $P_l(E_i) < P(E)$ resulting in $P_l(Q_i|E_i) > P(Q|E)$. For example, if $Q = Q_i = \{pf1 \cup pf2 \cup pf3\}$, $E = \{pf1 \cup (pf2 \cap pf4)\}$ and $E_i = \{pf1 \cup (pf2 \cap false)\} = \{pf1\}$ then $Pl(Q_i|E_i) = \frac{P(\{pf1\})}{P(\{pf1\})} = 1 > P(Q|E) = \frac{P(\{pf1\})}{P(\{pf1 \cup (pf2 \cap pf4)\})}$. Similarly one can miss proof $P_u(q|e) \geq P(q|e)$.

Thus, the proposed algorithm does not compute lower and upper bounded probabilities for queries with evidence. Our solution to this problem is to swap the divisors of the lower and upper iterations and compute the probabilities as follows: $P_l(q|e) = \frac{P_l(q|e)}{P_u(e)}$ and $P_u(q|e) = min(\frac{P_u(q|e)}{P_l(e)}, 1)$. Clearly, as $P_u(e) \geq P(e)$, $P_l(q \cap e) \leq P(q \cap e)$ then $\frac{P_l(q \cap e)}{P_u(e)} \leq \frac{P(q \cap e)}{P(e)}$ (similarly for the upper bound).

## 4    Experimental Results

For the purpose of this paper, we have implemented the proposed algorithm in MetaProbLog. MetaProbLog is an efficient implementation of ProbLog that is closely integrated with Yap Prolog [5] and is used in SkILL [4]. MetaProbLog supports both ROBDDs and sd-DNNFs as a knowledge compilation language. Previous experimental evaluations have shown that ROBDDs are able to solve more problems than sd-DNNFs in the context of MetaProbLog and sd-DNNFs only perform better in conditional queries [12,17]. For that reason, in our experiments we use ROBDDs.

We have experimented with 3 benchmark sets, namely Alzheimer, Smokers and Grid, which have been previously used for testing the performance of different ProbLog implementations. The Alzheimer benchmark set [8] was generated from a real-world biological dataset of Alzheimer genes. Due to the complexity and importance of this dataset, it has been established as the most used testing ground for ProbLog. We used three different queries (Q1, Q2, Q3) and their reversed instances $(\overline{Q1}, \overline{Q2}, \overline{Q3})$[2]. In order to see the scaling of the inference

---

[2] Q1 = p(hgnc_983,hgnc_620), $\overline{Q1}$ = p(hgnc_620,hgnc_983),
Q2 = p(hgnc_582,hgnc_620), $\overline{Q2}$ = p(hgnc_620,hgnc_582),
Q3 = p(hgnc_983,hgnc_582) and $\overline{Q3}$ = p(hgnc_582,hgnc_983).

methods based on the size of the graph, we increased the number of edges by 300 in each scale step starting from 1500 edges until 6000 edges (16 scale steps in total). The Smokers benchmark set [14] was introduced for testing multiple queries and queries with evidence. The scale parameter for Smokers is the number of persons in the social network, currently our dataset has up to 51 people. The Grid benchmark set [17] was constructed as a worst case scenario for ProbLog1 and MetaProbLog inference and is a fully connected grid that always contains the probabilistic information at the deepest step and, as such, it is the worst case scenario for our iterative algorithm.

The environment for our experiments was a Supermicro AS-2042G-72RF4 server with four AMD Opteron(tm) Processor 6376 (16 cores each, 64 cores in total) and 256 GB of RAM memory. The benchmarks where executed concurrently and each had a total of one hour for time out.

The foremost target of our approach is to enable us to compute an approximation in queries where exact inference is unable to compute any result. Furthermore, we would like our iterative inference method to be able to compute the exact inference and detect its computation when that is possible. Further than simply comparing our approach with the usual exact inference, we also used variable compaction for the Alzheimer dataset as presented in [12]. We noticed that variable compaction permitted us to compute more upper bounded queries and that, in general, variable compaction improved the performance (decreased the runtime) of the iterative inference method.

Table 1 presents the scaling results of our approach compared with exact inference. The queries Q1 to $\overline{Q3}$ are sorted from easier to hardest. One can notice that, for Alzheimer queries, exact inference usually times out at after 3000 edges. The presented iterative approach almost always computes results for all Alzheimer queries and in most cases computes the exact result for at least one scaling factor lower than what exact inference would compute. From a theoretical point of view, we were expecting iterative deepening to be able to compute the $N-1$ iteration of all benchmarks that exact inference was able to return the result. Theoretically, the complexity of computing iterations from 1 to $N-1$ is equal to $O(N)$ for iterative deepening strategies. Finally, we notice that computing upper bounded Boolean formulae is a significantly harder task than computing lower bounded Boolean formulae and some times even harder than computing exact Boolean formulae.

Regarding the Smokers datasets, we see similar behavior as with the Alzheimer dataset. The exact inference stops at queries with up to 40 people while our iterative deepening approach computed results for all our queries. Finally, for the Grid dataset our approach behaved as we expected. Our iterative deepening approach is able to compute the same queries as with exact inference. This was expected as the Grid problems push the probabilistic information very deep in the iterations and always time out on the knowledge compilation step. The results for the program sampling inference method show that it underperforms in the Alzheimer dataset problems, but it is ideal to solve problems like the ones introduced by the Grid dataset, where it easily solves the $15 \times 15$ graph.

**Table 1.** Highest scaling results for exact, program sampling, lower iterative, and upper iterative inference methods over the three datasets (columns **no**). For the Alzheimer dataset, we also present the results with variable compaction (columns **comp**). In parenthesis, we present the highest scaling factor at which the iterative inference detected that it has computed the exact probability.

| Dataset/query | Exact | | Program sampling | Lower iterative | | Upper iterative | |
|---|---|---|---|---|---|---|---|
| | no | comp | | no | comp | no | comp |
| Alzheimer Q1 | 6000 | 6000 | 6000 | 6000 (6000) | 6000 (6000) | 6000 (6000) | 6000 (6000) |
| Alzheimer $\overline{Q1}$ | 5100 | 3900 | 3300 | 6000 (3300) | 6000 (3300) | 2700 (2700) | 3900 (2700) |
| Alzheimer Q2 | 3000 | 3300 | 6000 | 6000 (3000) | 6000 (2700) | 6000 (3000) | 6000 (3000) |
| Alzheimer $\overline{Q2}$ | 3000 | 3300 | 2100 | 6000 (2400) | 6000 (2400) | 2400 (2400) | 3900 (2700) |
| Alzheimer Q3 | 3000 | 3000 | 2700 | 6000 (2400) | 6000 (2400) | 6000 (2400) | 6000 (2400) |
| Alzheimer $\overline{Q3}$ | 2400 | 2400 | 3900 | 5700 (2100) | 6000 (2100) | 6000 (2100) | 6000 (2100) |
| Smokers | 40 | – | – | 51 (40) | – | 51 (40) | – |
| Grid | $7 \times 7$ | – | $15 \times 15$ | $7 \times 7$ ($7 \times 7$) | – | $7 \times 7$ ($7 \times 7$) | – |

The second question we want to answer is how good is our approximations. Theoretically, it is difficult to answer this question, as we do not have a way to compute the amount of probabilistic information the next iterations would add. Practically, for most queries, we are able to compute both an upper and lower bound giving an indication of how good our approximation is. We use the same notion of precision as used in [18], but we also distinguish the queries where we are able to compute the exact probability. Table 2 shows the results.

For the Alzheimer dataset, we can see that there is a beneficial impact from enabling variable compaction. The impact comes from improved results in the upper bound computations. We also want to note that sometimes, even if the computed upper bounds are high, the computed lower bound probabilities are the exact probability but our system could not detect that (in brackets we present how the results would be affected if we could identify those cases).

In this regard, the Alzheimer $\overline{Q1}$ imposes an interesting problem for discussion. For that specific query, exact inference managed to compute the probability for graphs with up to 5100 edges. Our iterative deepening approach is able to compute the exact probability (as a lower bound) of that query for graphs with any number of edges in a identical execution time, but it fails to compute upper bound probabilities and it is also unable to automatically detect that the exact probability has been computed. The underlying reason for the complexity of this specific query is that it contains a complex graph that always leads to cycles but do not contributes to the query. The iterative deepening approach for the lower bound is able to drop this graph but is unable to detect that it is actually computing the exact probability. On the other hand, the upper bound computation is assuming that the complex graph contributes to the probability mass and always returns a probability of 1.0.

**Table 2.** Precision results of computed bounds by iterative deepening inference (columns **no**). For the Alzheimer dataset, we also present the results with variable compaction (column **comp**). In brackets are the results where exact probability is computed but is not detected. For program sampling we count the number of programs that reached a 95% confidence to be within a 0.01 interval.

| Precision | Alzheimer | | Smokers |
|---|---|---|---|
| | no | comp | no |
| Exact (<0.00001) | 40 (+9) | 41 (+9) | 304 |
| Almost exact ([0.00001, 0.01)) | 0 | 2 | 22 |
| Tight bounds ([0.01, 0.25)) | 29 | 26 | 27 |
| Loose bounds (>=0.25) | 27 (−9) | 27 (−9) | 4 |
| # **Queries solved by iterative deepening** | 96 | 96 | 357 |
| # **Queries solved by exact inference** | 48 | 46 | 305 |
| # **Queries solved by program sampling** | 55 | - | - |

## 5   Related Work

Lately, there has been a growing interest in combining probabilistic information with logic expressions, giving rise to different PLP systems, such as PRISM [16], IBAL [13], Alchemy [14], ProbLog [8] and PITA [15], among others. These systems use both exact and approximate inference methods in order to compute the marginal or/and conditional probabilities.

A similar inference method with our proposal is mentioned in [2]. Their iterative method is not described in detail and the authors only mention that it underperforms exact inference. By examining the provided source code, we have derived that their iterative method is used to generate growing subformulae that are given for knowledge compilation, i.e., their system handles the cycles before, at the logic part, assuming that the probabilistic derivations do not contain any cyclic information. Thus, their method does not generate a cyclic structure when representing the Boolean formulae like is in our proposal. As they conclude, exact inference or a $k$-best approximation is more appropriate in their setting (lack of cycles). Another similar approach is the *anytime (approximate) inference* method [18]. The main difference to our approach is that anytime inference fully constructs a CNF formula by executing the exact Boolean formula preprocessing step once and, then, performs incrementally the knowledge compilation step to a set of chosen subformulae. Theoretically, iterative deepening inference and anytime inference could be combined in order to improve the results of each other. Iterative deepening could be used in the Boolean formula preprocessing step and anytime inference in the knowledge compilation step and, in that way, the two approaches could be seen as the complement of each other. Finally [13] mentions the use of an iterative deepening algorithm in order to provide anytime inference for IBAL but the details of the algorithm are omitted from the paper.

# 6   Conclusions and Future Work

We have introduced a new approximate inference method for probabilistic logic programs based on a iterative deepening algorithm that, at each iteration, computes lower and upper bounds. Our algorithm is able to detect when an iteration would compute the exact probability either because the bounds converge or because the iteration examines the complete AND-OR graph. The proposed inference method can be used for any logic based system that collects SLG-derivations and needs to extract a cycle free Boolean formula from the derivations. This includes the PLP systems ProbLog1, ProbLog2, MetaProbLog, PITA and a version of PRISM that uses MTBBDs. Furthermore, some ASP systems use similar technology to handle Non-tight programs [9].

We also discuss how the new inference method is able to handle conditional queries and queries with general negation. Furthermore, our new inference method is compatible with all optimizations that the current system supports and, specifically, when it is combined with variable compaction, it is able to compute deeper iterations that enables us to get better bounds. The current implementation in MetaProbLog provides three new inference methods, namely: `problog_lower_iterative/2`, `problog_upper_iterative/2` and the combination of the two `problog_bounded_iterative/2`.

We performed a set of experiments on important applications of ProbLog that cover a wide range of different problems and we showed how our method enables us to solve queries that for exact inference were intractable. With the Alzheimer dataset, we presented the beneficial impact of variable compaction for our method. We used the Smokers dataset in order to compare our method against exact inference in the tasks of conditional and multiple queries. Our method clearly outperforms the exact inference being able to return results for all queries tests and returning the exact result for all but one query that exact inference could compute. Finally, we used the Grid dataset as a worst case scenario problem for our approach. Using Grid, we showed that in a worst case scenario our method performs similarly with exact inference, as expected.

For future work, we will extend the algorithm to use multi-threading in order to perform multiple knowledge compilations at the same time; investigate how to theoretically tighten the bounds of conditional queries; and take advantage of previous iterations compiled ROBDDs for incremental compilation. The development of this inference method was motivated by the SkILL system [4] and, as such, we intent to integrate the new method in SkILL. Finally, we are studying the combination of our approximate method with $T_P - Compilation$ [18] in order to boost even further the knowledge compilation step.

**Acknowledgments.** We want to thank the anonymous reviewers for their valuable comments. This work is partially funded by the ERDF through the COMPETE 2020 Programme within project POCI-01-0145-FEDER-006961, and by National Funds through the FCT as part of project UID/EEA/50014/2013.

# References

1. Akers, S.B.: Binary decision diagrams. IEEE Trans. Comput. **27**(6), 509–516 (1978)
2. Bragaglia, S., Riguzzi, F.: Approximate inference for logic programs with annotated disjunctions. In: Frasconi, P., Lisi, F.A. (eds.) ILP 2010. LNCS, vol. 6489, pp. 30–37. Springer, Heidelberg (2011). doi:10.1007/978-3-642-21295-6_7
3. Chen, W., Warren, D.S.: Tabled evaluation with delaying for general logic programs. J. ACM **43**(1), 20–74 (1996)
4. Côrte-Real, J., Mantadelis, T., de Castro Dutra, I., Rocha, R.: SkILL - a stochastic inductive logic learner. In: International Conference on Machine Learning and Applications (ICMLA), pp. 555–558 (2015)
5. Costa, V.S., Rocha, R., Damas, L.: The YAP prolog system. Theory Pract. Logic Program. (TPLP) **12**(1–2), 5–34 (2012)
6. Darwiche, A.: SDD: a new canonical representation of propositional knowledge bases. In: International Joint Conference on Artificial Intelligence (IJCAI), vol. 2, pp. 819–826 (2011)
7. Darwiche, A., Marquis, P.: A knowledge compilation map. J. Artif. Intell. Reason. (JAIR) **17**, 229–264 (2002)
8. Kimmig, A., Demoen, B., De Raedt, L., Santos Costa, V., Rocha, R.: On the implementation of the probabilistic logic programming language ProbLog. Theory Pract. Logic Program. (TPLP) **11**(2–3), 235–262 (2011)
9. Lierler, Y., Maratea, M.: Cmodels-2: SAT-based answer set solver enhanced to non-tight programs. In: Lifschitz, V., Niemelä, I. (eds.) LPNMR 2004. LNCS, vol. 2923, pp. 346–350. Springer, Heidelberg (2003). doi:10.1007/978-3-540-24609-1_32
10. Mantadelis, T., Janssens, G.: Dedicated tabling for a probabilistic setting. In: International Conference on Logic Programming (ICLP). Leibniz International Proceedings in Informatics (LIPIcs), vol. 7, pp. 124–133 (2010)
11. Mantadelis, T., Rocha, R., Kimmig, A., Janssens, G.: Preprocessing Boolean formulae for BDDs in a probabilistic context. In: Janhunen, T., Niemelä, I. (eds.) JELIA 2010. LNCS, vol. 6341, pp. 260–272. Springer, Heidelberg (2010). doi:10.1007/978-3-642-15675-5_23
12. Mantadelis, T., Shterionov, D., Janssens, G.: Compacting Boolean formulae for inference in probabilistic logic programming. In: Calimeri, F., Ianni, G., Truszczynski, M. (eds.) LPNMR 2015. LNCS, vol. 9345, pp. 425–438. Springer, Cham (2015). doi:10.1007/978-3-319-23264-5_35
13. Pfeffer, A.: IBAL: a probabilistic rational programming language. In: International Joint Conference on Artificial Intelligence (IJCAI), pp. 733–740 (2001)
14. Richardson, M., Domingos, P.: Markov logic networks. Mach. Learn. **62**(1–2), 107–136 (2006)
15. Riguzzi, F., Swift, T.: The PITA system: tabling and answer subsumption for reasoning under uncertainty. Comput. Res. Repository abs/1107.4747 (2011)
16. Sato, T., Kameya, Y.: PRISM: a language for symbolic-statistical modeling. In: International Joint Conference on Artificial Intelligence (IJCAI), pp. 1330–1339 (1997)
17. Shterionov, D., Janssens, G.: Implementation and performance of probabilistic inference pipelines. In: Pontelli, E., Son, T.C. (eds.) PADL 2015. LNCS, vol. 9131, pp. 90–104. Springer, Cham (2015). doi:10.1007/978-3-319-19686-2_7
18. Vlasselaer, J., Van den Broeck, G., Kimmig, A., Meert, W., De Raedt, L.: Anytime inference in probabilistic logic programs with Tp-compilation. In: International Joint Conference on Artificial Intelligence (IJCAI), pp. 1852–1858 (2015)

# Author Index

Printed in the United States
By Bookmasters